SECOND EDITION

SEX IS NOT A NATURAL ACT
and Other Essays

LEONORE TIEFER

A Member of the Perseus Books Group

Copyright © 2004 by Leonore Tiefer
Cartoon drawings for Parts One, Two, Three, Four, and Five are by Frank Irwin of Brooklyn, NY.

Published in the United States of America by Westview Press, A Member of the Perseus Books Group, 5500 Central Avenue, Boulder, Colorado 80301-2877, and in the United Kingdom by Westview Press, 12 Hid's Copse Road, Cumnor Hill, Oxford OX2 9JJ.

Find us on the world wide web at www.westviewpress.com

Westview Press books are available at special discounts for bulk purchases in the United States by corporations, institutions, and other organizations. For more information, please contact the Special Markets Department at the Perseus Books Group, 11 Cambridge Center, Cambridge, MA 02142, or call (617) 252-5298, (800) 255-1514 or email specialmarkets@perseusbooks.com.

Library of Congress Cataloging-in-Publication Data

Tiefer, Leonore.
    Sex is not a natural act / Leonore Tiefer.—2nd ed.
        p.   cm.
    Rev. ed. of: Sex is not a natural act and other essays. 1995.
    Includes bibliographical references and index.
    ISBN 0-8133-4185-X (pbk. : alk. paper)—ISBN 0-8133-4184-1 (hardcover : alk. paper)
    1. Sex.   2. Sexology.   I. Title.
HQ21.T574   2004
306.7—dc22
                                                                        2003022366

Typeface used in this text: Goudy

10   9   8   7   6   5   4   3   2   1

CONTENTS

Part Four:
The Medicalization of Sexuality

Part Five: The Creation of FSD

ACKNOWLEDGMENTS

In the first edition of this book (1995), I thanked the many feminist and sexologist colleagues who helped me figure out social constructionism. I thank them all deeply again, especially Ann Snitow and her seminar, Arthur Zitrin, and many friends at NYU, IASR, Montefiore, SSSS, SSTAR, and AWP.

I also gave praise to Frank Irwin for drawing the cartoons—he has updated and revised them for this edition, as well as adding a terrific new one for the final section. It's so good to have a politically savvy artist as a friend.

But the past eight years have seen many changes in sexology and in my career in sexology, and I have a whole raft of new friends and colleagues to thank—feminists, journalists, academicians, clinicians, and new colleagues in Germany, The Netherlands, India, England, New Zealand, France, India, Sweden, Denmark, Japan, and Croatia. Invitations to speak in these countries gave me perspective on sexuality in the U.S. as well as brilliant people with whom to discuss my ideas. Sexology is part of a global production of knowledge and practice, and I have aspired to some level of global understanding.

I am the sort of person who thinks best when she has to write something or give a talk. I must have gotten this from my mother, who only practices the piano if she has to perform. Let me thank my non-U.S. friends who have given me opportunities to reflect and pontificate in the last few years: Lynne Segal, Gunter Schmidt, Kiyomi Kawano, Saad Khoury, Alain Giami, Tricia Barnes, Paula Nicolson, Margret Hauch, Jagdish Bhatt, Peter Osborne, Jane Ussher, Lena Schonnesson, Sasha Stulhofer, Erwin Haeberle, Annie Potts, and many others. And I also benefitted from so many U. S. invitations and opportunities thanks to Ellen Kimmel, Suzanna Rose, Susan Campbell, Deborah Grant, Gil Herdt, Anke Ehrhardt, Joan Chrisler, Maureen McHugh, Kathryn Norsworthy, Joan Bertin, John Bancroft, Bruce Southworth, Jeanne Marecek, Loren Greene, Pam Connelly, Meika Loe, Pat Whelehan, Isabel Kaplan, and many others as well.

The Campaign for a New View of Women's Sexual Problems I convened in 2000 was a leap of faith since being an activist turns out to involve on the job training. We have accomplished more than I expected because of the help and encouragement of journalists, scientists, and so many more than I can list. But, thanks to all of you—especially to Linda, Jennifer, Lisa, Heather, Judy, Laura, Ellyn, Peggy, Meika, Marny, Carol E., and Carol T. Meika Loe, Marny Hall, and Carol Tavris have sung back-up to my every bleat these past few years—editing my clumsy language, helping me decide which road to take, and unfailingly cheering me on. Every campaign leader should have such a team. When I told Carol years ago that our friendship gave me immense pleasure because she finished my sentences correctly, I had no idea what sort of sentences I would be throwing her way. Her cleverness is my great good fortune.

The ideas in this book are an amalgam of feminism 101, science and technology studies, social science, psychotherapy insights, Unitarian Universalist values, cultural studies, constant comparative reading of *The New York Times* and the left-wing press, and a Bronx-hewn sense of humor and life perspective. I have benefitted from discussing sexual topics over the past two decades with the Keen's group (thanks especially Carol G. and Suzanne I.), and with the sex therapy study group the amazing Brunhild Kring and I convened over ten years ago. You are all my teachers. Finally, my family is smaller than most, but here, quality compensates for quantity. Loving thanks to them, and to everyone in my address book (the red leather one, not the computer one) I can't list by name.

LEONORE TIEFER

CREDITS

Part One

Chapter 1: "'Am I Normal?' The Question of Sex," in Carol Tavris, ed., *Everywoman's Emotional Well-being* (Garden City, N.Y.: Doubleday, 1986), 54–72. Copyright © 1986 by Nelson Doubleday, Inc. Published by arrangement with Doubleday Book & Music Clubs, Inc.

Chapter 2: "Social Constructionism and the Study of Human Sexuality," in P. Shaver and C. Hendrick, eds., *Sex and Gender* (Newbury Park, Cal.: Sage Publications, 1987), 70–94.

Chapter 3: "Sexual Biology and the Symbolism of the Natural." Paper presented at the International Academy of Sex Research, Sigtuna, Sweden, 1990. German translation published in *Zeitschrift fur Sexualforschung* 4 (1991): 97–108.

Chapter 4: "Historical, Scientific, Clinical, and Feminist Criticisms of 'The Human Sexual Response Cycle'," *Annual Review of Sex Research* 2 (1991): 1–23.

Part Two

Chapter 1: "Six Months at the *Daily News*." Selections from weekly "Your Sexual Self" column, the *New York Daily News*, 1980–81. Reprinted by permission.

Chapter 2: "The Kiss." Edited version of a lecture delivered in Bloomington, Indiana, October, 1998. The original version is on the Kinsey Institute website, http://www.kinseyinstitute.org/services/tiefer-talk.html

Chapter 3: "From Niagara to Viagra: Why It Is So Hard to Just Talk About Sex." Lecture delivered at Community Church of New York, March, 1999.

Chapter 4: "The Opposite of Sex." *Ms.* Magazine, August-September, 1999, pp. 60–65.

Chapter 5: "The McDonaldization of Sex." Lecture delivered at Community Church of New York, August, 2002.

Chapter 6: "Doing the Viagra Tango." *Radical Philosophy* No. 92, November/December 1998, pp. 2–5.

Part Three

Chapter 1: "An Activist in Sexology." Paper presented at the midcontinent regional meeting of the Society for the Scientific Study of Sex, Cincinnati, May, 1993, upon receipt of their 1993 Alfred C. Kinsey Award.

Chapter 2: "Biological Politics (Read: Propaganda) Is Alive and Well in Sexology." Forthcoming in *Feminism and Psychology*, 2004. London: Sage Publications (U.K.). http://www.sagepub.co.uk/home.aspx

Chapter 3: "Gender and Meaning in the Nomenclature of Sexual Dysfunctions." Paper presented at the American Psychological Association, Boston, August, 1990.

Chapter 4: "Some Harms to Women of Restrictions on Sexually Related Expression." *New York Law School Law Review*, vol. 38, nos. 1–4, pp. 95–101, 1993.

Chapter 5: "Towards a Feminist Sex Therapy." From *Women and Therapy*, 1996, 19: 53–64.

Chapter 6: "The Capacity for Outrage: Feminism, Humor and Sex." From *Sex and Humor: Selections from the Kinsey Institute*, edited by Catherine Johnson, Betsy Stirratt, and John Bancroft. Published by Indiana University Press, Bloomington, IN 2002.

Part Four

Chapter 1: "Sexism in Sex Therapy: Whose Idea Is 'Sensate' Focus?" Paper presented at the Society for Scientific Study of Sex, New York, 1981.

Chapter 2. "Women's Sexuality: Not a Matter of Health." In Alice Dan, ed., *Reframing Women's Health: New paradigms for multidisciplinary research and practice* (Newbury Park, CA: Sage, 1994), 151–162.

Chapter 3: "The Medicalization of Impotence: Normalizing Phallocentrism." *Gender and Society* 8 (1994): 363–377. Copyright © 1994 Sociologists for Women in Society. Reprinted by permission of Sage Publications, Inc.

Chapter 4: "Pleasure, Medicalization, and the Tyranny of the Natural." *Siecus Report*, April/May 2002, *30*, 23–26.

Chapter 5: "Sexology and the Pharmaceutical Industry: The Threat of Co-optation." *Journal of Sex Research*, 2000, *37*, 273–283.

Part Five

Chapter 1: "'Female Sexual Dysfunction' Alert: A New Disorder Invented for Women." Sojourner: The Women's Forum, October, 1999, p. 11.

Chapter 2: "A New View of Women's Sexual Problems." http://www.fsd-alert.org/manifesto.html.

Chapter 3: "The Selling of 'Female Sexual Dysfunction'." *Journal of Sex & Marital Therapy*, 2001, *27*, 625–628.

Chapter 4: "A New Sexual World——NOT!" *In The Family*, Summer, 2001, pp. 22–24.

Chapter 5: The Pink Viagra Story: We Have the Drug, but What's the Disease? *Radical Philosophy*, No. 121, September/October 2003, pp. 2–5.

INTRODUCTION TO THE SECOND EDITION: GOOD NEWS AND BAD NEWS

I've got good news and bad news.

The good news is that the 1st edition of this book sold so well that the publishers want to bring out a revision. This already is as rare as hens' teeth. Far better books have not had a 2nd edition, so I am definitely lucky.

The bad news is that the reason for my good fortune seems to be that the ideas in this book are still controversial despite my hope that the idea that sex isn't natural would sweep the nation. At the end of the introduction to the 1st edition (Tiefer, 1995), I wrote:

> Over the years, just as I have thought that sexology or popular thinking was about to shift away from biological determinism toward a more contextualized perspective, some big media splash about genes or hormones would depress me for a week. . . . Again, in the mid-1990s, I believe the new wave is finally coming in, and I am excited and optimistic. This collection will be useful, however, in case the pendulum swings back again. (p. 3)

Well, welcome back. The 1st edition of this book was published in 1995, right in the middle of the Human Genome Project, galloping advances in neuroscience, and a decade of general biomania. More to the point, it was published three years before the birth of Viagra ushered in a new era of sexual biomania.[1] The theme of this book was and is the social construction of sexuality, and the Viagra phenomenon offers a fabulous example of social construction in action.

The volcano of publicity around Viagra has probably changed sexual life irrevocably by raising the bar on what constitutes normal and adequate performance and planting the idea that sexual insecurity is abnormal and should be eliminated with medication. That's how social construction works: critical factors in the social environment shift and—bingo!—our expectations, behaviors, and relationships change. It's safe to predict that we will see more and more prescription drugs and over-the-counter supplements advertised to "treat" sexual deficiencies—and, of course, as with all advertised products, they will increase insecurity and the sense of sexual deficiency.

You know something like Viagra is a player in our image-driven culture because, as with 9/11 or Hollywood or McDonald's, it is used as a tool and metaphor for various causes ("McDonald's is the reason kids are fat," "Hollywood undermines modesty and monogamy," "9/11 has brought back family loyalty"). Viagra has already been used in campaigns around health care policy. Women who had been refused insurance coverage for oral contraceptives used Viagra's broad coverage to demand equality—and received it, when no other argument had worked. Likewise, Viagra has drawn public attention to how advertising costs contribute to high drug prices. Even though a lot of what one reads about Viagra seems to be jokey ("The weeds in my yard must have been taking Viagra"), the drug can also get serious subjects into the limelight.

Viagramania is a great example of how cultural events affect people's sexual lives. But Viagra and medicalization, much as they have obsessed me, are hardly the only examples of the social construction of sex. Huge social shifts such as global changes in gender roles, increases in leisure and longevity in the industrialized world, and the growth and influence of mass media have all deeply and irrevocably altered sexual life. A watershed event such as the approval of marriage for same-sex couples which occurred in the Netherlands in 2000 and Canada in 2003 shows just how much society and sexuality are changing.

Legal marriage for gays may be many years in the future for the U.S., however, which draws attention to the extraordinary range of cross-cultural variations that exist in sexual life. Issues like homosexuality, abortion, and comprehensive sex education are much more contentious in the U.S. than in other first-world countries. Comprehensive sex education (without "abstinence" promotion) is standard in Scandinavia and northern Europe. Prostitution was decriminalized in New Zealand in June 2003. Can you see this happening in the near future in the United States? Most Americans seem unaware of international variations, and how often the situation in the United States is bizarrely conservative, despite our all-sex-all-the-time popular culture. Awareness of cultural variation is a key element in a social constructionist perspective.

It is amazing how compartmentalized knowledge about sexuality is. Maybe it's because there are no multidisciplinary Departments of Sexuality Studies[2] where psychologists and anthropologists could share lunches with historians and team-teach seminars with cultural and religious studies scholars. Even professional conferences on sexuality are often narrow and profession-specific. As a consequence of the lack of cross-fertilization, people in one branch of sex research and theory are largely clueless about what's going on elsewhere.

But the problem with getting the big picture of sex is more than just academic compartmentalization or intellectual complexity. The bigger problem is that powerful conservative political groups opposed to reproductive rights, sexual empowerment, and sexual self-determination have discouraged and even prevented funding for sex education and scholarship (Irvine, 2002; Levine, 2002). If you want to understand how sexuality develops in children, for example, you are out of luck, since, in response to conservative legislators and lobbyists, the U.S. government refuses to fund that kind of research. And that's just one of many examples.

One reason sexuality medicalization has advanced so rapidly (see Parts Four and Five in this book) is because there are so few competing models for understanding sexuality, a situation I attribute to the fact that sex research is so politically squashed in the United States. As the corporate-controlled media and the pharmaceutical industry control even more public messages about sexuality, we will hear more about hot sex, sexual disorders, and new pills, but where will be the voices for sex as art, spiritual sex, cool sex, and the overselling of sex?

The future of sexuality in this country must include more sexuality policy, and I certainly don't mean repressive policy initiatives such as abstinence-only sex education or lock-up-child-molestors-forever criminal justice initiatives. I'm thinking about comprehensive sex education, including media literacy, consumer education, and cross-cultural awareness. In June, 2001, President Clinton's Surgeon General, David Satcher, issued a remarkable *Call to Action to Promote Sexual Health and Responsible Sexual Behavior* (http://www.surgeongeneral.gov/library/sexualhealth/default.htm). This report could be a beginning of progressive sexuality policy.

I have a fantasy of little sex-ed-book-and-videomobiles parked near schools, health clinics, libraries, malls, and laundromats, offering a cafeteria of information about sexuality to citizens of all ages. We have to enable people to get information about sex that doesn't come from the pharmaceutical industry, Hollywood, or Madison Avenue. There's no turning back the clock on sexuality, and realistic and positive sexual lives require new models and new policy initiatives.

I am having a strange career—that of a sexologist. It's not the sort of thing you can just study, get a degree in, and get hired to do, at least not yet, not in the United States. There are only a handful of academic programs in sexuality studies—nothing remotely adequate.

How did I learn about human sexuality? From my life and my friends' lives, of course, and from reading, writing, and working at various jobs over the past thirty-five years. Where do you work as a sexologist? I have taught sexuality courses to university, medical, and nursing students. I've done library research for public and professional lectures all over the world and have a long list of academic publications. I've evaluated over 2,500 individuals and couples with sexual complaints and provided sex therapy and psychotherapy for short (one or two sessions) and long (several years) periods of time. I've attended endless conferences on sexuality theory and research in the United States and abroad and participated in New York study groups for decades. I conducted laboratory research with hamsters and rats and questionnaire and interview research with patients and students. I've written for magazines and newspapers and been interviewed by journalists and documentary makers (you can learn a lot from being asked good questions). For decades I have saved newspaper and magazine articles on sexuality in a mismatched collection of filing cabinets in my New York apartment.

Although I earned a Ph.D. in physiological psychology in 1969 from the University of California at Berkeley with a dissertation on hormones and mating behavior in golden hamsters (*Mesocricetus auratus*), my ideas about sexuality subsequently underwent a complete transformation and I now believe that my dissertation and other similar biological work are largely useless for understanding human sexuality. In the 1970s, writings from the women's movement convinced me that the primary influences on women's sexuality are cultural norms internalized by women, reinforced by institutions and enacted in significant relationships. Hamsters had taught me nothing about social norms.

Fifteen years after my Ph.D. I returned to graduate school to respecialize as a clinical psychologist with a focus on human sexuality. During the 1980s, the deluge of new historical, feminist, and queer theory convinced me that human sexuality must be seen in light of competing ideological and economic interests. Hormones and life histories are far from enough to understand sex. No one can resist the influence of the mass media, for example, and we all live sexual lives circumscribed by politics. You and your generation have sexual choices I never did, and vice-versa. That's neither good nor bad—it's just social construction.

Working in urology departments for thirteen years, I could see what values and beliefs people draw on when their familiar sexual habits aren't working, and how the values of doctors come into the picture. Teaching in universities, I could see how the rapidly changing sexual culture affected students (and faculty). People do what they know about and what their peer group is doing, and they rely heavily on experts. Because sexuality is a subject of great emotional vulnerability, people get very distressed when their usual routines misfire, and they can be exploited by narrowly trained or fraudulent experts. There are too few places to turn for advice.

It makes me sad and frustrated to know that for many—perhaps most— people, sexual experience falls far short of what they hoped for and what they believe others experience. Sex is hyped in our culture, and secrecy makes things worse. Readers of self-help books and popular magazines can be misled by unrepresentative stories and too-brief vignettes. Stuff on the Internet seems to specialize in shock, and many new books normalize exotic practices. People looking for information can be misled into thinking that sex needs to be kinky to be interesting. It's hard to find useful information about how ordinary sexual routines develop and change, the roles of learning and expectation, how sexual reactions develop and how the whole thing links to personality and emotional needs. No wonder so many feel anxious and ill-prepared.

Despite the cacophony of messages about sex, many people still believe that "sex is natural"—that is, that sex is a simple and universal biological function that, without any training, all humans should experience, enjoy, and perform in roughly the same way. Many doctors believe this, too.

This book challenges the Catch–22 notion that "sex is natural." Naturalism positions sex as accessible and glorious yet at the same time makes it a mystery. In this book, I will dispute this perspective by logical argument, by reminding people of their real sexual life experience, by introducing ideas from other cultures and historical periods, and by suggesting metaphors and analogies designed to reframe sexuality as just another human potential (like music or spirituality or cuisine). I hope it helps people be less tongue-tied or giggly when discussing it. You'd be amazed at how much of sex therapy is about getting people to talk calmly and frankly about their sex lives, both about what they feel and want and about what they actually do. Once I can get a couple to talk with each other, the job is more than half done.

But, back to the bad news. Although reactions to the 1st edition of this book were generally very positive, and people said to me zillions of times, "Gee, I never thought of it that way," too many are still blinded by the idea that sex IS somehow natural and don't see the social constructions at work. They are unprepared, then, for the complicated realities of contemporary sex life. People don't understand the way advertising and the media set high but completely arbitrary sexual goals. They take too personally the anxiety that inevitably results from ignorance and insecurity. People become impatient and irritable at the thought that social and cultural studies are necessary for a good sex life, and I can understand that. But there is no alternative. If you lack "media literacy" and "consumer literacy," then you're going to be a patsy for mega-billion dollar industries that use the promise of good sex to sell their products.

We all want wonderful things to happen without effort, and occasionally they do. But because they often don't it helps to know that you're not the only person having trouble navigating the new sexual world. There is great potential for joy and deep connection in sex, but it requires some cultural sophistication to know which way the wind is blowing.

Notes

1. Viagra was approved by the U.S. Food and Drug Administration on March 27, 1998, which we will consider the birthday of Viagra. It was approved by the European Union on September 15, 1998.

2. San Francisco State University has a new department just like this as of 2002. Hallelujah, may its tribe increase.

part one

SEX IS NOT A NATURAL ACT: THEME AND VARIATIONS

My mother is a professional musician, and the metaphor of music has helped me explain sexuality to numerous audiences. Open a textbook on human sexuality, and nine times out of ten it will begin with a chapter on anatomy and physiology. This opening sets the stage for the assumption that "the biological bedrock," as it is often called, must be understood before we can look at anything else, such as what people want, what they experience, how they get their ideas about what sex ought to be, and so on. Furthermore, the biology presented in these texts always dwells on the anatomy and physiology of the genital organs, never of the tactile receptors of the cheek or lips or the physiology of aroma preferences. You'll find the physiology of arousal but not of pleasure, of performance but not of fantasy. So, it's not just biology that is being portrayed as fundamental, but a certain kind of biology.

Open a textbook of music, in contrast, and you will not find chapters on the bones, nerves, blood vessels, and muscles of the fingers (for playing the piano), the hands (to play cymbals or cello), or even the mouth or throat (for flute or singing). And what about the physiology of hearing or of the sense of rhythm? Why don't music texts start with biology? Isn't biology as fundamental to music as it is to sexuality?

It is, and it isn't. It depends on what you mean by *fundamental*. If you mean that music requires human physiology to produce and experience, of course this is largely true. But if you mean that the physiological aspect is the most human, the most complex, the most interesting, or the most important thing about experiencing music, well, then, we are going to have an argument! By privileging biology within the discourse of sexuality, and often by reducing sexuality to the biological, I think we've got the cart before the horse, as the musical analogy suggests. And by privileging genital physiology over any other aspect of bodily experience, sexology research and writing make further choices and, I think, further mistakes. Much of this collection examines these choices and their causes and implications.

But the rhetoric of sexuality as "natural" is not just about biology; it also relates to the expanding discussion of sexuality and health. As some of these writings will show, I worry a lot about the consequences of locating sexuality within the conceptual model and the material institutions of health and the health industry. I think the already-accomplished medicalization of male sexuality shows that sexuality is diminished and human interest only incompletely served by the medical model, at least at the present time. Maintaining that "sex is a natural act" identifies as experts those social actors who know a lot about body mechanics rather than those who understand learning, culture, and imagination.

Human sexuality is not a biological given and cannot be explained in terms of reproductive biology or instinct. All human actions need a body, but only part of human sexuality has to do with actions, and even that part only requires a body in the way that playing the piano does. What is done, when, where, by whom, with whom, with what, and why—these things have almost nothing to do with biology. Giving biology priority in our talking and theorizing about sexuality is called *essentialism* after the mistaken assumption that once you "strip away" all the cultural and historical trappings, the essence of sexuality that is left is biology. This type of thinking used to be called *biological determinism*, a perfectly good term.

So, if sex is not a natural act, a biological given, a human universal, what is it? I would say it's a concept, first of all—a concept with shifting but deeply felt definitions. Conceptualizing sex is a way of corralling and discussing certain human potentials for consciousness, behavior, and expression that are available to be developed by social forces, that is, available to be produced, changed, modified, organized, and defined. Like Jell-O, sexuality has no shape without a container, in this case a sociohistorical container of meaning and regulation. And, like Jell-O, once it is formed it appears quite fixed and difficult to re-form.

A kiss is not a kiss; in this perspective, your orgasm is not the same as George Washington's, premarital sex in Peru is not premarital sex in Peoria, abortion in Rome at the time of Caesar is not abortion in Rome at the time of John Paul II, and rape is neither an act of sex nor an act of violence—all of these actions remain to be defined by individual experience within one's period and place.

In Part One I attempt to articulate this antinaturalism perspective further. In these chapters I explain more about the naturalism perspective, where it comes from, how it tyrannizes, what the social constructionist alternative looks like, and how the new approach fits into current theory and research.

chapter 1

"AM I NORMAL?"
THE QUESTION OF SEX

Three times in my career I have written regular columns on sexuality for the public—a weekly column for six months for the *New York Daily News* in 1980–1981 and monthly columns for two national magazines, *Playgirl Advisor* and *Playgirl,* for a year and for four months, respectively. In each case I received stacks of letters from readers. The ones below, taken from the newspaper job in 1981, are representative:

My name is Arlene. I am eighteen years of age I have a friend [and] we have become very committed to each other in a friendship way, but he thinks that because we have developed this friendly relationship we ought to have a sexual relationship, too. But I am a bit confused [as] to what to do first before I have a sexual relationship with him. I am not sure if I really love him enough. What I am really afraid of is that once I get involved with him, all he will want to do is just have sex, and not be friends anymore.

I am forty-nine years old and my husband is fifty-five years old. My problem is that we have had sex twice in fourteen months. When I bring the matter up, which I have done twice in this period of time, my husband insists that there is nothing wrong, not in any way, physically or mentally. He says that he is more tired lately, or that our twenty-four-year-old daughter may come in. . . . Two years ago I had a hysterectomy and we both joked about freedom from contraceptives and how we could look forward to "really enjoying it." But, to the contrary, our sex life is almost nil. I miss those intimate moments, preliminary caresses, and the feeling of being desired.

I am a divorced woman who, in addition to a ten-year marriage, also has had two other sexually satisfying relationships. So I know I don't have a problem. In the past year, however, I have met several seemingly nice men who just don't make love very nicely, and it has created anxieties in me which were never there before. How common are things like this, for example?

a. Food, which I believe belongs in the kitchen, not on the body. (This man thought I was unimaginative and unenlightened.)

b. Such a preference for oral and manual sex that I felt like a masturbating machine, not a lover.

c. The weirdo who refused to ejaculate inside me, even with rubbers[1] "for the first two or three months until we know each other better." All he could say was, "Look, I've always done it this way. It frustrates me as much as it frustrates you, but I prefer not to just yet."

I know all about "consenting adults," but are these men normal?

God forbids all sex outside marriage—but you encourage it! Which leads to promiscuity and all sorts of trouble. Are you proud of yourself? Someday God will judge you. He will hold you accountable for everything.

There are three things to notice about these letters. First, they don't reveal that the writers themselves have any problems; rather, the partners have problems (2 and 3), the writer has a problem only because of her partner (1), or I, the expert, have a problem (4). This pattern also holds true in questions I've received during radio and TV shows. In part, people are understandably defensive and don't like to admit something is wrong with them. But, also, people who write are not just asking for help; they want to make a statement about how badly they're being dealt with and how they deserve some sympathy.

Second, notice that the question-writers want me to tell them things about their partners—people I've never laid eyes on! These women have been unable to get these men to give them straight answers, have not gotten any answers at all from them, or perhaps have not even been able to ask the men directly about the problem. The average person might not believe how many complex sexual problems are solved "merely" with improved communication, but anyone with any experience in long relationships probably realizes how difficult it is to change the communication patterns a couple has established.

Finally, note that in these letters the emphasis is not on performance (sexual "function") or pleasure so much as on psychological gratifications related to sex. The first woman wants to maintain her self-esteem and does not want to feel betrayed. The second woman misses intimacy, closeness, the feeling of being desired. The third woman wants her expectations met and wants to feel respected. The fourth writer wants me to subscribe to his or her moral vision of sexuality. Far more than is popularly realized, sexual activity is the means to gain or maintain important psychological feelings, and a challenge to one's sexuality is often a personal threat. Self-esteem, closeness, feelings of competence and well-being—these are the feelings sought from sex during modern times.

What Is Normal?

Why do people write letters like the ones above to medical sexuality "experts"? Why are radio phone-in shows on sexuality so immensely popular, night after night, coast to coast? The easy answer is that questions on sexuality have always existed in people's minds, but only recently has there been the opportunity to discuss such matters openly. Dramatic changes in broadcasting and publishing rules about explicit sexual language and imagery, this argument goes, have opened the door to public discussion of issues that have been on people's minds forever.

Another popular hypothesis to explain the explosion of public discussion about sex is that people are less willing nowadays to put up with sexual disappointment and sexual problems and less embarrassed to try and make things better.

Although I agree that as long as there have been human beings there have been questions about sex, I believe that the current deluge reflects less eternal inquisitiveness than a modern epidemic of insecurity and worry generated by a new social construction: the idea that sexual functioning is a central, if not *the* central, aspect of a relationship. Such an emphasis naturally leads to tremendous concern about sex and a greater need for advice, education, support, and a variety of repair services.

The new importance given to sexuality and emotional intimacy in relationships is one result of large social changes in how we view marriage and life:

- The purpose of marriage has shifted from economic necessity to companionship, resulting in dramatic changes in obligations and expectations.
- There has been a shift in how we measure a person's "success" to include physical vitality and life enjoyment along with material achievements.
- Divorce and "serial monogamy" have become increasingly acceptable, making people anxious about maintaining relationships.
- Changes in social attitudes and improvements in contraception have allowed women to view sexuality as separate from reproduction and as an avenue for self-expression and pleasure.
- People are relying on personal relationships to provide a sense of worth they lack in the public sphere due to increased technology, mobility, and bureaucracy.

These social changes provide the backdrop for reconstructing sexuality in modern life. But most people are not prepared for the increased importance of sex for relationships and personal identity. Sex, for the most part, is still a private and secret matter. The majority of people have never seen any genital sex acts but their own.[2] Most people do not talk honestly about sexual activity, and until recently there was no formal education in public schools about sex.

Imagine how you would feel if playing gin rummy, and playing it well, were considered a major component of happiness and a major sign of maturity, but no one told you how to play, you never saw anyone else play, and everything you ever read implied that normal and healthy people just somehow "know" how to play and really enjoy playing the very first time they try! It is a very strange situation.

Norms for sexual activity until recently came from religious authorities primarily concerned about moral boundaries. Sexual activities were governed by a right/wrong mentality, with homosexuality, masturbation, and having many partners among the wrongs and marital coitus, female sexual modesty, and a complete absence of self-disclosure between parents and children among the rights. During the nineteenth and twentieth centuries, religious authority over everyday activities has gradually eroded and the authority of science and science-based medicine to set norms has grown. Various forms of disapproved and deviant behavior (e.g., chronic lying, drinking, disobedience, and sexual "wrongs" of various sorts) came to be seen less as violations of God's law and more as the products of sick minds. The authority for interpreting deviations of behavior shifted almost imperceptibly, category by category, from the domain of sin and evil to that of disorder and abnormality.[3]

Five Meanings of Normal

Well, what is sexual normalcy? There are at least five ways to answer this question:

1. *Subjective:* According to this definition, I am normal, and so is anyone who is the same as me. Secretly, most of us use this definition a lot, but publicly, few will admit it.
2. *Statistical:* According to this definition, whatever behaviors are most common are normal; less frequent ones are abnormal. If you conduct a survey and ask people how many lies they have told, how often they have drunk alcohol, or what kinds of sexual activities they have engaged in over the past five years and graph the results on a curve, the most frequent responses will be those in the middle, with extreme highs and lows at the ends. The idea of normalcy as something that is not too high and not too low is based on the statistical viewpoint. In the United States today, "too little sex" has joined "too much sex" as cause for worry.

3. *Idealistic:* From this viewpoint, normal means perfect, an ideal to be striven for. Those who model their behavior on Christ or Gandhi, for example, are taking an ideal for their norm, against which they measure all deviations.

4. *Cultural:* Without realizing it, this is probably the standard most of us use most of the time. This measure explains why our notions of normalcy do not always agree with those of people from other countries, regions, cultures, religions, and historical periods. Bare breasts or men kissing in public is normal in one place but abnormal in another. It is common for deviant behavior to be perceived as dangerous and frightening in a culture that rejects it, although the same behavior may be as common and harmless as chicken soup a few tribes or national boundaries away. Mouth-to-mouth kissing is a good example. In much of Oceania, mouth-to-mouth kissing was long regarded as dirty and disgusting, and yet in Europe and North America it's a major source of intimacy and arousal.

5. *Clinical:* All the above definitions seem arbitrary, that is, they seem to depend on individual or group opinion rather than on "objective" evidence. The clinical standard, by contrast, uses scientific data about health and illness to make judgments. A particular blood pressure or diet or activity is considered clinically abnormal when research shows that it is related to disease or disability. It shouldn't matter to the clinical definition whether we are talking about the twentieth century or the tenth, about industrial Europe or rural Africa.

Using the clinical standard with regard to psychology is more difficult than using it for physiological matters because it is harder to prove psychological disease, deterioration, or disability. Who's to say, for example, that absence of interest in sex is abnormal according to the clinical definition? What sickness befalls the person who avoids sex? What disability? Clearly, such a person misses a life experience that some people value very highly and most value at least somewhat, but is avoiding sex "unhealthy" in the same way that avoiding protein is? Avoiding sex seems more akin to avoiding travel or avoiding swimming or avoiding investments in anything riskier than savings accounts—it's not trendy, but it's not sick, is it?

Are clinical standards that have been established for sexuality in fact based on valid and demonstrable standards of health and illness, or are they based on cultural and class opinion dressed up in scientific language? Sexual habits and preferences that do not conform to a procreative model for sex are the ones considered abnormal in medicine and clinical psychology. From lack of erection and orgasm to preference for masturbation and oral sex over intercourse to involvement of pain or items of clothing in sexual scripts—everything that is listed in contemporary psychiatric classification texts as abnormal refers to sexual practice that deviates from a preference for hetero-sexual coitus as the standard fare. Homosexual activities and affections would also still be included, except that political and scientific pressure forced the psychiatric community to "declassify" homosexuality in 1973.

A person's persistent interest in unconventional sexual expression and experience is often seen by clinicians as evidence of that individual's per-sonality immaturity, poor judgment, or extreme needs (e.g., for isolation or for humiliation). Although I agree that such patterns could be evidence of psychological problems, I would want corroborating evidence from other parts of a person's life. And I would want to see that there were negative consequences to the person's well-being other than a sense of shame or guilt from being different. The problem is that the very existence of stan-dards of normality breeds negative psychological consequences for those who deviate—that is known as the "social control" function of norms. And once norms become clinical standards, it's very difficult to identify those psychological problems that might not exist if social conformity weren't so important.

Why People Care About Being Normal

We don't want abnormal blood pressure because we don't want to feel ill or shorten our lives. But why do people want to be sexually normal if de-viance does not have harmful consequences? I think there are three inter-esting reasons.

- First, centuries of religious injunctions now transferred to medical lan-guage have convinced people that "abnormal" sexual desires, actions, or interests are always signs of mental or physical illness—in spite of the limited evidence for this assumption.

- The second reason connects adequate sexuality to relationship success and modern worries about divorce and breakup. Do sexual problems and dissatisfactions lead to divorce? Marriage counselors and therapists say that sexual dissatisfaction is often a *consequence* of marital troubles rather than a cause. An often-quoted study (published in the prestigious *New England Journal of Medicine*) of 100 self-defined "happy" couples found that there was some sort of arousal or orgasm dysfunction in the majority of cases but that the couples considered themselves happy both sexually and nonsexually nonetheless (Frank, Anderson, and Rubinstein, 1978). This is not to suggest that sexual problems or incompatibilities are trivial, but only that they are rarely the linchpin of relationships.
- The third, and I believe most important, reason that people stress the importance of sexual normality has to do with the need for social conformity. The current use of *normal* is code for socially okay, appropriate, customary, "in the ballpark." The average person uses the word in a kind of cultural-statistical way. How people feel about themselves depends to an enormous degree on the comparisons they make between themselves and others. Leon Festinger, a noted social psychologist, formulated this long-known aspect of human psychology into a formal theory in 1954.

Social comparison is the process by which people evaluate their own satisfactions and adequacy not in terms of some unique internal standard but by looking to see what others get and do. How else to decide "how we're doing"—in work, marriage, tennis, looks, health, church attendance, financial success, or any other social behavior? In the realm of sexuality, however, social comparison becomes difficult because people have no way to know *really* what other people are doing (or how they are doing it, or how they are feeling about it). Maybe that's one reason why exterior "sexiness" has become a stand-in for sexuality—at least people can measure their conformity to a stereotype of sexy looks. To evaluate their adequacy in terms of sexual behavior, people are forced to rely on depictions and discussions provided through books and other media—television, radio, magazines, and movies.

But the agenda of magazines or talk shows is not primarily to educate but rather to attract readers, viewers, and, not the least, advertisers, through providing something new and different. How often have you seen "latest findings" splashed across the cover of a magazine or paperback sex book? I think the public assumes that valid new information is continually emerging and that the media are serving a useful function by presenting it to the public. In fact, guests on *Oprah* and people quoted in magazine articles are usually just promoting their books or expressing their views— which may or may not be backed by valid evidence.

The media have created a class of sex "experts" who write magazine columns, give radio advice, talk on TV, and produce a seemingly endless number of question-and-answer books for the sexually perplexed. Is anyone with an M.D. or Ph.D. after his or her name qualified to speak authoritatively about physiology and medicine, normal and abnormal psychology, couple interactions, child-raising, or sexual abuse and assault? The audience has no idea where the expert's information comes from and only the faintest idea of what might qualify as valid research in this area. Thus it is that contemporary health professionals have replaced religious and moral leaders as sexual authorities in the public's pursuit of sexual "normalcy."

If magazines and nonfiction TV exaggerate the "new" in what they communicate about sexuality, soap operas, nighttime TV dramas, and movies exaggerate the sensational and passionate aspects. If the only knowledge of people's looks came from these media, we would rightly conclude that everyone in the world had perfect skin, hair, and teeth except ourselves. The information about sex from these sources suggests that (1) everyone wants a lot of it; (2) everyone breaks up relationships, families, and lives to get it; (3) everyone's sexual episodes are full of desperately urgent desire; and (4) the best sex is between strangers, especially strangers forbidden or prevented from consummating their desires. Even though we say that we don't take these images seriously, they shape our ideas of what is true and we end up suspecting that incredibly passionate sex is an immensely important part of many people's lives and perhaps therefore should be just as important in our own lives. A perpetual nagging disquiet is born in many people that shadows their own "ordinary" experiences.

Alfred Kinsey's revelations in 1948 and 1953 about the frequency of various sexual acts in America upset the commonly held belief that in private people were adhering to the official cultural sex norms (no premarital sex, no masturbation, no adultery, especially no adultery by wives, and so on). Prior to publication of those books, most people simply compared themselves to the official moral values and what they knew from rumor about neighbors and relatives. Some people tolerated more discrepancy from the norms than others, but at least they believed they knew where they stood. With the publication of Kinsey's surveys, that comfortable certainty disappeared. Fueled by the increasing emphasis on sexuality as a sign of social adequacy, a new era began in which the public seemed to acquire an insatiable appetite for information to answer the question, "Am I normal?"

Notes

1. These letters were written years before the risk of HIV transmission had inspired "safer sex" practices.

2. With technology and commercialization moving as fast as they are, I wonder if this assertion is still true for North Americans and Europeans.

3. At least the language shifted. It may be that the public has never surrendered the attitude that sexual transgressions really do represent moral violations.

chapter 2

SOCIAL CONSTRUCTIONISM
AND THE STUDY OF HUMAN SEXUALITY

In the past twenty years, scholarship on human sexuality has been undergoing a radical transformation, but only in some disciplines. Psychology seems not to have noticed that new theories have been proposed that are "potentially explosive in their implications for our future understanding and behavior in regard to sex" (Vicunus, 1982, p. 137). Yet there is an urgent need for new ideas and research in the psychology of sexuality. As feminist anthropologist Gayle Rubin (1984) put it,

There are historical periods in which sexuality is more sharply contested and more overtly politicized. In such periods, the domain of erotic life is, in effect, renegotiated. . . . Periods such as the 1880s in England and the 1950s in the United States recodify the relations of human sexuality. The struggles that were fought leave a residue in the form of laws, social practices, and ideologies which then affect the way sexuality is experienced long after the immediate conflicts have faded. All signs indicate that the present era is another of those watersheds. (Rubin, 1984, pp. 267, 274)

As I write, places of public sexual activity are closed "for health reasons" because of AIDS and quarantine is being discussed; censorship statutes are being passed to limit production and distribution of explicit sexual images to "protect" women and children; penal codes are specifying in ever greater detail illegal sexual activities between adults and children; and the U.S. Attorney General's Commission on Pornography (the Meese Commission) is blaming explicit sexual materials for sexual violence and abuse in our society.

History may show that the academic community did not, and perhaps could not, take a leadership role in these great sociosexual issues. Perhaps academia speaks with too fragmented a voice or on too slow a time scale. Most histories of sexuality (e.g., Weeks, 1981), however, agree that social scientists, physicians, mental health professionals, and other sexuality "experts" are increasingly relied on for advice and authority regarding social sexual policy. For this reason alone psychologists must familiarize themselves with the new scholarship on sex. Unfortunately, psychology has to date been dominated by a limited, medicalized perspective. I want to show how an alternative point of view emerging in other areas of scholarship offers exciting opportunities for psychologists.

The Social Constructionist Approach

Kenneth Gergen (1985) defined the social constructionist approach as a form of inquiry indebted to intellectual trends such as symbolic interactionism, symbolic anthropology, ethnomethodology, literary deconstructionism, existentialism, phenomenology, and social psychology. What these disciplines have in common is an emphasis on the person's active role, guided by his or her culture, in structuring the reality that affects his or her own values and behavior. This perspective is to be contrasted with empiricism and positivism, which ignore the active role of the individual in favor of the impact of external forces that can be objectively examined and analyzed.

Gergen identified four assumptions made by social constructionists:

1. The way professionals study the world is determined by available concepts, categories, and methods. Their concepts incline them toward or even dictate certain lines of inquiry while precluding others. For example, the assumption that there really are two and only two genders prevents scholars from designing studies to ask where gender conceptions come from and how they are promulgated or from looking at gender as a dependent rather than an independent variable (Kessler and McKenna, [1978] 1985).
2. Many of the concepts and categories people use in scholarship and everyday life vary considerably in their meanings and connotations over time

and across cultures. Gergen described considerable variation in concepts such as romantic love, childhood, mother's love, the self, and emotion. Accepting variation in meaning for these abstract notions makes questionnaire research or simple citation of earlier scholarship problematic.

3. The popularity and persistence of particular concepts, categories, or methods often depends more on their political usefulness than on their validity. For example, the positivist-empiricist model of statistics-driven, laboratory-based psychological research has been greatly criticized for its limitations and omissions, yet it persists because of prestige, tradition, and congruence with cultural values (Sherif, 1979; Unger, 1983).

4. Descriptions and explanations of the world are themselves forms of social action and have consequences. Gergen used as his illustration Carol Gilligan's (1982) discussion of the consequences of prominent theories of moral development to show how a system that ignored women's ethical values and ethical development became the academic standard by which moral function was judged.

Social Constructionism and Sexual Scholarship

Many scholars credit Michel Foucault's widely read 1976 essay with popularizing the view that ideas about sexuality arise in particular social-historical contexts. Foucault argued that, contrary to common belief, sexuality was not repressed during the long Victorian era only to gradually reawaken under the warming influence of twentieth-century permissiveness. Instead, he argued that there is no essential human quality or inner drive, sexuality, that is available to be repressed in one era and liberated in another. Rather, there is a human potential for consciousness, behavior, and physical experience that can be developed ("incited") by social forces of definition, regulation organization, and categorization. Sexualities and sexual experiences are produced, changed, and modified within an ever-changing sexual discourse. The modern view of sexuality as a fundamental drive that is very individualized, deeply gendered, central to personality and intimate relationships, separate from reproduction, and lifelong (literally womb-to-tomb) would be quite unrecognizable to people living in different civilizations.

Kenneth Plummer (1982) contrasted the popular drive-based view of human sexuality with the social constructionist dramaturgic metaphor of sexual script (Gagnon and Simon, 1973). Is sexuality better seen as a powerful universal biological drive that can be shaped to some degree by sociocultural forces and individual learning, or is it more akin to a "script" that is enacted in physical performance and created, not just shaped, within the sociocultural moment? The latter position leads to a vision of sexuality (1) as emerging within relationships and situations according to participants' expectations; (2) as needing to be constructed rather than controlled; (3) as available to satisfy needs for affection, protection, and gender-affirmation; and (4) as qualitatively different for children than it is for adults. The idea of a universal, inborn sexual drive is seen as a form of excuse and rationalization rather than a legitimate description.

Histories and anthropologies of sexuality are being revolutionized by the new constructionism. Whereas earlier scholarship tabulated cultural and historical variations in acts and attitudes (Ford and Beach, 1951; Lewinsohn, 1958), newer works in history (Weeks, 1981) and anthropology (Ortner and Whitehead, 1981) trace the variation and meanings of the categories and concepts themselves. There's no point in making a cross-cultural table of age at first intercourse, for example, without discussing differences in the meaning of intercourse—and differences in choreography as well. Acts of intercourse, for example, even if they all involve contact between men's and women's genitalia, have no more in common necessarily than haute couture coats and bearskins. And the experience of such acts conducted in wildly different sociocultural settings will have about as much in common as the experience of wearing the Paris coat and the bearskin. As one of the "new" histories put it, "In any approach that takes as predetermined and universal the categories of sexuality, real history disappears" (Padgug, 1979, p. 5).

Most sex researchers, grounded in biology or the decontextualized study of the individual, accept universal categories no matter how much sexual variety they document. As Jeffrey Weeks has pointed out, "Even in the case of writers like Kinsey, whose work radically demystified sexuality, and whose taxonomic efforts undermined the notions of 'normality,' the [naturalistic] concept is still traceable in the emphasis on sexual 'outlet' as opposed to beliefs or identities" (Weeks, 1982, p. 295).

Kinsey, originally a zoologist, uncritically accepted the common idea of an evolutionarily determined drive as the bedrock of sexuality. Only recently has biological determinism been seriously challenged: "Biological sexuality is only a precondition, a set of potentialities, which is never unmediated by human reality, and which becomes transformed in qualitatively new ways in human society" (Padgug, 1979, p. 9).

Patricia Miller and Martha Fowlkes (1980) have suggested that the sociological perspective on sexuality has been limited because the few sociologists who have been interested in sex have focused on deviance and social control and have studied prostitutes, nudists, transvestites, and homosexuals far more than "ordinary" heterosexuals and couples. Now that feminists and gay and lesbian scholars have entered the academy in significant numbers, they can make "dominant" forms of sexuality the object of analysis.

Aspects of the
Social Constructionist Approach

Analysis and Challenge of Categories and Concepts

The most basic, and also most difficult, aspect of studying sexuality is defining the subject matter. What is to be included? How much of the body is relevant? How much of the life span? Is sexuality an individual dimension or a dimension of a relationship? Which behaviors, thoughts, or feelings qualify as sexual—an unreturned glance? any hug? daydreams about celebrities? fearful memories of abuse? When can we use similar language for animals and people, if at all?

As Kinsey, with Wardell Pomeroy and Clyde Martin, plaintively wrote in describing their method,

> In spite of the long list of items included in the present [interview] study [anywhere from 300 to 521 items per interview], and in spite of the fact that each history has covered five times as much material as in any previous study, numerous students have suggested, and undoubtedly will continue to suggest after the publication of the present volume, that we should have secured more data in the fields of their special interests. Specifically it has been suggested that the following matters should have had more thorough investigation:

racial ancestry . . . somatotypes . . . hormonal assays . . . physical examination
of the genitalia . . . marital adjustment . . . early childhood and parental relations . . . motivations and attitudes . . . cultural and community backgrounds
. . . [and] sperm counts. (Kinsey, Pomeroy, and Martin, 1948, p. 56)

It seems that when sex researchers discuss "terminology," naturalism
and essentialism have prevented them from seeing that the discussion of
language is not a search for the "real" or "clearest" variables and terms but
an exercise in boundary setting. What should we choose, for the purposes
of a particular study, to construe as sexual?

Herant Katchadourian's (1979) psychological review of "the many
meanings of sex," for example, failed to note that all the terms discussed
(gender identity, drive, partner choice, desire, sexual experience, arousabil-
ity) described individual issues. By contrast, Michel Foucault and Richard
Sennett (1982) explicitly problematized the individualized focus of sexuality language. Their examination took them to early Christian theology and
nineteenth-century medicine. Theology, preoccupied with sexual purity
and personal obedience, and medicine, preoccupied at that time with sexual excess and insanity, construed sexuality as an individual matter within
the discourses of personal responsibility and individual disease. Theirs is a
discussion of sexual constructionism, showing how concepts are fluid, responsive, and constructed within particular contexts. There is no expectation that "the" definition of sexuality is being sought or found.

Paul Robinson (1976) examined how William Masters and Virginia
Johnson's (1966) commitment to equal sexual rights for women led them to
force their physiological findings into a procrustean conceptual bed. After
selecting a homogeneous sample and testing subjects in an environment
where the definition of sexual behavior was physical arousal and orgasm,
Masters and Johnson "found" similar patterns between men and women,
which they described in terms of a fixed four-stage "human sexual response
cycle." The persistence of this arbitrary and ill-fitting model illustrates Gergen's claim about how politics determine many categories in sexology.

Imagery and Metaphor

What kinds of things is sexuality (or sexualities) like? Sociologists John
Gagnon (1973) and William Simon (1973) intended the metaphor of dra-

matic scripts to draw our attention to learned, planned, external sources. Ethel Person (1980), a psychoanalyst, changed the metaphor to a "sex print . . . in the sense of fingerprint, unchangeable and unique . . . an individualized script that elicits erotic desire" (p. 620). She focused on the learned sources of eroticism, but with Freudian early-life determinism. Ironically, Simon (1973) had intended to exclude psychoanalytic ideas of irreversibility with a metaphor that would underscore "a continuing potential for reorderings of meanings . . . a reordering that has permanent consequences in the sense that later changes are at the very least as significant in informing current behavior as were the original or earlier meanings, and, in many instances, more significant" (p. 70).

Metaphors such as script and fingerprint, like drive and instinct, direct the attention of researchers, scholars, and readers to distinct sexual possibilities. This is what Gergen meant by saying that descriptions of the world are themselves forms of social action and have consequences. The 1973 struggle within the American Psychiatric Association over continuing to classify homosexuality as a mental disorder seemed often to be primarily about imagery in discourse about sexuality, with both proponents and opponents of "declassification" arguing that the presence of homosexuality in the official listing carried a powerful message to young people, parents, legislators, teachers, and homosexuals (Bayer, 1981).

Historical Dimensions of Sexuality Language

Historical studies are dear to social constructionists because they can point the way to analyses of cultural meanings and changing personal experiences. There's been a great deal of work on historical shifts in the construction of homosexuality, and methods developed in that work should prove extremely useful in studying all aspects of sexual experience, behavior, and identity (Plummer, 1981).

Mark Elliott (1985) counted the frequency of the terms impotence and frigidity in the psychological literature between 1940 and 1983. He found that each term appeared in titles indexed in Psychological Abstracts between two and eight times per year until 1970, when titles with impotence escalated dramatically. I have written at length about the numerous social forces contributing to this change and about the consequences of the "growth" of "impotence" for sexuality discourse and men's experiences.

Historical work is providing the greatest impetus to social constructionism in sexuality, as this work emphatically destabilizes essentialist notions.

Methods for Studying Sexuality

Gergen (1985) asserted that a constructionist analysis must "eschew the empiricist account of scientific knowledge . . . the traditional Western conception of objective, individualistic, ahistorical knowledge . . . [and embrace criteria such as] the analyst's capacity to invite, compel, stimulate, or delight the audience. . . . Virtually any methodology can be employed so long as it enables the analyst to develop a more compelling case" (pp. 271, 272, 273).

This suggestion is completely in sync with feminist complaints about the limitations and biases in positivist scholarship. To understand sexuality, scholars need to use and respect multiple methods and researcher points of view and to see experimental, correlational, participatory, and clinical methods as complementary, not competing (Carlson, 1971). Individual constructions of sexuality involve an interplay of individual and social processes that cannot be adequately explored with only one method.

Suppose scholars were to start with an idiosyncratic speculation about the psychology of sexuality such as the following:

> It is the recollection rather than the anticipation of the act that assumes a primary importance in homosexual relations. That is why the great homosexual writers of our culture can write so elegantly about the sexual act itself, because the homosexual imagination is for the most part concerned with reminiscing. . . . This is all due to concrete and practical considerations and says nothing about the intrinsic nature of homosexuality. (Foucault, 1982/1983, p. 19)

Following Gergen's lead, scholars who accepted this view would not tend to formulate empirical research to decide whether and under what circumstances it was "true" that homosexuals felt and believed this way. Rather, they would want to explore the now and then, the here and elsewhere, the who, what, when, where, and why of this speculation, without the goal of identifying once-and-for-all-truths about homosexuals. What does clinical work on the nature of fantasy have to teach us? What about theories on the nature of representation? What about cultural variations in myth and the encouragement of individual imagination? How might claims about imagination be affected by mass availability of erotic images?

Unfortunately, both the methodological eclecticism of constructionism and its tendency to place the subject at the center of the method conflict with the quest for "rigor" of many sex researchers. An important conference sponsored by the National Institute of Mental Health underscored sexology's commitment to "unambiguous concepts," "objective measurement," "operationalism," and all possible forms of scientific "control" (Green and Wiener, 1980). Nevertheless, even in that setting, one could find suggestions for more constructionist scholarship, including life histories and analyses of diverse kinds of relationships, and some workers expressed a preference for studying real situations rather than laboratory analogs.

The Medicalization of Sexuality

The major obstacle to a social constructionist approach to sexuality is the domination of theory and research by the biomedical model. As Catherine Riessman (1983) defined it, "The term medicalization refers to two interrelated processes. First, certain behaviors or conditions are given medical meaning—that is, defined in terms of health and illness. Second, medical practice becomes a vehicle for eliminating or controlling problematic experiences that are defined as deviant" (p. 4).

The ideological support for medicalization is essentialist, naturalist, biological thinking. The major constructionist project is to define and locate sexuality in personal, relational, and cultural, rather than physical, terms. This is a real uphill battle.

Analyzing the Privileged Position of Biology in Sexuality

Here's the beginning of a psychoanalytic essay about sexuality:

> The scientific picture of sexual behavior has become so distorted that we must make a serious attempt to rediscover the obvious. In any attempt of this kind, it is always well to begin again at the beginning, in this case with a brief reexamination of the evolutionary differentiation of the sexes, and

the physiologic basis of sexual activity. . . . In the most primitive protozoa, the individual propagates by itself. (Rado, 1949, p. 159)

In the beginning we always seem to find the birds and the bees: biology and reproduction, the genes and the genitals. The privileged position of biology in sexual discourse is based on the assumption that the body dictates action, experience, and meaning. Why has biological reductionism retained such a grip on sexology when it has long been dethroned from other aspects of psychology? I think there are two reasons. The contemporary reason, the political one, has to do with legitimacy for sex research. Sex is dirty, or at least risqué, but emphasizing the biological bases makes it a more reputable subject of study.

But the more profound answer has to do with Western Judeo-Christian discourse, wherein sex came to be located in the body, separated from the spirit and the mind (Petras, 1973). Foucault and Sennett (1982) argued that the Christian moral agenda of self-purification became linked with an antimasturbation preoccupation in the eighteenth century, which was in turn translated into the medical idea that sexuality exists in the individual prior to any sexual relationship or activity.

Jeffrey Weeks (1985) illuminated the deep faith of early sexologists that in the struggle between sexual ignorance and enlightenment the surest weapon would be biological science. He told how German sexologist Magnus Hirschfeld, founder of sexology journals, research institutes, and international congresses, saw his Berlin Institute seized and its papers burned by the Nazis in 1933 and yet could still write: "I believe in Science, and I am convinced that Science, and above all the natural Sciences, must bring to mankind, not only truth but with truth, Justice, Liberty and Peace" (Hirschfeld, 1935, cited in Weeks, 1985, p. 71). Feminists have also traced the reliance on biological theories to a displaced search for divine guidance. "The laws which Science was uncovering would turn out to be the expression of the will of God—revelations of the divine Plan. Thus, science would provide moral guidelines for living" (Ehrenreich and English, 1978, p. 66).

Sexual biology, at first the study of instincts, later the study of brain centers, germ plasm, hormones, and fetal development, and most recently the study of vaginal blood flow, molecular genetics, nipple enlargement, and clitoral histochemistry, would reveal nature's direction for human sexual conduct. Biological science promised that *what is* would provide direction for *what ought to be*.

Biology's privileged position within contemporary sexuality discourse thus descended from early researchers' hope that "objective science" would replace oppressive orthodoxies of the past. Yet the emphasis on biological variables can create its own oppressive constructions. An example of this is the impact of Masters and Johnson's (1966) research on female sexuality. At the same time that their description and measurement of female orgasm documented some women's physical capacities and changed some old prejudices, their exclusive focus on measurable bodily states mechanized and trivialized sexual experience and mystified social and psychological aspects of sexuality, including those which operated in the laboratory during their research (Segal, 1983).

Increasing Importance of Sexual "Adequacy"

The social support for sexual medicalization arises in part from the increasing importance of sexuality itself in modern life. Like fitness, sexuality has gained importance as part of society's glorification of youth and health, its "denial of death." German sexologist Gunter Schmidt (1983a) identified three "compensatory" functions that sexuality serves in our time:

> [Sexuality] is supposed to hold marriages and relationships together because they scarcely fulfill material functions any longer; it is supposed to promote self-realization and self-esteem in a society that makes it more and more difficult to feel worth something and needed as an individual; it is supposed to drive out coldness and powerlessness in a world bureaucratized by administration, a world walled-up in concrete landscapes and a world of disrupted relationships at home and in the community. . . . All discontent—political, social and personal—is meant to be deflected into the social and relationship sector in order to be compensated. (Schmidt, 1983a, pp. vii–viii)

In a world where gender remains very important while the proofs of gender adequacy become more elusive, sexual knowledge and performance, for both men and women, need to serve the function of proving gender adequacy, too.

The Media and the Hegemony of Sexual Medicine

As sexual interest and adequacy gain in social importance, weaknesses in one's preparation become more significant. The major source of information for the young has become mass media, both because of parents' silence and because of the dearth of sex education in the current conservative climate (Gagnon, 1985). In the twentieth century, mass media shape popular consciousness by providing language, experts, information, and fictional scripts.

Nonfiction media are dominated by a health model of sexuality, with physicians, psychologists, or other health specialists the authorities. Sex enters the print media either because of a newsworthy event ("new" research or technology, sexual crimes, escapades of celebrities) or in the form of a feature article in which authorities give their opinions of issues of normal "adjustment" ("How to Have Great New Sex with Your Same Old Spouse," Sarrel and Sarrel, 1983) or of deviance ("The Anguish of the Transsexuals," Churcher, 1980). Perhaps because of the history of censorship, the media are more comfortable with the aspects of sexuality that seem least like pornography, that is, closer to medicine and public health.

Even the science articles focus on sensational new developments, typified by "the 'G' spot" flurry of 1981 and 1982. A trade book about the "G" spot (Ladas, Whipple, and Perry, 1982), based on skimpy research that even prior to publication had been contradicted in professional journals and scientific meetings, became a bestseller in 1982. Newslike reports of a scientific "discovery," an area of unusual erotic sensitivity on the anterior wall of the vagina that related to an alleged ability of women to ejaculate fluid at orgasm, appeared in numerous women's magazines, newspapers, and sex-oriented magazines. The authors of the book appeared widely on national television. Seven book clubs purchased the book before publication. The insatiability of the media for the commercial potential of sexual topics results in an endless search for news and advice, whereas disconfirming evidence receives little or no publicity. The combination of scientific (read: biological) "news" and health-expert advice in the nonfiction media reinforces the impression that sex is very important without providing the kind of information ordinary readers or viewers can actually use. People end up with the directive to consult a professional expert—not the most empowering message.

The romantic and passion-filled portrayals of sexuality in the fiction media (e.g., movies, soap operas, television series like *Dynasty*) stroke the public's expectations. If sex can provide such power, meaning, and material rewards, if it can make or break relationships, if it is such a large part of people's lives, then the public's dependence on experts and authorities for guidance in this maelstrom increases. A constructionist approach to sexuality can elucidate how individuals, couples, and social groups are affected by the media's various messages.

Political and Economic Aspects of Professional Expansion

Cultural authority in the area of sexuality is not passively conferred on health authorities; it is actively sought, consolidated, and maintained. Through individual and group efforts, professionals take measures to ensure their autonomy, promote their economic opportunities, and increase their public status (Larson, 1977).

In sexology, professional expansion and control within health fields have been promoted through specialty organizations with restricted memberships, registries of "approved" service providers, advertising by institutional public relations offices, frequent conferences that define professional boundaries, awards, media contacts, and numerous specialized journals and newsletters. The development of "impotence" diagnosis and treatment as a subspecialty within urology illustrates many aspects of professional medicalization, as does having sexual dysfunctions defined as psychiatric disorders by the American Psychiatric Association.

Consider as an example the construction of the condition of "anorgasmia." Based on her wide familiarity with sexual patterns around the world, Margaret Mead (1955) observed, "There seems to be a reasonable basis to assuming that the human female's capacity for orgasm is to be viewed much more as a potentiality that may or may not be developed by a given culture, or in the specific history of an individual, than as an inherent part of her full humanity" (p. 166). Like playing the piano or grinding corn for tortillas, producing an orgasm is probably a universal human potential that depends on opportunity, training, and goals. But, rather than making orgasms an arbitrary matter of talent and predilection, professional interests in medicalization have made them a matter of health and disorder. Social constructionist research can analyze how people internalize the medicalized messages of sexuality professionals and how these messages contribute to their sexual scripts and expectations.

The Public's Role in the Medicalization of Sexuality

The public is also not merely a passive player reflexively responding to the proselytizing of health experts and the media. Rather, medicalized discourse about sexuality seems to be actively sought to provide both authoritative direction and self-protective attributions. The dearth of sex education plus the high importance attributed to sexuality leave the public eager, even desperate, for information from respected authorities. The morally neutral discourse of "objective medical science" provides ideal cover for sexual claims and desires that might otherwise be questioned. Feminists, for example, embraced Masters and Johnson's (1966) "proof" that women were entitled *by their biology* to sexual activity, pleasure, and orgasm. The gay community cites the American Psychiatric Association's 1973 declassification of homosexuality as evidence of its biological normalcy.

Sexuality and Psychology

Any research that emphasizes individual and group variations in sexual meaning and experience will undermine the universalistic assumptions central to the medical model. How, from the vast range of physical and mental possibilities, do people come to call certain ones sexual? How do these sexual activities come to be invested with personal meaning? How do these individual constructions change over the lifetime of a person or a relationship? We assume that the contemporary commercialization of sexuality, which has made images so much more available to the public, has changed scripts and expectations, but how? How do people incorporate what is in the culture into their own life course?

Research is needed to examine the psychological experience of words used very often in sexology: *pleasure* and *intimacy*. Pleasure is often rated as the most important element of sexual satisfaction, yet we cannot assume a universal inborn experience and there is no research concerning how people apply a "pleasure" label to aspects of sexual relations. The sex therapy literature is full of claims about the importance of intimacy to clinically healthy sexual performance, although it seems safe to assume that the vast majority of genital unions over the centuries have occurred without the presence of anything remotely like our modern idea of "self-in-intimacy."

Studies of how body image develops and influences sexual experience are also needed—do people compare themselves to cultural ideals of sexiness and, invariably falling short, suffer? Or are ideas of sexiness more dependent on early personal experiences of being praised by doting adults? What factors buffer feelings of inadequacy and which ones add fuel to the fire?

Medicalized discourse, with its smooth, superficial prescriptions for sexual experience, sets up norms and deviations without regard to the range of possible pathways and outcomes for sexual development. If constructionists succeed in reframing sexuality as constructed in interaction as a result of expectations and negotiations, psychology may move to the forefront of sexuality analysis.

John Gagnon, a social constructionist sex researcher for the past thirty years, believes that "people become sexual in the same way they become everything else. Without much reflection, they pick up directions from their social environment. They acquire and assemble meanings, skills and values from the people around them" (Gagnon, 1977, p. 2). Perceiving sexual behavior in this "ordinary" way conflicts with the popular perception of deeply buried instincts and raging hormones. The medicalized discourse has held sway because it offers respectability to sex researchers, entrepreneurs, and customers alike, but it does not offer a route to a rich understanding. It's time to give the social constructionist perspective an opportunity to develop a more compelling case.

SEXUAL BIOLOGY AND
THE SYMBOLISM OF THE NATURAL

Uses of Nature and
Naturalism in Sexology

I thought for years that sex was natural, but now I realize that I never stopped to think about exactly what I meant by that statement and what evidence existed for the claim. Let's consider some uses of naturalism language in writings about sexuality.

> The whole of sexual experience for both the human male and female is constituted in two . . . separate systems . . . that coexist *naturally*. . . . The biophysically and psychosocially based systems of influence that *naturally* coexist in any woman [can] function in mutual support. . . . Based on the manner in which an individual woman internalizes the prevailing psychosocial influence, her sexual value system may or may not reinforce her *natural* capacity to function sexually. One need only remember that sexual function can be displaced from its *natural* context temporarily or even for a lifetime in order to realize the . . . import [of the sexual value system]. . . . It seems more accurate to consider female orgasmic response as an acceptance of naturally occurring stimuli that have been given erotic significance by an individual sexual value system than to depict it as a learned response. (Masters and Johnson, 1970, pp. 219, 297, emphasis added)

> Present-day legal determinations of sexual acts which are acceptable, or *natural*, and those which are "contrary to *nature*," are not based on data

obtained from biologists, nor from *nature* herself. (Kinsey, Pomeroy, and Martin, 1948, p. 202, emphasis added)

It is an essential part of our conceptual apparatus that the sexes are a polarity, and a dichotomy in *nature*. (Greer, 1971, p. 15, emphasis added)

The *nature* of the society in which a people live clearly plays a significant part in shaping the patterns of human sexual behavior. . . . Human societies appear to have seized upon and emphasized a *natural*, physiological determined inclination toward intercourse between males and females, and to have discouraged and inhibited many other equally *natural* kinds of behavior. We believe that under purely hypothetical conditions in which any form of social control was lacking, coitus between males and females would prove to be the most frequent type of sexual behavior. (Ford and Beach, 1951, p. 19, emphasis added)

This *natural* instinct which with all conquering force and might demands fulfillment. (Richard von Krafft-Ebing, *Psychopathia Sexualis*, 1886, quoted in Weeks, 1985, p. 69, emphasis added)

Raymond Williams (1976), the historian of culture, identified three uses of the term *nature* and located their origins in seventeenth-century Enlightenment political debates. He began his discussion, by the way, by saying that *nature* is "perhaps the most complex word in the language" (p. 219).

According to the first use, *nature* refers to the *essential quality* of something. For the author of the fourth quotation above, for example, "the nature of the society in which a people live" means the essential quality of the society. Nature here is a metaphor for what is bottom, bedrock, fundamental. Once the essence of something is its *nature*, then other uses of *nature* acquire the connotation of basic, bedrock.

The second use Williams identified is nature as an *inherent force* directing the world. This meaning can be seen in the second quotation's use of the phrase "contrary to nature." This legal term, which is still in use, means that some sexual act is opposed to a higher force directing the world, nature here as successor or stand-in for God. Don't fool with Mother Nature. Power is connoted here.

The third use is *nature* as *material world*, particularly as *fixed* material world. This meaning seems to be the most common one in the sexological quotes above: The third quote says the sexes are a dichotomy in nature, that is, they are a fixed dichotomy in the material world; the first quote says female orgasm is natural, that it definitely exists in the material world. Nature "herself" is referred to in the second quote: "Present-day legal determinations . . . are not based on data obtained . . . from nature herself"; in other words, the existence of a material world that lies outside of human intervention is assumed. Independence, objectivity, and a contrast with human culture are connoted here.

The term *nature* is often used in sexology for its rhetorical power. By emphasizing that something is *in nature*, an author gives whatever is being discussed solidity and validity. That special rhetorical power often seems to call on nature *by contrast with culture*, as if anything human-made can be the result of trickery, but something prior to and outside of human culture can be trusted. The laws of nature, for example, are thought to be above human politics, while the laws of people are polluted with politics (Schiebinger, 1986). The term confers the authority of something before or underneath culture, something prior to culture. Sexual nature, then, sounds like something solid and valid, not human-made.

But there are two more aspects of the rhetorical power conveyed to orgasm or intercourse or certain sexual acts or instincts by calling them *natural*. The first is *universality*. Part of the rhetorical power comes from generalizing what's natural and therefore presocial into what's natural and therefore *universal*. Because human culture has not yet interfered with something that is natural, the allegedly natural act or instinct is thought to be part of the essence of being human and therefore universal to the human condition.

Finally, the quality of *biological* is implied, since what else is *universal, presocial*, and of the *essence* but *biology*? It is biology that is contrasted with culture when a sexologist uses the term *nature*. *Natural orgasm* is universal and a biological thing; *natural intercourse* is universal and a biological thing; *natural sexuality* is universal and a biological thing.

I submit that the term *natural* is used so frequently in sexologic discourse because of *rhetorical needs for justification and legitimacy*. *Nature* and *natural* are used to persuade, not to describe or to give information. In the quotations above, the rhetorical efforts are most apparent in the language of Masters and Johnson, where presocial, universal, and biological connotations of *nature* help support their theses about the importance and propriety of men's and, especially, women's sexuality.

But sexologists use the rhetoric of naturalism not just to endorse the value of sexuality but to increase their own respectability as scholars of sexuality. Respectability is a chronic problem in this field. Many sex researchers will sympathize with the tone of these words by George Corner, a leading sex endocrinologist of the twentieth century:

> In 1922 the National Research Council was called upon by influential groups . . . to bring together existing knowledge and to promote research upon human sex behavior and reproduction. . . . The Committee for Research in Problems of Sex, with financial support from the Rockefeller Foundation, successfully undertook to encourage research on a wide range of problems of sex physiology and behavior. The younger readers of this book will hardly be able to appreciate the full significance of [this]. . . . It represented a major break from the so-called Victorian attitude which in the English-speaking countries had long impeded scientific and sociologic investigation of sexual matters and placed taboos on open consideration of human mating and childbearing as if these essential activities were intrinsically indecent. To investigate such matters, even in the laboratory with rats and rabbits, required of American scientists . . . a certain degree of moral stamina. A member of the Yerkes Committee once heard himself introduced by a fellow scientist to a new acquaintance as one of the men who had "made sex respectable." (Corner, 1961)

This quotation highlights an important point about how the language of naturalism, with its implications of biological universality, allows researchers to keep the focus of their work on some phenomenon called "sexuality" even while replacing human subjects with rats and rabbits (Hall, 1974). We sex researchers study "sexual" behaviors in all these species and believe we are studying some uniform and universal phenomenon, albeit manifested in somewhat differing form across species. This paves the way for studies of "homosexuality" and "courtship" in animals and "mating behavior" and "copulation" in humans. It's all sexuality, after all, in one big happy mammalian family.

Origins of the Use
of *Nature* and *Naturalism*

I alluded earlier to seventeenth-century European sources that used the language of naturalism (Williams, 1976). Let me say a little more about this period in order to demonstrate that these terms originated in a *particular* time for *particular* purposes and thereby shed some light on the rhetoric involved in contemporary uses of such language.

Philosophers and historians of science remind us that a call for a scientific approach to knowledge—an approach dedicated to studying "the laws of nature" objectively—arose during the Enlightenment to reinforce democratic politics in Britain and Europe (Bloch and Bloch, 1980). Writers of the period called on nature for a source of authority and legitimacy other than mysticism or monarchy; laws of nature were to compete with laws of kings and popes.

Political philosophers of the sixteenth and seventeenth centuries invoked a hypothetical state of nature, subject to the laws of nature, to support political theories based on individuals' free and rational acceptance of the social contract. Such theories were intended to support the right of the people to resist the doctrine of the divine right of kings as well as to resist abuses of power by the church. Recourse to the concept of the state of nature and its laws represented an effort to invoke a presocial design for the world (Williams's second definition) that would trump the mere historical legitimacies of states. Appeals to the reason and dignity of man as given by nature supported claims for individual human rights and aspirations and for equality (Schiebinger, 1986).

At the same time, nature, this time the mere material world, to use Williams's third meaning, was invoked throughout the writings of seventeenth-century scientists such as Francis Bacon and René Descartes as something waiting to be tamed and controlled through man's use of reason (Lloyd, 1984). Emancipated from ignorance and fear, making use of the new economic and technological opportunities of the time, man (often the male of the human species and not the generic *man*) would master nature, rip the veil from nature, and so on. The rhetorical uses of nature as presocial, universal, and biological thus arose as political rhetoric in this intense cauldron of social change and have shaped our language and imagery since.

Feminist Challenge to
the Language of Naturalism

Throughout the current women's movement, the language and implications of naturalism have been a special target of attack (Lowe and Hubbard, 1983). Feminist scholars have attacked the ideology of male supremacy based on assumptions about male and female nature as prime supports for sex-role stereotyping and women's social, economic, and political oppression. Feminists have implicitly recognized the political dangers of the use of naturalism language—on the one hand, *natural* was used in the normative sense to imply good, healthy, and moral, yet at the same time it connoted something biologically based, fixed, and presocial. That is, feminists worried that through the use of naturalism metaphors, what is would be assumed to be what should be. Reflecting these fears, the title of one book was *Woman's Nature: Rationalizations of Inequality* (Lowe and Hubbard, 1983).

The explosive rise of sociobiology in the mid-1970s seemed to be a backlash confirming the feminists' fears. Biological, evolutionary, and animal research was recruited to justify the status quo. Donald Symons' (1979) sociobiology text, for example, argued that "there is a female human nature and a male human nature and these natures are extraordinarily different, though the differences are to some extent masked . . . by moral injunctions" (p. v).

And what are these different sexual natures? Symons compiled field and laboratory studies and made generous generalizations from these studies to support his conclusion that there are "natural" differences in how men and women experience desire, jealousy, sexual pleasure, orgasm, and wishes for partner variety. Perversely, Symons's book seems unusually open-minded in its discussion of language, including issues concerning natural language and the idea of a natural environment, the semantics of ultimate causation, and the relation of human culture to evolution. Symons even concluded his book with this caution: "Tendencies to equate 'natural' and 'good' and to find dignity in biological adaptation can only impede understanding of ultimate causation and distort perceptions of nonhuman animals, preliterate peoples, and history" (Symons, 1979, p. 313).

Yet, as reviewers in *Science* (Shapiro, 1980), *The Quarterly Review of Biology* (Hrdy, 1979), and *The New York Review of Books* (Geertz, 1980) all pointed out, Symons's "freewheeling" search for universals through a random pastiche of evidence from academic scholarship to Frank Harris and Shere Hite frequently violated his own cautionary note. He ended up, as might be predicted, even criticizing feminist political demands. Thus is it always, feminists would say, when nature is valorized.

In the 1960s and 1970s, feminist theory and research were directed to patiently correcting ideas about women by identifying the causes of gender differences in the multiple influences of socialization and social structure as contrasted with any "natural" inevitability of biological determinism. This painstaking social science accumulation was and continues to be productive.

But, as Ruth Bleier (1986) finally concluded, research on and claims about sex differences, especially those linked to biology, are, like Banquo's ghost, impossible to kill. If it isn't the size of brains, then it's mathematical ability; if it isn't impulses toward aggression, then it's interhemispheric transfer of information; if it isn't preferences in types of play activities, then it's pleasure in genital sexuality. A modern society built on sex differences requires continual infusions of supportive science, and the media, as Lynda Birke (1986) and others have shown, feeds on conceptual simplicity and polarizations. Thus, studies with positive sex differences are frequently featured in *The New York Times*, and if the evidence can be attributed to biological factors, the study will often make the front page.

In the 1980s a new strategy of feminist scholarship emerged, not to correct false ideas of female nature, not to show the social distortion of natural female capacity by institutionalized oppression, but to challenge the whole notion of naturalism through the idea of social construction. Feminist primatologist Donna Haraway (1986) discussed this shift in an essay entitled "Primatology Is Politics by Other Means."

> The past, the animal, the female, nature: these are the contested zones in the discourse of primatology. . . . [But] rarely will feminist contests for scientific meaning work by replacing one paradigm with another, by proposing . . . alternative accounts and theories. Rather, as a form of narrative practice or storytelling, feminist practice in primatology has worked more by altering a "field" of stories or possible explanatory accounts, by raising the cost of defending some accounts, by destabilizing the plausibility of

some strategies of explanation. . . . Feminist science is about changing possibilities. (Haraway, 1986, pp. 115; 81)

While Haraway supports efforts to challenge existing theories of gender
difference by showing female primates capable of competition, mobility,
aggression, and sexual assertion, she argued that showing that females are
"just like and therefore just as good as males" is ultimately a doomed strategy that perpetuates the focus on gender as difference and on male norms.

Narrative analysis, however, along with other forms of postpositivist research (Guba, 1990), conflicts with sexology's continuing needs for legitimacy. Recall George Corner's (1961) comment that studying the sex
physiology and behavior of rats and rabbits was the only way early researchers had of getting into otherwise risqué and taboo sex research. Writing about psychology, Carolyn Sherif (1979) argued that reductionism
wouldn't disappear until the prestige hierarchy in science changed; "What
psychology defined as basic was dictated by slavish devotion to the more
prestigious disciplines. Thus, a physiological or biochemical part or element
was defined as more basic than a belief that Eve was created from Adam's
rib, not because the former can necessarily tell us more about a human individual, but because physiology and biochemistry were more prestigious than
religious history or sociology" (p. 100).

Following the lead of scholars examining the particularities of the Enlightenment origins of science, feminists eager to "destabilize the plausi-
bility of these strategies of explanation" have challenged the definition of
the experimental "subject," the role of technology, and the role of quan-
tification as they allowed the new field of psychology, particularly in the
United States, to differentiate itself from philosophy (e.g., Hornstein,
1989). Psychology strove to gain scientific respectability with displays of
technique and language demonstrating alliance and identification with
better-established fields. The history of sex research will tell the same tale
about the inclusion and exclusion of methods and theories as part of the
quest for legitimacy.

Thus, biological sex research is a target for feminist analysis and deconstruction not only because of its ties to notions of male and female nature
but because it dominates the scientific prestige hierarchy and prevents alternate forms of knowledge from achieving legitimacy.

Postmodern
Scholarship and "Denaturalization"

Scholars in many disciplines identify postmodernism as a contemporary shift in worldview and the construction of reality. As one leading feminist author has said, "Postmodern discourses are all 'deconstructive' in that they seek to distance us from and make us skeptical about beliefs concerning truth, knowledge, power, the self and language that are often taken for granted within and serve as legitimation for contemporary Western culture" (Flax, 1987, p. 624). *Discourses,* of course, can be scientific or academic treatises or they can be diaries, poems, productions on the analyst's couch, lullabies, or filmscripts. Postmodernism is about challenging absolutes in favor of multiple points of view. It's about honoring the contexts of observations and concepts and contesting objectivity and privileged access to the "way things really are." It's about acknowledging change and the difficulty of definitive pronouncements. It's about permanent instability.

William Simon (1989), discussing postmodernism as it affects sex research, identified the "emergent consensus about the absence of consensus" (p. 18) as the central theme of postmodernism, "a sense of being forced to an unexpected and often discomforting pluralism" (p. 19). Such a skeptical position concerning truth, knowledge, power, the self, and language will inevitably challenge concepts of nature and naturalism. Simon argued that in fact postmodernism *is about* denaturalization: "In effect . . . what is implied is the reading of the sexual 'against the grain,' i.e., reinterpreting the predominant biological explanatory concepts as metaphorical illusions" (p. 24).

This perspective has so far had its strongest impact on the history of sexuality (Duggan, 1990) and the notion of sexual object choice or sexual identity (e.g., Boswell, 1990). The postmodern boom in scholarship, especially in the interpretive disciplines of anthropology and history, offers a powerful opportunity to challenge the "naturalistic" categories, concepts, and metaphors about sexuality.

I view my scholarship in sexology as a version of postmodernism. It is committed to diversity and relativism and regards human physiology as providing a set of physical possibilities unlabeled as to use or meaning. Penile erection, for example, that centerpiece of much contemporary sex research, might or might not have anything to do with pleasure or procreation or display or domination or anxiety or hypochondriasis or ego-satisfaction or intromission into another person. It all depends on the context and how that physical possibility is socially constructed.

Conclusion

The perspective that biological sex research is more basic than other approaches because it examines something closer to nature, that is, something presocial and thus more generalizable than anything learned or influenced by culture, can be traced to European Enlightenment constructions of nature and the natural world, which served the particularities of Enlightenment politics, and its persistence can be traced to the rhetoric used in scientific and sexological claims to legitimacy. But this construction is coming under challenge from many directions. Historian Ludmilla Jordanova (1989) wrote:

> Over the last 20 years or so historians have become aware of the need to unpack the processes through which "naturalization" takes place, whereby ideas, theories, experiences, languages, and so on, take on the quality of being "natural," permitting the veiling of their customary, conventional and social characteristics. Understanding such naturalization is integral to the project of delineating and explaining the precise nature of scientific and medical power. (Jordanova, 1989, p. 5)

Biological sex research, the language of sex as a "natural act," is popular in large part because it accesses and maintains prevailing scientific authority. But there are other equally persuasive and more inclusive ways to construe sexuality, if we can manage to shake loose of that prestige hierarchy of knowledge. Postmodernism offers feminism a powerful ally for the shaking.

HISTORICAL, SCIENTIFIC, CLINICAL, AND FEMINIST CRITICISMS OF "THE HUMAN SEXUAL RESPONSE CYCLE" MODEL

The sexuality that is measured is taken to be the definition of sexuality itself.

—LIONEL TRILLING

The Human Sexual Response Cycle Metaphor: A Universal Machine Without a Motor

The idea of the human sexual response cycle (HSRC) by that name was initially introduced by William Masters and Virginia Johnson (1966) to describe the sequence of physiological changes they observed and measured during laboratory-performed sexual activities such as masturbation and coitus. The goal of their research was to answer the question: "What physical reactions develop as the human male and female respond to effective sexual stimulation?" (Masters and Johnson, 1966, p. 4). Although they coined terms for their four stages, it appears that the metaphor of "the" overall sexual "cycle" was assumed from the very outset. They wrote: "A more concise picture of physiologic reaction to sexual stimuli may be presented by dividing *the human male's and female's cycles* of sexual response into four separate phases. . . . This arbitrary four-part division of *the sexual response cycle* provides an effective framework for detailed description of physiological variants in sexual reaction" (p. 4, emphasis added).

The cycle metaphor indicates that Masters and Johnson envisioned sexual response from the start as a built-in, orderly sequence of events that would tend to repeat itself. The idea of a four-stage cycle brings to mind examples such as the four seasons of the annual calendar or the four-stroke internal combustion engine. Whether the cycle is designed by human agency or "nature," once begun it cycles independently of its origins, perhaps with some variability, but without reorganization or added stages, and the same cycle applies to everyone.

The idea of a sexual response cycle has some history, although its precursors focused heavily on an element omitted from the HSRC—the idea of sexual drive. In his intellectual history of modern sexology, Paul Robinson (1976) saw the origin of Masters and Johnson's four-stage HSRC in Havelock Ellis's theme of "tumescence and detumescence."[1]

But the language of tumescence and detumescence was popular even prior to Ellis. In his analysis of Freud's theory of the libido, Frank Sulloway (1979) discussed nineteenth-century German and Austrian sexological ideas in circulation while Freud was writing. Sulloway pointed out that many sexological terms associated with Freud, such as *libido* and *erotogenic zones*, were in widespread use in European medical writings by the turn of the century, and he credited Albert Moll (then "possibly the best-known authority on sexual pathology in all of Europe" though "an obscure figure today") with originating a theory of two sexual drives—one of attraction and the other of detumescence (Sulloway, 1979, p. 302).

It is significant that, despite this long heritage of sexologic theorizing about sexual "energy," Masters and Johnson's model of sexual response did not include initiating components. Their omission of sexual drive, libido, desire, passion, and the like would return to haunt clinical sexology in the 1970s. Actually, in avoiding discussion of sexual drive, Masters and Johnson were following a trend peculiar to sexologists (in contrast to psychiatrists and psychoanalysts) during the twentieth century. Perhaps because of the history of elaborate but vague nineteenth-century writings, perhaps because of the subjective connotations of *desire*, talk of sex drive seemed to cause nothing but confusion for modern sexual scientists interested in operational definitions. Kinsey used the term only in passing, and meant by it "sexual capacity," the capacity to respond to stimulation with physical arousal (e.g., Kinsey, Pomeroy, Martin, and Gebhard, 1953, p. 102). Sexologists could compare individuals and groups in terms of this hypothetical internal mechanism, capacity, by looking at their frequencies of sexual behavior, thresholds for response, and so on with no reference to internal experience.

Frank Beach (1956), writing during the time Masters and Johnson were beginning their physiological observations, argued that talking about sex *drive* is usually circular and unproductive and approvingly noted that even Kinsey "equates sexual drive with frequency of orgasm." Beach suggested that sexual *drive* had nothing to do with "genuine biological or tissue needs" and that the concept should be replaced by sexual *appetite*, which is "a product of experience, . . .   [with] little or no relation to biological or physiological needs" (Beach, 1956, p. 4). Although the concept of appetite never caught on in sexology, the recent rediscovery of "desire" indicates that ignoring the issue of initiation of sexual behaviors did not solve the problem.

By omitting the concept of drive from their model, Masters and Johnson eliminated an element of sexuality that is notoriously variable within populations and succeeded in proposing a universal model seemingly without much variability. In what I think is the only reference to sexual drive in their text, Masters and Johnson indicated their belief that the sexual response cycle was actually an inborn drive to orgasm: "The cycle of sexual response, with orgasm as the ultimate point in progression, generally is believed to develop from a drive of biologic origin deeply integrated into the condition of human existence" (Masters and Johnson, 1966, p. 127). The cycle of sexual response, then, reflects the operation of an inborn program, like the workings of a mechanical clock. As long as the "effective sexual stimulation" (i.e., energy source) continues, the cycle proceeds through its set sequence.

Scientific Criticisms of the HSRC Model

Masters and Johnson proposed a universal model for sexual response. At no point did they talk of "a" human sexual response cycle, but only of "the" human sexual response cycle. The critique of the HSRC model begins with a discussion of the generalizability of Masters and Johnson's research results. Analysis of their work shows that the existence of the HSRC was assumed before the research began and that this assumption guided subject selection and research methods.

Subject Selection Biases:
Orgasm with Coital and Masturbatory Experience
In a passage buried four pages from the end of their text, Masters and Johnson revealed that for their research they had established "a *require-ment* that there be a positive history of masturbatory and coital orgasmic experience before any study subject [could be] accepted into the program" (Masters and Johnson, 1966, p. 311, emphasis added). This requirement in and of itself would seem to invalidate any notion that the HSRC is universal. It indicates that Masters and Johnson's research was designed to identify physiological functions of subjects who had experienced *particular,* preselected sexual responses. That is, rather than the HSRC being the best-fit model chosen to accommodate the results of their research, the HSRC actually guided the selection of subjects for the research.

Two popularizations of Masters and Johnson's physiological research commented on this element of subject selection but disregarded its implications for HSRC generalizability:

> Men and women unable to respond sexually and to reach orgasm were also weeded out. Since this was to be a study of sexual responses, those unable to respond could contribute little to it. (Brecher and Brecher, 1966, p. 54)

> If you are going to find out what happens, obviously you must work with those to whom it happens. (Lehrman, 1970, p. 170)

"Unable to respond"? If you want to study human singing behaviors, do you only select international recording artists? One could just as easily argue that there are many sexually active and sexually responsive men and women who do not regularly experience orgasm during masturbation and/or coitus whose patterns of physiological arousal and subjective pleasure were deliberately excluded from the sample. No research was undertaken to investigate "human" sexual physiology and subjectivity, only to measure the responses of an easily orgasmic sample. The "discovery" of the HRSC was a self-fulfilling prophecy, with the research subjects selected so as to compress diversity. The HSRC cannot be universalized to the general population.

The apparently identical performance requirements for male and female research subjects masked the bias of real-world gender differences in masturbatory experience. Masters and Johnson began their physiological research in 1954. In 1953, the Kinsey group had reported that only "58 percent of the females" in their sample had been "masturbating to orgasm at some time in their lives" (Kinsey, Pomeroy, Martin, and Gebhard, 1953, p. 143). Married women, the predominant subjects in Masters and Johnson's research, had even lower masturbatory frequencies than divorced or single women. This contrasts with the 92 percent incidence of men with masturbatory experience reported by the same researchers (Kinsey, Pomeroy, and Martin, 1948, p. 339). Masters and Johnson had to find men and women with similar sexual patterns despite having been raised in dissimilar sociosexual worlds. Obviously, because of this requirement the women research participants were less representative than the men.

Subject Selection Biases: Class Differences

Just as Masters and Johnson chose subjects with certain types of sexual experiences, they deliberately chose subjects who did not represent a cross-section of socioeconomic backgrounds. They wrote: "As discussed, the sample was weighted *purposely* toward higher than average intelligence levels and socioeconomic backgrounds. *Further selectivity* was established . . . to determine willingness to participate, facility of sexual responsiveness, and ability to communicate finite details of sexual reaction" (Masters and Johnson, 1966, p. 12, emphasis added). Masters and Johnson's popularizers disparaged the possible bias introduced by this selectivity with such comments as, "The higher than average educational level of the women volunteers is hardly likely to affect the acidity of their vaginal fluids" (Brecher and Brecher, 1966, p. 60).

But one cannot simply dismiss possible class differences in physiology with an assertion that there are none. *Could* differences in social location affect the physiology of sexuality? The irony of assuming that physiology is universal and therefore that class differences make no difference is that no one conducts research that asks the question.

In fact, Kinsey and his colleagues had shown wide differences between members (especially males) of different socioeconomic classes with regard to incidence and prevalence of masturbation, premarital sexual activities, petting (including breast stimulation), sex with prostitutes, positions used in intercourse, oral-genital sex, and even nocturnal emissions. For example, "There are 10 to 12 times as frequent nocturnal emissions among males of the upper educational classes as there are among males of the lower classes" (Kinsey, Pomeroy, and Martin, 1948, p. 345). Kinsey noted, "It is particularly interesting to find that there are [great] differences between educational levels in regard to nocturnal emissions—a type of sexual outlet which one might suppose would represent involuntary behavior" (p. 343). Given this finding, doesn't it seem possible, even likely, that numerous physiological details might indeed relate to differences in sexual habits? Kinsey also mentioned class differences in latency to male orgasm (p. 580). The more the variation in physiological details among subjects from different socioeconomic backgrounds, the less the HSRC is appropriate as a universal norm.

Subject Selection Biases: Sexual Enthusiasm

Masters and Johnson concluded their physiological research text as follows: "Through the years of research exposure, the one factor in sexuality that consistently has been present among members of the study-subject population has been a basic interest in and desire for effectiveness of sexual performance. *This one factor may represent the major area of difference between the research study subjects and the general population*" (Masters and Johnson, 1966, p. 315, emphasis added).

Masters and Johnson do not explain what they mean by their comment that "the general population" might not share the enthusiasm for sexual performance of their research subjects and do not speculate at all on the possible impact of this comment on the generalizability of their results. Whereas at first it may seem reasonable to assume that everyone has "a basic interest in and desire for effectiveness of sexual performance," on closer examination the phrase "*effectiveness* of sexual *performance*" seems not so much to characterize everyone as to identify devotees of a particular sexual style.

We get some small idea of Masters and Johnson's research subjects from the four profiles given in Chapter 19 of *Human Sexual Response* (1966).

These profiled subjects were selected by the authors from the 382 women and 312 men who participated in their study. The two women described had masturbated regularly (beginning at ages ten and fifteen, respectively), had begun having intercourse in adolescence (at ages fifteen and seventeen), and were almost always orgasmic and occasionally multiorgasmic in the laboratory. For the first woman, twenty-six and currently unmarried, it was explicitly stated that "sexual activity [was] a major factor in [her] life" (Masters and Johnson, 1966, p. 304) and that she became a research subject because of "financial demand and sexual tension" (p. 305). No comparable information was given about the second woman, who was thirty-one and married, but she and her husband had "stated categorically" that they had "found [research participation] of significant importance in their marriage" (p. 307).

The unmarried male subject, age twenty-seven, was described as having had adolescent onset of masturbation, petting, and heterosexual intercourse as well as four reported homosexual experiences at different points in his life. The married man, age thirty-four, had had little sexual experience until age twenty-five. He and his wife of six years had joined the research program "hoping to acquire knowledge to enhance the sexual component of their marriage" (Masters and Johnson, 1966, p. 311). The researchers noted, "[His] wife has stated repeatedly that subsequent to [research project] participation her husband has been infinitely more effective both in stimulating and satisfying her sexual tensions. He in turn finds her sexually responsive without reservation. Her freedom and security of response are particularly pleasing to him" (p. 311).

Every discussion of sex research methodology emphasizes the effects of volunteer bias and bemoans the reliance on samples of convenience that characterizes its research literature (e.g., Green and Wiener, 1980). Masters and Johnson make no attempt to compare their research subjects with any other research sample, saying, "There are no established norms for male and female sexuality in our society . . . [and] there is no scale with which to measure or evaluate the sexuality of the male and female study-subject population" (Masters and Johnson, 1966, p. 302). Although there may not be "norms," there are other sex research surveys of attitudes and behavior. For example, volunteers for sex research are usually shown to be more liberal in their attitudes than socioeconomically comparable nonvolunteer groups (Hoch, Safir, Peres, and Shepher, 1981; Clement, 1990).

How might the sample's interest in "effective sexual performance" have affected Masters and Johnson's research and their description of the HSRC? The answer relates both to the consequences of ego-investment in sexual performance and to the impact of specialization in a sexual style focused on orgasm, and we don't know what such consequences might be. I cannot specify the effect of this sexually skewed sample any more than I could guess what might be the consequences for research on singing of only studying stars of the Metropolitan Opera. The point is that the subject group was exceptional, and only by *assuming* HSRC universality can we generalize its results to others.

Experimenter Bias in the Sexuality Laboratory

Masters and Johnson made no secret of the fact that subjects volunteering for their research underwent a period of adjustment, or a "controlled orientation program," as they called it (Masters and Johnson, 1966, p. 22). This "period of training" helped the subjects "gain confidence in their ability to respond successfully while subjected to a variety of recording devices" (p. 23). Such a training period provided an opportunity for numerous kinds of "experimenter biases," as they are known in social psychology research, wherein the expectations of the experimenters are communicated to the subjects and have an effect on their behavior (Rosenthal, 1966). The fact that Masters and Johnson repeatedly referred to episodes of sexual activity with orgasm as "successes" and those without orgasm or without rigid erection or rapid ejaculation as "failures" (e.g., Masters and Johnson, 1966, p. 313) makes it seem highly likely that their performance standards were communicated to their subjects. Moreover, they were candid about their role as sex therapists for their subjects: "When female orgasmic or male ejaculatory failures develop in the laboratory, the *situation is discussed* immediately. Once the individual has been *reassured, suggestions* are made for improvement of future performance" (p. 314, emphasis added).

Another example of the tutelage provided is given in the quotation from the thirty-four-year-old man described in Chapter 19 of their book. He and his wife had entered the program hoping to obtain sexual instruction and seemed to have received all they expected and more. Masters and Johnson appeared to be unaware of any incompatibility between the roles of research subject and student or patient. Again, this reveals their preexisting standards for sexual response and their interest in measuring in the laboratory only sexual patterning consisting of erections, orgasms, ejaculations, whole-body physical arousal, and so on, that is, that which they already defined as sexual response.

In addition to overt instruction and feedback, social psychology alerts us to the role of covert cues. Research has shown that volunteer subjects often are more sensitive to experimenters' covert cues than are nonvolunteers (Rosenthal and Rosnow, 1969). One could speculate that sex research volunteers characterized by a "desire for effective sexual performance" may well be especially attentive to covert as well as overt indications that they are performing as expected in the eyes of the white-coated researchers.

The Bias of "Effective" Sexual Stimulation

As mentioned near the beginning of this chapter, Masters and Johnson set out to answer the question, "What physical reactions develop as the human male and female respond to effective stimulation?" (Masters and Johnson, 1966, p. 4). What is "effective" sexual stimulation? In fact, I think this is a key question in deconstructing the HSRC. Masters and Johnson stated, "It constantly should be borne in mind that the primary research interest has been concentrated quite literally upon what men and women do in response to effective sexual stimulation" (p. 20).

The *intended* emphasis in this sentence, I believe, is that the authors' "primary" interest was not in euphemism, and not in vague generality, but in the "literal" physical reactions people experience during sexual activity. I think the *actual* emphasis of the sentence, however, is that the authors were interested in only one type of sexual response, that which people experience in reaction to a particular type of stimulation. Such a perspective would be akin to vision researchers only being interested in optic system responses to lights of certain wavelengths, say, red and yellow, or movement physiologists only being interested in physical function during certain activities, such as running.

In each of the book's chapters devoted to the physical reactions of a particular organ or group of organs (e.g., clitoris, penis, uterus, respiratory system), Masters and Johnson began by stating their intention to look at the responses to "effective sexual stimulation." But where is that specific type of stimulation described? Although the phrase appears dozens of times in the text, it is not in the glossary or the index, and no definition or description can be found. The reader must discover that *"effective sexual stimulation" is that stimulation which facilitates a response that conforms to the HSRC.* This conclusion is inferred from observations such as the following, taken from the section on labia minora responses in the chapter on "female external genitalia": "Many women have progressed well into plateau-phase levels of sexual response, had the effective stimulative techniques withdrawn, and been unable to achieve orgasmic-phase tension release. . . . When an obviously effective means of sexual stimulation is withdrawn and orgasmic-phase release is not achieved, the minor-labial coloration will fade rapidly" (Masters and Johnson, 1966, p. 41).

Effective stimulation is that stimulation which facilitates "progress" from one stage of the HSRC to the next, particularly that which facilitates orgasm. Any stimulation resulting in responses other than greater physiological excitation and orgasm is defined by exclusion as "ineffective" and is not of interest to these authors.

This emphasis on "effective stimulation" sets up a tautology comparable to that resulting from biased subject selection. The HSRC cannot be a scientific *discovery* if the acknowledged "primary research interest" was to study stimulation defined as that which facilitates the HSRC. Again, the HSRC, "with orgasm as the ultimate point in progression" (Masters and Johnson, 1966, p. 127), preordained the results.

Clinical Criticisms of the HSRC Model

The HSRC model has had a profound impact on clinical sexology through its role as the centerpiece of contemporary diagnostic nomenclature. In this section, I will first discuss how contemporary nomenclature came to rely on the HSRC model and then describe what I see as several deleterious consequences.

HSRC and the DSM Classification of Sexual Disorders
I have elsewhere detailed the development of sexual dysfunction nosology in the four sequential editions of the American Psychiatric Association's

Diagnostic and Statistical Manual of Mental Disorders (DSM) (Tiefer, 1992b). Over a period of thirty-five years, the nosology evolved from not listing sexual dysfunctions at all (APA, 1952, or *DSM-I*) to listing them as symptoms of psychosomatic disorders (APA, 1968, or *DSM-II*), as a subcategory of psychosexual disorders (APA, 1980, or *DSM-III*), and as a subcategory of sexual disorders (APA, 1987, or *DSM-III-R*).

The relation of this nosology to the HSRC language can be seen in the introduction to the section on sexual dysfunctions (identical in both *DSM-III* and *DSM-III-R*):[2]

> The *essential feature* is inhibition in the appetitive or psychophysiological changes that characterize *the complete sexual response cycle.* The complete sexual response cycle can be divided into the following phases: 1. Appetitive. This consists of fantasies about sexual activity and a desire to have sexual activity. 2. Excitement. This consists of a subjective sense of sexual pleasure and accompanying physiological changes. . . . 3. Orgasm. This consists of a peaking of sexual pleasure, with release of sexual tension and rhythmic contraction of the perineal muscles and pelvic reproductive organs. . . . 4. Resolution. This consists of a sense of general relaxation, well-being, and muscular relaxation. (APA, 1987, pp. 290–291, emphasis added)

In fact, this cycle is not identical to Masters and Johnson's HSRC (although it, too, uses the universalizing language of "the" sexual response cycle). The first, or appetitive, phase was added when sexologists confronted clinical problems having to do with sexual disinterest. In their second book (1970), Masters and Johnson loosely used their HSRC physiological research to generate a list of sexual dysfunctions: premature ejaculation, ejaculatory incompetence, orgasmic dysfunction (women's), vaginismus, and dyspareunia (men's and women's). These were put forth as deviations from the HSRC that research had revealed as the norm. By the late 1970s, however, clinicians were describing a syndrome of sexual disinterest that did not fit into the accepted response cycle. Helen Singer Kaplan argued that a "separate phase [sexual desire] which had previously been neglected, must be added for conceptual completeness and clinical effectiveness" (Kaplan, 1979, p. xviii). *DSM-III* and *DSM-III-R* then merged the original HSRC with the norm of sexual desire to generate "the complete response cycle" presented above.

Clearly, the idea and much of the language of the nosology derived from Masters and Johnson's work, and in fact they are cited in the *DSM* footnotes as the primary source. Is it appropriate to use the HSRC to generate a clinical standard of normality? Is it appropriate to enshrine the HSRC as the standard of human sexuality such that deviations from it become the essential feature of abnormality?

Let us briefly examine how sexual problems are linked to mental disorders in the *DSM* and how the HSRC was used in the sexuality section. The definition of mental disorder offered in *DSM-III* specifies:

> In *DSM-III* each of the mental disorders is conceptualized as a clinically significant behavioral or psychological syndrome or pattern that occurs in an individual and that is typically associated with either a painful symptom (distress) or impairment in one or more areas of function (disability). In addition, there is an inference that there is a behavioral, psychological or biological dysfunction. (APA, 1980, p. 6)

In an article introducing the new classification scheme to the psychiatric profession, the APA task force explained their decisions. With regard to sexual dysfunctions, the task force members had concluded that "inability to experience the normative sexual response cycle [emphasis added] represented a disability in the important area of sexual functioning, whether or not the individual was distressed by the symptom" (Spitzer, Williams, and Skodol, 1980, pp. 153–154). That is, deviation from the now-normative sexual response cycle was to be considered a disorder even if the person had no complaints.

The diagnostic classification system clearly assumed that the HSRC was a universal bedrock of sexuality. Yet I have shown that it was a self-fulfilling result of Masters and Johnson's methodological decisions rather than a scientific discovery. It was the result of a priori assumptions rather than empirical research. Arguably, a clinical standard requires a greater demonstration of health impact and universal applicability than that offered by Masters and Johnson's research.

In fact, it is likely the case that the *DSM* authors adopted the HSRC model because it was useful and convenient. Professional and political factors that probably facilitated the adoption include professional needs within psychiatry to move away from a neurosis disorder model to a more concrete and empirical model, legitimacy needs within the new specialty of sex therapy, and the interests of feminists in progressive sexual standards for women (Tiefer, 1992b). Thus, the enshrinement of the HSRC and its upgraded versions as the centerpiece of sexual dysfunction nomenclature in DSM-III and DSM-III-R is not scientifically reliable and represents a triumph of politics and professionalism.

Sexuality as the Performances of Fragmented Body Parts

One deleterious clinical consequence of the utilization of the HSRC model as the sexual norm has been increased focus on segmented psychophysiological functioning. Just for example, consider the following disorder descriptions, which appear in DSM-III-R:

1. "partial or complete failure to attain or maintain the lubrication-swelling response of sexual excitement [Female Arousal Disorder]"
2. "involuntary spasm of the musculature of the outer third of the vagina that interferes with coitus [Vaginismus]"
3. "inability to reach orgasm in the vagina [Inhibited Male Orgasm]"

In the current nosology, the body as a whole is never mentioned but instead has become a fragmented collection of parts that pop in and out at different points in the performance sequence. This compartmentalization lends itself to mechanical imagery, to framing sexuality as the smooth operation and integration of complex machines, and to seeing problems of sexuality as "machines in disrepair" that need to be evaluated by high-technology part-healers (Soble, 1987). If there is a sexual problem, check each component systematically to detect the component out of commission. Overall satisfaction (which is mentioned nowhere in the nosology) is assumed to be a result of perfect parts-functioning. Recall that subjective distress is not even required for diagnosis, just objective indication of deviation from the HSRC.

This model promotes the idea that sexual disorder can be defined as deviation from "normal" as indicated by medical test results. A bit of thought, however, will show that identifying proper norms for these types of measurements is a tricky matter. How rigid is rigid? How quick is premature? How delayed is delayed? The answers to these questions are more a product of expectations, cultural standards, and particular partner than they are of objective measurement. And yet a series of complex and often invasive genital measurements are already being routinely used in evaluations of erectile dysfunction (Krane, Goldstein, and DeTejada, 1989). Norms for many of the tests are more often provided by medical technology manufacturers than by scientific research, and measurements on nonpatient samples are often lacking. Despite calls for caution in use and interpretation, the use of sexuality measurement technology continues to escalate (Burris, Banks, and Sherins, 1989; Kirkeby, Andersen, and Poulson, 1989; Schiavi, 1988; Sharlip, 1989).

This example illustrates a general medical trend: While reliance on tests and technology for objective information is increasing, reliance on patients' individualized standards and subjective reports of illness is decreasing (Osherson and AmaraSingham, 1981). The end result may be, as Lionel Trilling (1950) worried in a review of the first Kinsey report, that "the sexuality that is measured is taken to be the definition of sexuality itself" (p. 223). Although it seems only common sense and good clinical practice to want to "rule out" medical causes prior to initiating a course of psychotherapeutic or couple treatment for sexual complaints, such "ruling out" has become a growth industry rather than an adjunct to psychological and couple-oriented history-taking. Moreover, there is a growing risk of iatrogenic disorders being induced during the extensive "ruling out" procedures.

The HSRC has contributed significantly to the idea of sexuality as proper parts-functioning. Masters and Johnson's original research can hardly be faulted for studying individual physiological components to answer the question, "What physical reactions develop as the human male and female respond to effective sexual stimulation?" But once the physiological aspects became solidified into a universal, normative sequence known as "the" HSRC, the stage was set for clinical preoccupation with parts-functioning. Despite Masters and Johnson's avowed interest in sexuality as communication, intimacy, self-expression, and mutual pleasuring, their clinical ideas were ultimately mechanical (Masters and Johnson, 1975).

Exclusive Genital (i.e., Reproductive) Focus for Sexuality

"Hypoactive sexual desire" is the only sexual dysfunction in the *DSM-III-R* defined without regard to the genital organs. "Sexual aversion," for example, is specifically identified as aversion *to the genitals*. The other sexual dysfunctions are defined in terms of *genital* pain, spasm, dryness, deflation, uncontrolled responses, delayed responses, too-brief responses, or absent responses. The *DSM* locates the boundary between normal and abnormal (or between healthy and unhealthy) sexual function exclusively on genital performances.

"Genitals" are those organs involved in acts of generation, or biological reproduction. Although the *DSM* does not explicitly endorse reproduction as the primary purpose of sexual activity, the genital focus of the sexual dysfunction nosology implies such a priority. The only sexual acts mentioned are coitus, (vaginal) penetration, sexual intercourse, and noncoital clitoral stimulation. Only one is not a heterosexual coital act. Masturbation is only mentioned as a "form of stimulation." Full *genital performance during heterosexual intercourse is the essence of sexual functioning,* which excludes and demotes nongenital possibilities for pleasure and expression. Involvement or noninvolvement of the nongenital body becomes incidental, of interest only as it impacts on genital responses identified in the nosology.

Actually, the HSRC is a whole-body response, and Masters and Johnson were as interested in the physiology of "extragenital" responses as genital ones. Yet the stages of the HSRC as reflected in heart rate or breast changes did not make it into the *DSMs*. As Masters and Johnson transformed their physiological cycle into a clinical cycle, they privileged a reproductive purpose for sexuality by focusing on the genitals. It would seem that once they turned their interest to sexual problems rather than sexual process, their focus shifted to *sexuality as outcome*.

There is no section on diagnosis in Masters and Johnson's second, clinical, book (1970), no definition of normal sexuality, and no hint of how the particular list of erectile, orgasmic, and other genitally focused disorders was derived. The authors merely described their treatments of "the specific varieties of sexual dysfunction that serve as presenting complaints of patients referred" (Masters and Johnson, 1970, p. 91). But surely this explanation cannot be the whole story. Why did they exclude problems like "inability to relax, . . . attraction to partner other than mate, . . . partner chooses inconvenient time, . . . too little tenderness" or others of the sort later labeled "sexual difficulties" (Frank, Anderson, and Rubinstein, 1978)? Why did they exclude problems like "partner is only interested in orgasm, . . . partner can't kiss, . . . partner is too hasty, . . . partner has no sense of romance," or others of the sort identified in surveys of women (Hite, 1976)?

In fact, the list of disorders proposed by Masters and Johnson seems like a list devised by Freudians who, based on their developmental stage theory of sexuality, define genital sexuality as the sine qua non of sexual maturity. Despite the whole-body focus of the HSRC physiology research, the clinical interest of its authors in proper genital performance as the essence of normal sexuality indicates their adherence to an earlier tradition. The vast spectrum of sexual possibility is narrowed to genital, that is, to reproductive performance.

Symptom Reversal as the Measure of Sex Therapy Success

A final undesirable clinical consequence of the HSRC and its evolution in the DSM is the limitation it imposes on the evaluation of therapy success. Once sexual disturbances are defined as specific malperformances within "the" sexual response cycle, evaluation of treatment effectiveness narrows to symptom reversal.

But the use of symptom reversal as the major or only measure of success contrasts with sex therapy as actually taught and practiced (Hawton, 1985). Typical practice focuses on individual and relationship satisfaction and includes elements such as education, permission-giving, attitude change, anxiety reduction, improved communication, and intervention in destructive sex roles and life-styles (LoPiccolo, 1977). A recent extensive survey of 289 sex therapy providers in private practice reinforced the statement that "much of sex therapy actually was nonsexual in nature" and confirmed that therapy focuses on communication skills, individual issues, and the "nonsexual relationship" (Kilmann et al., 1986).

Follow-up studies measuring satisfaction with therapy and changes in sexual, psychological, and interpersonal issues show varying patterns of improvement, perhaps because therapists tend to heedlessly lump together cases with the "same" symptom. It is erroneous to assume that couples and their experience of sex therapy are at all homogeneous, despite their assignment to specific and discrete diagnostic categories based on the HSRC. Citing his own "painful experience" (Bancroft, 1989, p. 489) with unreplicable results of studies comparing different forms of treatment, John Bancroft suggested that there is significant prognostic variability among individuals and couples even within diagnostic categories. He concluded, "It may be that there is no alternative to defining various aspects of the sexual relationship, e.g., sexual response, communication, enjoyment, etc. and assessing each separately" (p. 497).

It might be thought that using symptom reversal as the measure of success is easier than evaluating multiple issues of relationship satisfaction, but this is not true, since *any* measure of human satisfaction needs to be subtle. That is, it is indeed easy to measure "success" with objective technologies that evaluate whether a prosthesis successfully inflates or an injection successfully produces erectile rigidity, of a certain degree. When evaluating the human success of physical treatments, however, researchers invariably introduce complex subjective elements. The questions they select, the way they ask the questions, and their interpretations of the answers are all subjective (Tiefer, Pedersen, and Melman, 1988). In evaluating patients' satisfaction with penile implant treatment, asking the patients whether they would have prosthesis surgery again produces different results from evaluating postoperative satisfaction with sexual frequency, the internal feeling of the prosthesis during sex, anxieties about the indwelling prosthesis, changes in relationship quality, and so on.

The present diagnostic nomenclature, based on the genitally focused HSRC, results in evaluation of treatment success exclusively in terms of symptom reversal and ignores the complex sociopsychological context of sexual performance and experience. The neat four-stage model, the seemingly clean clinical typology, all result in neat and clean evaluation research—which turns out to relate only partially to real people's experiences.

Feminist Criticisms of the HSRC Model

Paul Robinson (1976) and Janice Irvine (1990) have discussed at length how Masters and Johnson deliberately made choices throughout *Human Sexual Response* and *Human Sexual Inadequacy* to emphasize male-female sexual similarities. The most fundamental similarity, of course, was that men and women had identical HSRCs. The diagnostic nomenclature continues this emphasis by basing the whole idea of sexual dysfunction on the gender-neutral HSRC and by scrupulously assigning equal numbers and parallel dysfunctions to men and women. (Desire disorders are not specified as to gender; other dysfunctions include one arousal disorder for each gender, one inhibited orgasm disorder for each gender, premature ejaculation for men and vaginismus for women, and dyspareunia, which is defined as "recurrent or persistent genital pain in either a male or a female.")

Yet, is the HSRC really gender-neutral? Along with other feminists, I have argued that the HSRC model of sexuality, and its elaboration and application in clinical work, favors men's sexual interests over those of women (e.g., Tiefer, 1988a). Some have argued that sex role socialization introduces fundamental gender differences and inequalities into adult sexual experience that cannot be set aside by a model that simply proclaims male and female sexuality as fundamentally the same (Stock, 1984). I have argued that the HSRC, with its alleged gender equity, disguises and trivializes *social* reality, that is, gender inequality (Tiefer, 1990a) and thus makes it all the harder for women to become sexually equal in fact.

Let's look briefly at some of these gender differences in the real world. First, to oversimplify many cultural variations on this theme, men and women are raised with different sets of sexual values—men toward varied experience and physical gratification, women toward intimacy and emotional communion (Gagnon, 1977; Gagnon, 1979; Gagnon and Simon, 1969; Simon and Gagnon, 1986). By focusing on the physical aspects of sexuality and ignoring the rest, the HSRC favors men's value training over women's. Second, men's greater experience with masturbation encourages them toward a genital focus in sexuality, whereas women learn to avoid acting on genital urges because of the threat of lost social respect. With its genital focus, the HSRC favors men's training over women's. As has been mentioned earlier, by requiring experience and comfort with masturbation to orgasm as a criterion for all participants, the selection of research subjects for *Human Sexual Response* looked gender-neutral but in fact led to an unrepresentative sampling of women participants.

Third, the whole issue of "effective sexual stimulation" needs to be addressed from a feminist perspective. As we have seen, the HSRC model was based on a particular kind of sexual activity, that with "effective sexual stimulation." Socioeconomic subordination, threats of pregnancy, fear of male violence, and society's double standard reduce women's power in heterosexual relationships and militate against women's sexual knowledge, sexual assertiveness, and sexual candor (Snitow, Stansell, and Thompson, 1983; Vance, 1984). Under such circumstances, it seems likely that "effective sexual stimulation" in the laboratory or at home favors what men prefer.

The HSRC assumes that men and women have and want the same kind of sexuality since physiological research suggests that in some ways, and under selected test conditions, we are built the same. Yet social realities dictate that we are not all the same sexually—not in our socially shaped wishes, in our sexual self-development, or in our interpersonal sexual meanings. Many different studies—from questionnaires distributed by feminist organizations to interviews of self-defined happily married couples, from popular magazine surveys to social psychologists' meta-analyses of relationship research—show that women rate affection and emotional communication as more important than orgasm in a sexual relationship (Hite, 1987; Frank, Anderson, and Rubinstein, 1978; Tavris and Sadd, 1977; Peplau and Gordon, 1985). Given this evidence, it denies women's voices entirely to continue to insist that sexuality is best represented by the universal "cycle of sexual response, with orgasm as the ultimate point in progression" (Masters and Johnson, 1966, p. 127).

Masters and Johnson's comparisons of the sexual techniques used by heterosexual and homosexual couples can be seen to support the claim that "effective sexual stimulation" simply means what men prefer. Here are examples of the contrasts:

> The sexual behavior of the married couples was far more performance-oriented. . . . Preoccupation with orgasmic attainment was expressed time and again by heterosexual men and women during interrogation after each testing session. . . . [By contrast] the committed homosexual couples *took their time* in sexual interaction in the laboratory. . . . In committed heterosexual couples' interaction, the male's sexual approach to the female, . . . rarely more than 30 seconds to a minute, were spent holding close or caressing the total body area before the breasts and/or genitals were directly stimulated. This was considerably shorter than the corresponding time

interval observed in homosexual couples. (Masters and Johnson, 1979, pp. 64–65, 66)

After describing various techniques of breast stimulation, the authors reported that heterosexual women enjoyed it much less than lesbians but that "all the [heterosexual] women thought that breast play was very important in their husband's arousal" (p. 67). The authors repeatedly emphasized that the differences between lesbian and heterosexual techniques were greater than between heterosexual and male homosexual techniques.[3]

The enshrinement of the HSRC in the DSM diagnostic nomenclature represented the ultimate in context-stripping, as far as women's sexuality is concerned. To speak merely of desire, arousal, and orgasm as constitutive of sexuality and ignore relationships and women's psychosocial development is to ignore women's experiences of exploitation, harassment, and abuse and to deny women's social limitations. To reduce sexuality to the biological specifically disadvantages women, feminists argue, because women as a class are disadvantaged by social sexual reality (Laws, 1990; Hubbard, 1990; Birke, 1986).

Finally, the biological reductionism of the HSRC and the *DSM* is subtly conveyed by their persistent use of the terms *males* and *females* rather than *men* and *women*. There are no men and no women in the latest edition of the diagnostic nomenclature, only males and females and vaginas and so forth. In *Human Sexual Response*, men and women appear in the text from time to time, but only males and females make it to the chapter headings, and a rough count of a few pages here and there in the text reveals a 7:1 use of the general animal kingdom terms over the specifically human ones. A feminist deconstruction of the HSRC and of contemporary perspectives on sexuality could do worse than begin by noticing and interpreting how the choice of vocabulary signals the intention to ignore culture.

Conclusion

I have argued in this chapter that the human sexual response cycle (HSRC) model of sexuality is flawed from scientific, clinical, and feminist points of view. Popularized primarily because clinicians and researchers needed norms that were both objective and universal, the model is actually neither objective nor universal. It imposes a false biological uniformity on sexuality that does not support the human uses and meanings of sexual potential. The most exciting work in sex therapy evolves toward systems analyses and interventions that combine psychophysiological sophistication with respect for individual and couple diversity (e.g., Verhulst and Heiman, 1988). Subjective dissatisfactions are seen more as relative dyssynchronies between individuals or between elements of culturally based sexual scripts than as malfunctions of some universal sexual essence.

Defining the essence of sexuality as a specific sequence of physiological changes promotes biological reductionism. Biological reductionism not only separates genital sexual performance from personalities, relationships, conduct, context, and values but also overvalues the former at the expense of the latter. As Abraham Maslow (1966) emphasized, studying parts may be easier than studying people, but what do you understand when you're through? Deconstructing and desacralizing the HSRC should help sex research unhook itself from the albatross of biological reductionism.

Notes

1. Robinson suggests that Masters and Johnson's "scheme of four phases" is "irrelevant" and "merely creates the impression of scientific precision where none exists" (Robinson, 1976, p. 130). The reader is referred to his dissection of the model's stages.

2. The same introduction persists in the *DSM-IV* (APA, 1994). See Part 3, Chapter 3, note 1, for further information about *DSM-IV*.

3. Again, it must be emphasized that subject selection plays a large role, as acknowledged by Masters and Johnson: "Study subjects were selected because they were specifically facile in sexual response. . . . The carefully selected homosexual and heterosexual study subjects employed in the Institute's research programs must be considered representative of a cross-section of sexually adult men and women in our culture" (Masters and Johnson, 1979, pp. 61–62).

part two

POPULAR WRITINGS
ON THE THEME

I am fortunate to have the gift of gab. It's nothing I get credit for. Like being funny, being able to produce and perform large numbers of words easily has just been part of me for as long as I can remember. It probably comes from wanting to get attention from my somewhat depressed father. The gift of gab certainly helped me as a college professor, it helps as a therapist (I like to say more than "mm . . . hmm . . . tell me more about that"), and it certainly has helped me as a public speaker and spokesperson for my political views. Of course, in all honesty, I have to admit that it's gotten me in trouble, too.

The essays in this section—some published, some public lectures, one magazine interview—are efforts at deconstruction, although I had never heard of this term when I wrote most of them. I can see now that my theme in these popular writings was often to challenge conventional meanings and relocate authority away from experts. I kept trying to take the familiar and make it unfamiliar.

There are even two sermons in this section—talks delivered on Sunday mornings from the pulpit of Community Church of New York. It would be a long story to explain how a feminist sexologist ended up as an active member of a Unitarian-Universalist congregation, but suffice it to say that secular humanism offers a very hospitable "faith environment" for a Jewish atheist and I'm not the only one there. The UUs developed a comprehensive sex ed curriculum in the 1970s, and colleagues I would meet at sexology conferences would often turn out to be UUs. These sermons were a kind of community-based adult sex education that we need in this country to compensate for sexual ignorance and misinformation.

As a sexologist, I have had a love-hate relationship with mass media. In the 70s and early 80s I occasionally wrote articles about sexuality for magazines and newspapers, but when I had to deal with journalists I would grit my teeth. "Could you tell me what's new about transgender, or female orgasm, or sexless marriages?" they'd begin, and when I would answer, "Well, how much do you already know?" they would say, "Well, not much. I heard you were an expert and I was hoping you could tell me." They would always be "on deadline" and needed my time immediately! If I did take time to explain some of the complexities of the topic, I would invariably find little of my perspective in the final article. Some throwaway line I'd tossed out would be quoted, but not the careful analysis, and no complexity.

After Viagra was approved in 1998 and I decided to play a public role to raise awareness about medicalization, I changed my tune and made myself more available to the media. I learned that there are many types of journalists (and TV producers and documentary-makers), and that I could get along well with some of them. Most, though, I still believe, suffer from a kind of "naïve realism" about sex. They deny that the media are major players in the process of social construction and that media create categories and set values. The journalists I met seemed uninterested in the political, historical, or cultural aspects of their subjects and never thought about how different groups (e.g., Kenyans/Muslims/gay men) might have different views on a topic, why such views change, and what political or socioeconomic interests might promote change. This is yet another reason to despair about the lack of sophisticated sexuality education in this country. Most journalists, who are college grads, don't "get it" about how sexual life is constantly in flux and that they are part of the social construction.

chapter 1

SIX MONTHS
AT THE *DAILY NEWS*

In 1980 I was invited to write a weekly 200-word column for the *New York Daily News*, which advertises itself as the largest-circulation daily in the country. I knew they wanted something popular and a little titillating, not academic or political, but I thought I would see if I could find some way to present the ideas I was interested in anyway. The *News* called the column "Your Sexual Self," exactly the sort of privatized perspective I planned to preach against! I had to repeatedly resist the editors' request that I answer readers' questions in the column. I got lots of mail, but none of it ever commented on the columns; it all wanted advice. The *News* called it quits after six months; I have selected a few of those columns to include here.

The Myth of Spontaneity

Nowadays we are expected to be sexually spontaneous. Scheming and playing games are out. But good sex doesn't strike like lightning. Only in romantic novels do lovers swoon from a single glance or pant from a passing touch. Getting turned on in real life is more like warming up an engine than flicking on a light switch.

Such is the power of our ignorance on this subject that many people suspect organic or hormonal weakness if they are not aroused at a moment's notice. Even those informed about the importance of mental preparation may wrongly label themselves psychologically undersexed. Not to mention the names they hurl at their partners.

In fact, seasoned lovers often deliberately put themselves in the mood. Thinking about sex usually tops their list of preliminaries. Like John Travolta, leisurely and lovingly combing his hair before going out to disco in *Saturday Night Fever,* anyone can tune into sensual, sexual feelings by imagining good times ahead. Relaxing, mentally and physically, is important. A shower works for some, a quiet time alone for others.

Some people complain that all this groundwork is too mechanical and time-consuming. Working at sex, they say, defeats the whole purpose. Ironically, these same people don't grouse over warming up for tennis or deny themselves an appetizer before dinner. One of the real reasons people are shy about making preparations for sex is that it seems sinful. Planning for sex runs counter to much of our early learning. Willfully conjuring up a lusty fantasy is wicked. Even sex within marriage can be tainted for some by too voluptuous an attitude.

People may also avoid planning because whenever you plan you risk disappointment. What if you dab on a little perfume and he isn't interested? What if you shave just before bed and she laughs at your obviousness? The risks feel greatest when you are insecure about yourself or your partner. This can make any negative thing feel like a catastrophe. In fact, I believe the risks in warming yourself up for sex (not every time—let's not get compulsive about this) are trivial compared to the possible benefits. Being embarrassed isn't shattering.

In our rush to celebrate spontaneous sex, we may have forgotten a childhood phenomenon—that waiting for Christmas was a big part of the fun. Can we abandon the trickery of seduction without losing the delicious excitement of the tease? Can we remember that a few solitary moments in the bullpen can make all the difference when we finally get into the game?

Bring Back the Kid Stuff

Poor little petting. Lost in the great big world of grownup sex. Somewhere along the line, kissing and tickling, rubbing and hugging became mere preliminaries to the main event.

A lot more is being lost than you might at first realize. Deprived of touch, many of us get a kind of itchy skin hunger. Sexual petting has been one of the primary ways adults can obtain the comforts of touch. While petting, many lovers murmur of their admiration and affection, talk baby-talk, or whisper and giggle—in a way that's not possible during intercourse. Exchanging endearments creates a special emotional bond. You may smile at the memory of a lover's nickname long after you've forgotten the physical details of sex together. Before we can value such indulgence, however, petting would have to lose the stigma of being kid stuff. As most of us grew up, intercourse was rated X: For Adults Only. It acquired the lure of the forbidden and the status of the big leagues.

At a time when lovers complain about insufficient variety, petting should become more popular. The skin is the largest sex organ, yet many of us have learned to regard as sexual only a tiny percentage of the available acreage. On the Polynesian island of Pnape, partners spend hours petting and nuzzling before they begin to think about intercourse.

Couples who seek out sex therapists because of sexual disinterest or difficulty in sexual function are often thunderstruck to hear that the first homework assignment of the treatment is to pet with each other. They can't imagine how avoiding intercourse and just playing around will help. They want help with "real" sex. Therapists explain that petting will lead their clients to discover (or rediscover) a wide variety of erotic sensations while positive emotions generated by the mutual stroking will strengthen the couple's attachment.

But, as clients soon realize, it may be easier to have intercourse than to hug and kiss! The task is better defined: a clear goal, a standard method, easy-to-locate equipment, and a socially defined endpoint. It can be accomplished with a minimum of communication. With petting, the script is more vague. Over what path do the hands and mouth wander? What words are said? How do you know when you're through?

You can have successful intercourse with a stranger, but you have to like someone to enjoy petting. Because the physical sensations are less intense, much of the reward must come from the closeness. It's joyless and burdensome to cuddle and embrace with someone you neither know well nor want to know better. The petting assignment is very revealing for many couples.

Calling kissing and hugging "foreplay" reveals their status as means to an end. Anything that is sometimes an appetizer and sometimes the main dish is worthy of a name other than foreplay. Let's save that one for something more appropriate—like golf.

Shedding Light on Sex in the Dark

Sex is the only game we play in the dark. Are we ashamed to watch what we're doing, or is darkness necessary to liberate our intimate passions?

In the darkness, lovers are safe from the prying eyes of children, parents, neighbors—and each other. To the extent that you want to deny others knowledge of you as a sexual person, you will welcome the protection of the dark.

Under cover of darkness, we are all beautiful. Flab, sag, spots, and wrinkles are mercifully hidden. With the contortions and grimaces of sexual exertion out of focus, we seem graceful as gazelles. To the extent that you find earthy images of skin and sweat distracting, you seek the camouflage of darkness.

In the permissive darkness, sin is softened. Taboos occur without witness. To the extent that your upbringing stressed the prohibitions surrounding sex, you may require the tolerance afforded by darkness.

Concealed by darkness, cracks in the ceiling—or your life—lose their immediacy. It's just the two of you, close together, with the colored lights flashing in your heads. The details of existence fade away.

Blinded by darkness, we are forced to use our other senses. We rediscover touch, aroma, sound. Covered with clothes, we are chronically deprived of the variety of pleasures and comforts available through touch. To the extent that vision distracts you from concentrating on other sensations, you will prefer darkness.

Screened by darkness, we become bold. Our words and our rhythms reveal a lusty eagerness we might deny by day. Shyness can be slain by the dark. In the privacy of darkness, we can exaggerate and improve our actual experience through imagination. Our wishes fulfilled, we feel deeper love and greater passion. Through illusion, we become more involved in reality. To the extent that imagination enriches the moment, darkness is a friend.

The trouble with darkness is that you can't see what you're doing. You can't see how your partner is reacting. You can't gaze into each other's eyes. Travelers ignorant of the territory tend to stick to familiar and well-marked routes. Sex in the dark often becomes routine. Many people protest that seeing themselves and their partners is immodest. But we're talking here about moonlight and 40-watt bulbs, not airport runway approach beacons.

Yet many of us have the greatest difficulty believing that anyone would enjoy seeing our genitals. We've been told they're cursed, or dirty. Many women are so paralyzed by shame they even avoid medical examination "down there." Modesty is often shame in disguise.

Perhaps because of the taboos on showing and looking, such acts can be the final revelation of trust between lovers. Like all proofs of acceptance, they must be mutual—forced, they become empty gestures of intimacy.

Sex Is an Unnatural Act

I have a T-shirt that reads, "Sex is a natural act." I used to think it was at least amusing, at best profound. If people would only relax and let their natural reactions flow, I thought, sex would be more of a pleasure and less of a Pandora's box.

I'm wiser now. I think the sentiment of the T-shirt distorts the truth. The urge to merge may be natural for birds and bees, but the biological takes a back seat in our own species. We humans are the only ones with a sex drive that isn't solely related to procreation.

Originally, the message that sex is natural was meant to relieve guilt feelings—you can't be blamed for doing what is healthy and normal. Such permission was extremely useful for a time. It enabled many people to break free from choking inhibitions.

But the message was taken too literally. I now meet people who believe hormones control their sex life. They feel no pride when sex is good and have no idea what to do when it is not. Letting Mother Nature do the driving sounds like the lazy person's dream; actually it makes you feel powerless and ignorant.

Belief that sexuality comes naturally relieves our responsibility to acquire knowledge and make choices. You don't have to teach your kids anything special—when the time comes, they'll know what to do. You don't have to talk with your partner about your love life—it'll all just happen automatically.

What happens automatically is often brief, routine, and more in the category of scratching an itch than indulging a beautiful expression. Such a sexual style may satisfy a person for whom sex has a low priority. It is unreasonable to expect mutual pleasure, variety, or emotional intimacy without some information and a lot of practice. If all you need for fulfilling sex comes already built in, then any difficulties must be due to physical breakdown. Many couples seek medical help when what they need is a course on communication. Sexual enrichment workshops mixing film, lecture, discussion, and time for private practice present an approach to sex that emphasizes the relationship.

You can't ignore the way worry and anger affect desire. You need to learn how to give suggestions and feedback without putting each other down. There's no way but trial and error to identify forms of effective stimulation. Most important, the attitude that sex is a natural act implies that great sex occurs early in a relationship and stays constant throughout. A dynamic vision of continuing change and adjustment is more realistic—it's not failing memory that leads some older couples to report that sex keeps getting better.

Unfortunately, most sex education has not caught up with what people need in the 1980s. High school and college classes dwell at length on statistics, plumbing, and contraception. Students rarely read about connections between sexuality and feelings. Nor do they discuss what influences sexual attraction or how psychological needs are met through sex. Often students enter a course and leave it still thinking that love will guide the way to sexual happiness.

Limiting instruction to issues like birth control and venereal disease prevention may promote public health goals, but it does little to enrich the quality of sexual experience. Techniques of pregnancy prevention don't work to prevent sexual disappointment.

Natural sex, like a natural brassiere, is a contradiction in terms. The human sex act is a product of individual personalities, skills, and the scripts of our times. Like a brassiere, it shapes nature to something designed by human purposes and reflecting current fashion.

Sex as Communication?
Save Your Breath!

It seems that every new sex book proclaims, "Sex is the ultimate form of communication." What does this mean? How can I figure out if it's true if I can't figure out what it means?

I go to my local guru. He tells me it means that people are most honest, most open, most truly themselves during sex. I ask why. You never really know a person until you've had sex together, he says. I say, I thought you never really knew a person until you got drunk together, or until one of you got cancer. Same thing, he says. Extreme situations cause people to reveal themselves. I'm dubious. Sex may be an extreme situation, but it makes as many people clam up as open up.

I go to another guru. This one tells me that sex is the ultimate form of communication because sex allows a person to express the broadest range of intimate feelings. People fumble for words, she says. They get tongue-tied and choked by emotion. Ah, but in bed they can let themselves go. Love, fear, tenderness, trust, generosity, sensitivity, respect, even anger. But what about those people whose sexual vocabulary is a one-note song? What about those who can emit volumes over breakfast, but only paragraphs in bed? Is sex the ultimate form of communication for them, too?

Another guru, another explanation. This one tells me sex offers the best hope for communication because words can lie, but bodies tell the truth. But I know bodies can lie. Or, rather, that reading body language can lead as often to misunderstanding as revelation. People mistake fatigue for rejection or disinterest. Physical arousal doesn't necessarily reflect desire for the partner in one's arms. Behavior isn't that easy to interpret; smiles and caresses can be as deceptive as words.

Maybe the best approach is to abandon the jargon. What does one person tell another by means of sex? Is the message unique to sex? Can it be delivered better for some people in words, other gestures of tenderness, or intimacy or devotion?

The truth seems to be that people express themselves during lovemaking just as they do by all their activities. There tends to be a lot of consistency to the messages, as couples in sex therapy frequently discover. If one partner dominates sex so the other can't get a move in edgewise, it's a safe bet the same thing occurs during a discussion of how to discipline little Billy.

The gurus' basic error is overgeneralization. To claim sex is the ultimate form of communication sounds as if something fundamental about sex were being revealed that was true for all people. In fact, some people express their feelings better with caresses than words, but others don't. Some people reveal more of their inner feelings in sex than over coffee; others don't. Some people are closer to their lovers than to other companions, but many are not.

Like all generalizations, this one bulldozes individual differences. And like all hype about sex, it makes most of us wonder what we're missing. The word "ultimate" is the tipoff. No one human activity could possibly be the ultimate everything to anyone. We're just not that much alike.

Free Love and Free Enterprise

Every war has its profiteers, and the sexual revolution is no exception. Did you notice the moment when the movement to decrease sexual guilt and ignorance suddenly became big business? The question now is whether the run for the bucks will completely obliterate the original liberatory impulse.

Imagine a sex show at the New York Coliseum. Products and services once available only to decadent aristocrats are now accessible to everyone. Let's tour around and assess the impact of this commercial boom.

The first booth salutes the information explosion. Textbooks and visuals for schools and professional training line one wall; popular books, magazines, and TV presentations on sex cover the other. Soon every citizen will have been interviewed and observed and will have written a book about the experience. Yet, though many of the materials repeat the same points over and over, the public's appetite for such materials seems inexhaustible. Will we ever overcome our ignorance?

The second booth advertises help for the sexually troubled. Lists of disorders reach from floor to ceiling. Different schools of treatment challenge each other's success statistics and argue about causes and cures. Their standards for adequacy make most people feel inadequate, generating perpetual business. Fortunately, for a price, they're all available to treat your "problem." It's a little confusing, though, when you see ads for treatment in newspapers or telephone directories and have no idea about the qualifications of the providers. Can you be helped by a sexual surrogate? Don't look to science for an answer.

The next booth moves us into the world of stuff. Under the banner "Bare-handed sex is boring," we find equipment to enhance the senses and the imagination. Massage oils and flavored lotions lie next to vibrators and dildos. Alarming displays of bondage equipment are shown along with phony organ enlargers. There are life-size "sex partners" in different colors of plastic. Underwear comes in sequined, leather, very skimpy, and edible versions. There are records and tapes of love sounds (orgasmic sighs and ocean waves), satin sheets, aromatic candles, incense, mirrored beds with built-in bars, fluffy rabbit-fur mitts. Parents worry where they'll put their toys so the kids don't find them.

A fourth booth displays aphrodisiacs—substances that allegedly arouse desire or intensify experience. Few have been scientifically tested, and those few have proven ineffective. Nevertheless, the supply of potions and pills expands as people chase their rising expectations. Next door is the hygiene and fitness booth. Leotards, instruction books, and gym business cards promise that if you change your body, you'll build up your chances for sexual success.

The sixth booth is for the vast world of visual erotica. Some educational, some offensive, some conventional, some unusual—but who can draw the lines? The flood of sexually explicit material for the home market looms on the horizon. Since the major use of pornography has always been for masturbation, sex experts and commercial interests seem in collusion as they sing the praises of solo sex.

Another booth is plastered with brochures that promise the zing of sex away from home. Bring your honey to a hot-tub motel (with waterbed, whirlpool, and X-rated TV movies), or make it with a stranger in a local orgy room. There's something about the unfamiliar that makes us pay attention and feel more intensely. Bring your checkbook and check it out.

The final booth contains the business cards of people who want to have sex with you—for a price. "Dates" are available for out-of-town visitors to fill a lonely evening. Bars with runways have dancers who strip or parade to inflame your fantasies. Models will pose, and participate. Massages can be had without sex—or with. And prostitutes of every age and talent are available, as they have always been.

Commercial interests exist to make a profit. Contributions to human well-being are incidental. Sexual commercialism surely exploits and preys upon insecurity, but it also stimulates and expands the imagination. It's difficult to find the line between moralistic or embarrassed kneejerk rejection ("What do they need *that* for?") and simplistic and indiscriminate acceptance ("Everybody should do their own thing"), but we owe it to ourselves to try.

chapter 2

THE KISS

A knowledge of oral sex has become unexpectedly useful if you want to follow the news of the day.[1] Because our tour of the kiss today might seem unusual, I need to establish my credentials at the outset. I once won a kissing contest. This isn't why (or how) I became a sexologist, but at least it puts to rest the claim that those who can't do, teach.

The Psychobiosocial Approach

Many of us who study sexuality take a psychobiosocial approach to our subject. This allows us to think of any sexual activity, such as erotic kissing, as a tapestry tightly woven of three different kinds of yarn. There are psychological factors such as memories and hopes and fears, biological factors such as hormones and genetic influences, and social factors such as religious values, the opinion of your neighbors and the messages you get from the movies.

Sex researchers who use the psychobiosocial model to examine kissing are trying to answer questions such as:

What is the origin of kissing?
How does kissing differ around the world?
How do events of childhood affect adult kissing?
Do animals kiss?

A social constructionist, of course, also wants to know about the symbolism and significance of the kiss, and how it is used within various political and sociocultural regimes.

Let me start with an overall psychobiosocial theory of kissing. What links the deliciousness of erotic kissing to the social importance of kisses of greeting, farewell, and congratulation? Why do so many cultural ceremonies involve kissing objects of reverence such as the Pope's ring or the King's robe?

Our experience of security and sensuality begins in infancy as we are held while we nurse. The sucking experience, the use of tongue and lips, the aroma of body and skin, the touch on the face—psychobiosocial theory suggests that every kiss from infancy on reverberates with deeply felt echoes of emotional comfort and sensual pleasure. The lips and tongue have large representations in the brain—every infant must suckle to survive. As we suckle, we feel and we don't forget.

Humans' vertical posture and the emotional power of eye contact for all primates brings other elements into the kiss. Even in cultures where mouth-to-mouth kissing is disapproved, reverberations of attachment and sensuality occur when cheeks rub together or the aroma of a beloved's face is inhaled. Biting, nibbling, nipping, or blowing on the lips and face may be part of a sexual script. Attachment and pleasure reverberate even when only one mouth is doing the work. After all, in infancy, it's only one mouth.

Because kissing can arouse powerful memories and longings, kisses have power and can endanger, as is well-known in legend and literature. Where people cannot choose their own mates or the free expression of sexuality is taboo or a sin, kisses symbolize social chaos. Thus, we have all learned about dangerous love kisses that mortally bond the "wrong" pair (Romeo and Juliet, Tristan and Isolde).

The power of kisses is also shown when kisses of betrayal are the ultimate symbol of violating trust and intimacy (Judas' kiss of betrayal or the deathly kiss of the vampire). In religious stories, dangerous kisses are those that transgress social boundaries (witches kiss the devil to signal allegiance or Christian martyrs kiss lepers to enact their sacrifice). Dangerous kisses can easily become eroticized in fantasy and ritualized practice.

Kisses bond, perhaps because they recruit infant feelings of being soothed and comforted. It's this safeness component of kissing, how kissing can reduce tension, that is expressed not only intimately, but in the reverent kisses meant to soothe or appease those with power (kissing the Bible, the Torah, the dice for luck).

Research with bonobos, members of the chimpanzee family, shows how kisses reduce conflict in situations of fear or competition in this highly social primate species. Bonobos of every social status, whether female, male, or infant, respond to kisses by reducing aggressive behaviors. Likewise, kisses are ever present in human social situations where people must make sure harm is left outside the door. We touch lips or cheeks to signify I'm safe to you and you're safe to me. Much social and ceremonial kissing, of course, has become completely ritualized, and the emotional component is only a dim reverberation.

A Clinical Story

Let's look at some specific stories about kisses. I want to start with a clinical example from my sex therapy practice to illustrate the psychobiosocial model at work.

A few years ago, a married couple came to see me with a common complaint—premature ejaculation. Their sexual life was unsatisfying and although they had been married only four years, they were having sex very infrequently. Sex felt very uncomfortable and they couldn't get turned on together and conduct a sexual encounter without tears and frustration. But, they had no idea why. They were in their middle 30s, lower middle-class, both healthy and employed, he was Italian-American and she was Burmese-American. (Burma is now known as Myanmar.) They had become attracted to each other, decided to marry and assumed sex would just happen "naturally."

After several therapy sessions discussing the specifics of their sex life, the premature ejaculation was attributed to infrequent sex, and dismissed as a problem. The couple's discomfort and difficulty in getting turned on together became the primary problem. He accused her of not loving him because she lacked ardor during foreplay, though she insisted she loved him very much. She accused him of not loving her because he didn't understand why she was so withdrawn during foreplay. The therapist proposed, to their surprise, that the heart of their problem was a cultural discrepancy in kissing. Social, psychological, and physical arousal factors were all interacting.

The wife had an aversion, common in her native region, to mouth-to-mouth kissing. Many Asian (and African and South American) groups view mouth-to-mouth kissing as dirty, dangerous, and disgusting, something akin to sticking one's tongue in another's nose and wiggling it around. It turned her off to imagine, anticipate, or experience it, and she felt confused and unhappy when she saw how much her husband enjoyed it. Though she deeply loved her husband, ardor during foreplay was impossible for her under the circumstances. The husband, by comparison, had learned and practiced and fantasized within European social rules where deep kissing is highly intimate and erotic. He wanted to kiss, he needed to kiss, and he felt rejected and discouraged by his wife's negative reactions.

Their gender socialization compounded the difficulty. The couple had both learned that men are supposed to take the lead in sex and that women are supposed to be modest and fairly unassertive. It is common for Asian women not to express their sexual likes and dislikes, and the wife had never mentioned her feelings about kissing. Neither member of the couple realized how much physical arousal and sexual satisfaction were the result of psychology (learning, expectancy, and fantasy) and social customs.

Moreover, even after we all "realized" what the difficulty was, it took them a long time to overcome deeply ingrained beliefs and habits and create a mutually agreeable sexual life together. Those of you who have lived in a culture very different from the one you grew up in will know what I mean. He couldn't suddenly stop wanting to kiss any more easily than she could suddenly start wanting to. Although they wanted to be close, their sexual scripts were intimately connected to lifelong feelings of comfort and familiarity. It took a lot of motivation and practice over many months for them to create a new sexual script and then to feel spontaneous in its enactment.

The Kiss as Symbol

The kiss lends itself to generous symbolic use. There are many nonsexual uses of kissing such as social greeting and farewell, religious kisses of peace, kisses of respect for the Torah or another icon as it is carried into a house of worship, kissing the statue of a religious or secular leader to show loyalty, kissing dice for luck in a casino, kisses that symbolize sexual awakening as in fairy tales like "Sleeping Beauty" or kisses that symbolize protection as in legends like *The Ring of the Nibelungs*. There is the Sammy Sosa (Dinah Shore) kiss that connects a celebrity to the public. And there are the scary kisses—the Judas kiss of betrayal, the Mafia kiss that means death, the devil's kiss that signifies eternal damnation *(Don Giovanni, Faust)*. From loyalty and luck to disloyalty and damnation. This kiss is powerful medicine. Oh, yes, don't forget mothers' kissing the hurt away—the kiss as alternative health care (or placebo).

A Political Story

Let me tell a story of the kiss as symbol and place it in the context of sexual politics. And I don't mean President Clinton's impeachment and *those* sexual politics, but in the context of the political contests that over the past three decades have come to be called the "Sex Wars."

Recent battles in the "Sex Wars" have been fought on abortion laws, abortion funding, public sex education, public funding of art, funding of sex research, conferences on sexuality at public universities, zoning of erotic bookstores and places of entertainment, limits on sexually explicit materials on newsstands and in bookstores, restriction of sex on the internet, limits on sexually explicit rock lyrics, etc. etc.

Rodin's famous 1889 sculpture *The Kiss* is no stranger to censorship.[2] Although many have regarded it as "the kiss of kisses" and a sculptural masterpiece, others have seen its voluptuousness, its frank eroticism, and its depiction of transgressive sexual activity as another example of how immoral artists rationalized their images of nudity and lust with classical stories. It's been banned; it's been covered with cloth. It's a powerful symbolic kiss.

Rodin's sculpture immortalizes an erotic moment from Dante's *The Divine Comedy,* completed in 1321. As Dante travels through the realms of the dead in search of his muse, Beatrice, he encounters Paolo and Francesca entwined in an embrace. Francesca da Rimini, the daughter of the 13th-century ruler of Ravenna, had been married to a political ally of her father's, but fell in love with her husband's brother, Paolo, who was also married. In some versions of the story[3] Francesca's husband was lame and deformed, and she was tricked into an engagement by first meeting the handsome brother Paolo under false pretenses. In *The Divine Comedy* Dante learns that Paolo and Francesca, though passionately attracted, had resisted their desires until one day, reading about the adulterous love of Lord Lancelot and Queen Guinevere, they restrained themselves no longer. One kiss, and they were goners.

For transgressing the bonds of marriage, they were murdered by Francesca's outraged husband and eternally doomed to try to repeat the adulterous kiss which was their downfall. In Rodin's sculpture, you can see a book, presumably the story of Lancelot and Guinevere, clutched in Paolo's left hand. So, Rodin's sculpture is an oft-censored work of art depicting a transgressive kiss, a kiss that itself was inspired by another work of art depicting other transgressive kisses. *The Divine Comedy* explicitly blames Francesca's corruption on her erotic reading matter.

Disputes about eros and danger aren't ancient history. In 1997 *The Kiss* was excluded from a traveling exhibit of Rodin's work by Brigham Young University because the nudity was regarded as "offensive to community morals and religious views." Many other portrayals of kisses have been banned because they show people of the same sex or because they depict kissing buttocks or genitals. Art censorship is a major focus of U.S. conservative political groups.

Taming the Danger

Do you have any idea how many greeting cards depict kisses between animals, angels, or children? What is the symbolism here? What is the politics? Some would say these pictures show innocence, sweetness, harmlessness, kisses for the sheer pleasure of affection, with no awareness of future heartbreak or loss.

"Innocent" images depict kissing without sexuality; they attempt to deny the sexual power of kissing. In a society where kisses like Rodin's give offense and lead to censorship, commercial depictions of kissing will try to avoid offense by de-eroticizing and taming the kiss. In the world of greeting cards, airbrushed and trivialized images make the kiss into a product. "Cute" may not be offensive, but just try to imagine a world of "cute" sexuality.

A Commercial Story

Who owns the kiss? Well, the Hershey chocolate company owns part of the kiss. I called the company to ask if they have a trademark on the word "kisses," but they said the legal department only replies by mail, and I never received any letter. Hershey's website says that they do have a trademark on the plume extending out of the wrapper, and on the familiar foil configuration.

Hershey's kisses were introduced in 1907 and the little squirts of chocolate were handwrapped until 1921 when automated wrapping machines entered the picture. The Hershey's website reports that they think "the candy was named for the sound or motion of the chocolate being deposited during the manufacturing process." I find that a sensual notion—kiss as squirt.

I want to tell a more serious story about the kiss as product. French photographer Robert Doisneau took a famous 1950 photo of a kiss in Paris, and called it *The Kiss at City Hall*.[4] Seemingly oblivious to the bustle of Paris, to onlookers, to whatever else is going on, two lovers sense only each other as they walk along. A thick scarf encircles his neck as he leans down to her upturned face.

In 1988, Jean-Louis and Denise Lavergne saw this photo, and thought they recognized themselves. They had been in that very street in April, 1950 and had a diary to prove it. Madame Lavergne still had the skirt and jacket she wore that day and Monsieur Lavergne recognized the blue scarf his sister had given him for Christmas. They contacted Doisneau, and he, they said, was charming to them, and said, "you are now in my family."

They were delighted to be part of the history of romance, Paris, youth, freedom, passion, and the kiss. The couple was filmed for a TV documentary about Doisneau, but when the footage of them wound up on the cutting-room floor, they were upset that their romance story wouldn't be in the film. So—and don't say America is the only land of litigation—they went to court to prove that they were the legendary couple. Under a 1985

French privacy law, they claimed their image had been stolen from them by the photographer, and they demanded financial compensation.

Whereupon an actress named Françoise Bornet stepped forward to say that she and her boyfriend were the couple in the photo, and that, although she had been paid a small sum to pose for the picture, she now wanted more, plus a percentage of future proceeds. The agency that handled Doisneau's photos produced what it said were the contact sheets of the original shoot which showed that several versions of the photo had been taken—all with models. Like the famous American World War II photo of the raising of the flag on Iwo Jima, this document of love had been posed.

Doisneau's tale allows us, finally, to add social construction to our psychobiosocial story of the kiss. Our romantic liplocks, in reality and fantasy, partake of infantile attachment, brain neuroanatomy, mammalian conflict reduction, cultural variation, and all sorts of learning experiences—yes. But, as with all aspects of sexuality, a hefty dose of symbolism spices up the mix. And symbolism, as we all know, can be created or altered for all kinds of human purposes—not the least of which are political ideology and cold hard cash.

Notes

1. This talk was given in October, 1998, in the middle of the Clinton/Lewinsky scandal.

2. See the sculpture as well as the story about the 1997 censorship on: http://www.ncac.org/cen_news/cn68rodin.html

3. Such as *Francesca da Rimini*, the 1914 opera by Riccardo Zandonai, libretto by Tito Ricordi.

4. See the photograph on: http://www.masters-of-photography.com/D/doisneau/doisneau_kiss_full.html. I am indebted to Adrianne Blue's 1996 book *On Kissing: From the Metaphysical to the Erotic* (London: Victor Gollancz) for this story.

FROM NIAGARA TO VIAGRA: WHY IT IS SO HARD TO JUST TALK ABOUT SEX

Joking Around

What is it with all this joking about sex? I'm going to tread on dangerous ground here, because people don't like to be told that humor is often not about humor, that there's more going on in a joke than just wit or amusement. I mean, sex is really not all that funny, is it? Somerset Maugham, the novelist, joked that "the posture is ridiculous" but that's true of washing the kitchen floor, and I haven't heard too many standup routines about that.

I think it is embarrassment that makes people laugh. Most people admit that they are embarrassed to talk about sex, making it easier to crack a joke than to have an honest conversation. But why are we so embarrassed and uncomfortable to talk about sex? The simplest answer is that we are unfamiliar with hearing sexual words spoken out loud in regular conversation. Who grew up hearing discussions of masturbation or kissing? Who hears people put into regular words their feelings about having or losing sexual desire?

Sex educators for little kids recommend naming genital parts like vulva, clitoris, penis, scrotum, and anus in the same way toes and eyes get named. Most parents don't do this because they are embarrassed, and as a consequence people are unfamiliar with words for many sexual parts of their body.

But unfamiliarity is only part of the reason for embarrassment. Behind the embarrassment, most people feel using sexual words is shameful, as if it's not a nice thing to do. To talk about sexual daydreams and feelings in a straightforward fashion feels like it breaks some taboo and you are a bad person.

Many peoples of the world are embarrassed to talk about sex. A recent *Denver Post* column described a vigorous publicity campaign in Uganda of billboards, TV ads, and clinic pamphlets to get parents to talk about sex with their kids.[1] A Zimbabwean woman said to the reporter, "African parents are shy. . . . Traditional African parents don't talk about sex to their children. . . . The custom is for the aunties to talk to the children. But as families move to the cities, the aunties are not available to fulfill their role."

In some parts of the world, however, like Scandinavia and The Netherlands, talk is more open between the generations and school-based sex education is much more open, too. In The Netherlands, for example, discussions of every aspect of sex begin in elementary school and continue through all the grades. Dutch teens, like teens in many countries, tend to have sex when they fall in love—but they tell their parents that they've begun to do so. Surprisingly, Dutch teens tend to start their sex lives later in adolescence than do Americans, British, Germans, and French, contradicting the claim that sex education makes kids experiment and start having sex earlier. Moreover, The Netherlands has low rates of teen pregnancy and sexually transmitted diseases (U.S. rates for both are the worst in the industrialized world).

U.S. family research by the Kaiser Foundation repeatedly shows that kids want to talk with their parents about sexuality, but that parents are barely comfortable with factual information, and won't talk about the questions kids are really interested in like how you know when you're ready for sex or how to handle peer pressure.

Many people say that these topics are *private*, and that you don't need to talk about them, but I think that this privacy argument is an excuse to avoid the embarrassment and feelings of shame honest talk would produce. So, let's go back to this shame. Where does it come from? Well, think back to when you first were curious about sexual anatomy or activities. What happened in *your* life?

My friend Mary Ann Silchenstedt told me a story about when she was eight years old and a neighbor's dog had puppies. Little Mary Ann was all excited and asked her mother how the puppies got here. Her mother just looked at her, so Mary Ann repeated the question. "The puppies weren't here yesterday and they're here today, so where'd they come from?" Whereupon her mother *slapped her across the face*.

In one form or another, that's been the experience of most of us. A slap, or shocked silence, or some extremely brief answer. Every day, kids are asking (or thinking about asking), "Mom, how old were you the first time you had sex?" "Dad, what did the President do with Monica Lewinsky?" "Mom, do girls masturbate?" "Dad, can a girl be a fag?" "Mom, did you ever want to do it with anybody but Dad?" And every day, teaching moments are evaded and avoided. "You are too young to even think about such things." "Where did you get such a question?" "That's the dumbest question I ever heard." "You'll find this stuff out when the time is right." Or the ever-popular, "Here—read this book." Soon there are no more questions. And then parents say proudly, "My kids never ask about that stuff." Whenever someone refers to sex as "that stuff" it's probably a clue that it's a taboo subject. And thus the embarrassment gets passed down through the generations.

It's possible that silence and embarrassment were appropriate in earlier times, with no divorce or contraception, shorter life spans, less travel, and less sexy advertising. But, so many things about our sex lives have changed. At the turn of the 21st century, people expect that good sex will be a central part of their adult lives, but are we doing anything as a society to bring such an outcome about other than keeping our fingers crossed?

Consequences of Embarrassment and Silence

There are two tragic consequences of this history of silence and embarrassment. The first has to do with personal anguish, and the second with how ignorance leaves us vulnerable to exploitation.

On the personal level, our inability to talk about sexuality often prevents a beautiful sexual life. Sexuality is a human potential that is part of our birthright, a unique sensual part that grows through education and life experience. As with spirituality or the love of music, the seeds of sexuality are there in all of us, but they need positive nurturance. Sex below the neck is diminished if it isn't linked to a brain that knows what's going on.

It's like dancing without any training. Everyone can sort of shuffle around and occasionally manage a little twirl. But to get pleasure in any sustained way, practice, communication, and know-how are needed.

Ignorance is a prison that keeps a person anxious. I could easily tell you hundreds of stories about the consequences of ignorance from my many years as a sex therapist about people who don't understand their own sexual feelings or those of their sexual partners or spouses, or who have questions they've never been able to ask anyone.

There's the story of the couple where the wife had been molested by her grandfather, and though her husband was very sympathetic, he couldn't understand that this meant she had to learn from scratch a positive attitude and habits about sex free from fear, shame, anxiety, and anger. He felt that since the molestation was a long time ago and it didn't involve intercourse and he was a very different person that his wife's reaction to him should be more loving. For a long time, his wife was unable to put into words that his insistence and entitlement actually reminded her of her grandfather, and mobilized all that negative fear, shame, anxiety, and anger. He found it very threatening to give up a sense of entitlement, and talking remains the key to their marital intimacy.

And then there's the story of the loving but asexual interracial couple for whom the restoration of their sex life required talking more than they wanted about racial prejudice. They felt that their relationship was close and warm and therefore insulated against racism, but it had gotten into their heads in too many ways. Their parents' negative racial messages still affected them. Cultural stereotypes about the sexuality of blacks and Jews still affected them. And their unwillingness to talk about race was itself a consequence of the deep pain of racism. Their sexual desires were held hostage until a lot of candid discussion could occur.

And then there are the stories of the overweight wife who hated her body and her husband (who liked her body), and the very anxious husband who could only have sex when he could put his work worries out of his mind (though this regimentation was hopelessly unromantic for his wife). I have interviewed over 2,000 couples at this point, and it is impossible to summarize all their stories, except to say that being able to talk to each other and put feelings into words was essential to overcoming their problems, and that this learning was both very difficult and ultimately very rewarding.

But, let me turn to the second consequence of embarrassment and silence—vulnerability to exploitation.

From Niagara to Viagra

Behind the history of both honeymoon jokes about Niagara Falls and Viagra jokes about heavy-duty bedsprings, winking pharmacists, and king-sized everythings, is the disappointing reality disguised by inflated symbols.

Why is Viagra so immensely popular? I think it's because it promises a magical solution to a society crippled by sexual ignorance, shame, and embarrassment. People with sexual questions have to deal with busy doctors who can't or won't take the time to really talk with them, and managed care companies that like patients to take up little time in doctor's offices and just leave with a prescription. Pharmaceutical companies are happy to exploit people suffering from limited sex education and histories of shame and embarrassment. Inflated promises are what the ever-growing Madison Avenue part of their companies is all about.

Bob Dole and all the subsequent ads imply that Viagra (and the other drugs for both men and women that are coming down the road) will restore romance and self-respect, but will it be that simple? Here is a recent story on an internet Viagra chatline:

> I am a 37 year old man with erectile problems for 2 years. I have used 50 mg. Viagra 4 times. All of those times have resulted in a very good erection and intercourse. The side effects are headache, upset stomach, stuffy nose, and facial flushing. My 3rd time with Viagra my stomach got so upset I had to run into the bathroom and that wasn't good. . . . [Now here is my routine]: About 30 mins after taking Viagra I take 2 Tylenol and a Tums and start drinking water. After about 15 mins I take another Tums and use a nasal spray for my stuffiness. I will continue this combination and it will work for me.

This sounds more like a Jackie Gleason routine rather than a romantic evening, but I think it is close to the reality of what life with these drugs will be like. Will this young man go on like this indefinitely? How does his sexual partner feel about the whole drama with the Tums and the nasal spray and the Tylenol?

Viagra is not selling anywhere near as well in Germany or the Netherlands or other countries where there are less conservative sexual politics and more sex education. My sex therapist friends in Germany regard the American mania about Viagra with the same amusement they regarded the disguised salaciousness of the Starr Report or the hypocrisy of abstinence-only sex curricula in the age of AIDS. American politics about sexuality is a mystery and a joke to the rest of the civilized world.

Our sexuality, one of our original blessings, is being exploited by politics and exploited by profits. As people of liberal faith, we should mobilize the same vigor for sexual liberty that we bring to other areas of social justice work. I hope we are not too embarrassed to march on behalf of true sexual liberation.

Notes

1. *Denver Post* column, 3/2/99, by Diane Carmen.

THE OPPOSITE OF SEX

Interview by
Moira Brennan in *Ms.* Magazine

The sexual experience notoriously defies clear-cut categorizing. What constitutes pleasure, what turns a person on, when and why—these are some of life's kaleidoscopic questions. In the best of circumstances, it can be a hell of a lot of fun trying to answer them. In the worst, it can be a source of tremendous frustration and anxiety.

Which is why the announcement in February, 1999, by a University of Chicago team of medical researchers that 43 percent of women and 31 percent of men are suffering from sexual "dysfunction" prompted concern. On one hand, the numbers seemed alarmingly high. On the other, the question quickly arose, "Says who?" It's the nature of sex to "function" on many levels—physical, emotional, intellectual, among others. Were scientists looking at all these aspects? And if not, which one were they looking at when they pronounced judgment? And what were their criteria? If someone told them, "I don't climax with my partner but always do when I masturbate," did that make the respondent dysfunctional, or was her partner just in need of education?

Questions about sex are charged with anxiety, defensiveness, and a few centuries of shame thrown in for good measure. But as feminists know all too well, the more you search for the "normal," the more you box people into narrow lives and narrow expectations. So not surprisingly, feminists are among the leaders in the effort to redefine sexual function and take it away from the medical establishment—a group still predominantly led by white men who seem to believe biology is destiny.

Looking for someone to comment on the Chicago study, and the larger, insistent questions about sexuality so many of us obsess about, we turned to . . . well, a doctor. But a doctor with a difference. Despite her own long career as a psychologist at Albert Einstein College of Medicine in New York City, and a sex therapist in private practice, Leonore Tiefer is an iconoclastic feminist thinker who takes nothing about human sexuality for granted. Her approach is to question everything—and to be as provocative, encouraging, and daring as she can be in the process. In her latest book, *Sex Is Not a Natural Act* (Westview Press), she points out that Western industrialized society is in love with the scientific method—to the detriment of our sex lives. This perspective leads us to break sexuality down into analyzable parts, and to see it as a merely biological drive, causing us to miss the immense impact of culture on our desires. Tiefer has even gone so far as to argue that there may be no biological sex drive at all: what influences people's desire most, she says, is the culture that surrounds them.

In Tiefer's view, sex can be ecstatic or boring, but it can also be something in the middle: a way to comfort others, to find relief from the drudgeries of our lives; an affirmation of our ability to please someone else, as well as an affirmation of our own desirability. Her goal is to decrease people's anxiety about sex, to put its importance into reasonable perspective.

This kind of approach highlights the dangers of medicalization and the mania for "quick fixes" like Viagra. Of course, the feminist and lesbian and gay rights movements have been challenging the masculinist, coitus-centered definition of sex for decades—often successfully. But Tiefer reminds us that there are many struggles yet to be won, and that we need to remain vigilant in a world where the power to define things still rests in the hands of white, heterosexual men.

mb In your book, you raise some very provocative questions about our understanding of sex—the very idea of its being "natural," for example. Why are these questions important for feminists?

lt People come at sex with a variety of goals, and sex can be very useful in meeting a lot of different needs. But there is a tendency in this culture to view sex with a very narrow focus—simply as a biological act, or as the domain of the beautiful, or as shameful. I believe that sex is fundamentally a cultural phenomenon. It doesn't exist in a fixed way but is created in relation to whatever is going on in the culture at a given moment.

This is a valuable approach for feminists, because a lot of social issues converge around sex, from reproduction to violence to objectification to disempowerment in intimate situations. It's not about whether someone can achieve orgasm or get an erection, but what are the forces—the social forces, the economic forces—at play? It's rich territory for social criticism as long as we're asking the right questions.

mb What do you think are the "right" questions that we should be asking?

It One of the problems I think we need to address is what sexuality is. People use the phrase "my sexuality" as though they are only sexual in one way. They say that really comfortably, but I'm not so comfortable with that, because the sexuality that I have with one person is very different than what I have with another person. My experience—I think everybody's experience as they get older—is one of enormous fluctuation in my sexual life. Sexuality is more situational, like friendship. You have the potential for friendship, but it's not like you walk around saying, "Gee, my friendship is really going strong today."

What you put in a category is an important part of how you experience it. When you see the gynecologist, who fiddles with your genitalia, we don't call that sexuality. There's no arousal. There's no orgasm. So what makes something "sexual"? The idea is always to ask, what is this? How does it work in my life? Who says so? Does the way I am looking at it make me happy?

mb Is there any way we can increase people's understanding of sexuality?

It It's the same way as with everything else, through the discussion of real experience. The personal is political. And through much more comprehensive sex education, increasing people's knowledge. If people could know a lot more about sex in psychological, physiological, sociological ways, they would be more protected against misinformation and hysteria. The effects of advertising, for example. We don't teach that in sex ed, and yet it has a profound impact on the sexual experience. And pleasure for the sake of pleasure. Certain commercial interests promote pleasure when it's linked to a product they're selling, but very few people are really trying to bring about an understanding of product-free pleasure. This is an era where Pfizer, the maker of Viagra, is trying to wring every nickel out of every human being on the face of this globe. I want people to be prepared to deal with that.

Nor do I see any members of the clergy writing op-eds or sermons about how we need more comprehensive sex education so that people will be able to better launch into their adult spiritual capabilities, because sex is such a great avenue to spirituality. I recently gave a sermon at my Unitarian Universalist Church called "From Niagara to Viagra: Why Is It So Difficult to Just Talk About Sex?" and my point was that whether it's honeymoon jokes or jokes about Viagra, people can make cracks, but they can't just talk. I started off by saying that I'd been going to this church for 15 years, and I had never heard a single word about sex from the pulpit. I was really glad and really scared to be doing it. But the congregants were wildly enthusiastic. People are parched for this kind of stuff.

mb On the other hand, we are inundated by talk of sex in the news, in the movies. That can also feel oppressive.

lt Well, we live in a sexualized culture as compared to earlier periods of repression and inhibition. The overemphasis on sex by the media is a phase. The behaviors and feelings of people have not changed as much as the commercialization of society, which has exploded. The visibility of sex in the media and its influence on how we understand sex is only 30 or 40 years old. If we were better educated about everything that has changed—the way birth control has shifted the role of sex, the way divorce has done the same thing, the way a good sex life has become synonymous with "success"—maybe we wouldn't feel as oppressed.

All this is complicated by the fact that political conservatives have taken advantage of the anxieties created by this overemphasis on sex. The right, from abstinence education to attacks on *Roe* v. *Wade*, is very invested in not allowing a discussion about things that they think are morally impure. They believe the mere talking about it is permissive. And there is something about the power of secrecy to generate shame and the power of openness to reverse that. So they're right—if we just say words, or allow teachers or books to say certain words, we could be generating the kind of society the right is opposed to: relativistic, morally open, diverse.

We're also inundated with the idea that sex is just biology and can be "fixed" by medicine. That causes a kind of fragmentation in people's thinking. If your focus is on a particular body part as the source of the problem, it prevents you from seeing sex as an act that involves your entire emotional, sensual, intellectual makeup—your whole self. The benefit of bringing a bigger picture to the act of making love is that it can remind you that it's you who is there making love, not some body part that does or does not live up to a medical norm. It's a perspective that honors uniqueness, which is one of the great things we can bring to sex. It's about allowing more humanistic values to be part of the discussion.

mb Is it hard for people to apply those values to sex?

It We don't value our uniqueness in the sexual encounter partly because so much of sex is a secret. You don't see your mother and father making love, but if you did you wouldn't be so inclined to think that you need to look like Michelle Pfeiffer in order to have sex. The cultural messages, whether they are coming from religion or commercialism, are influential in part because they're not counteracted by your own observation. I'm not advocating that everybody watch their parents have sex. But if you stopped to think, you might say to yourself, "I've never seen ordinary people make love. What do they do with a big stomach? How do they undress each other?" I have films of every conceivable kind of person—able-bodied and disabled, fat and thin, old and young—making love, and I can't show them to my medical students because the climate now says any explicit image is pornography and it's degrading. But the lack of this kind of bridge between people's own experience and the culture serves to depress us about sexuality. I think people are depressed constantly about their bodies, attractiveness, and physical expression. It's not so much about what you do with your genitalia that's the problem—it's learning how to feel like a desirable person, and to see that other people are desirable.

mb Do you think our understanding of sex also affects our understanding of gender?

It Gender affirmation is a phenomenally important element in the current construction of sexuality—at least for heterosexuals, who have been the bulk of my clients. Reproduction used to be the essence of gender affirmation for women. And for men it was employment. Now there are fewer and fewer ways of proving gender, and yet it's as important as it ever was. So how do you prove your gender? You've got to be able to have sex—not just any old sex, but coitus. Talking about this in the context of feminism is crucial. It's men's investment in a particular kind of masculinity that is fueling Viagra. Part of the work of feminists has been to question accepted notions about masculinity, whereas you could say Viagra is affirming them.

I worked in the urology department for many years and guys would come in and say, "I'm impotent," and I'd say, "So how is that a problem for you?" And they'd look at me like I was nuts. They'd say, "What? I can't have sex!" And I'd say, "And why do you want to have sex?" in an extremely conversational tone of voice, making eye contact, all of that. And they would say to me, "What do you mean? *Everybody* has sex."

They simply didn't have any answer for these questions. They couldn't answer them because the vocabulary is impoverished, profoundly impoverished. Sometimes somebody would be able to cough up a few words, and they'd say, "It means I'm normal."

Not being able to have an orgasm is like the epitome of not being normal. It's the epitome of not being a man or not being a woman. So I would tell them that there are ways to cope with this. Let's be a man in other ways. No, they couldn't accept that. To them, this was the proof.

I always say to people, orgasm is very American. Because it's a score. It's short. You know when you've had it. You can put the notch on your belt.

mb How successful have you been when you ask people to reconsider these notions?

It It's very hard. I have to admit very modest success. I think my patients would say that I revolutionize their thinking, but from my point of view it's a tiny revolution compared with how I've revolutionized my own thinking. And they don't come for a course on radical sexual thinking. They come to learn how to have an orgasm. I start out by telling them, "Here are 18,000 reasons why it's not as important as you think," but you can't talk somebody out of wanting to have an orgasm. You have to teach them to have an orgasm, and then show them how trivial it really is. It's just a reflex. It's the symbolism that makes it feel so good. The symbolism imbues it with dessert and wedding and Nobel Prize, all at once.

I try to give people the sense that what's valuable about their sexuality is their story—their own symbolism—rather than how closely they approximate the "healthy norm." People haven't been taught the words for their own stories. There's no vocabulary for anything other than technique. People have a very, very hard time describing the yearnings, the longings, the feelings of gratification surrounding sex.

I don't think there's any one way to experience sex. I'm not offering a road map. I say you can use sex in all kinds of ways for any human motive.

Solace, nurturance, celebration. And people do. They just don't think of it that way. They look at S/M and they say, "It needs whips and chains, it needs rubber—it's weird." They don't realize that submitting themselves to another person's desire is just one form of pleasure, one that's available to all of us from time to time. Imagine coming home and saying, "This was a really awful day. I don't want to be in charge of myself anymore. You do it. Do me." That sort of subordination could be a welcome relief. Ritual can work the same way. People go to weddings and things are familiar, they have a certain order and that's comforting. Sex is often ritualized without thinking about it, but I think it can be more intentionally ritualized. You might decide to celebrate the opportunities offered by a sexual encounter the way you'd celebrate the opportunities offered by a Thanksgiving dinner. During the day, you rarely get an opportunity to express yourself, nobody listens to you, so you get home and you need some affirmation. Sex can do that. The stroking. The relaxing. Approval. When somebody touches you and kisses you and licks you and says you're beautiful, that's approval. The trouble is, for a lot of women it's very hard to accept that somebody thinks they're beautiful. Somebody wants to lick their whole body: what makes a woman feel entitled to that? You've got to feel secure in yourself first.

mb Do you think part of the reason we don't talk more honestly about sex is because people want to retain some sense of mystery? And is that important?

It People have conflicting wishes when it comes to sex. They want unpredictability and control at the same time. So they tell themselves that if they know too much they will lose the mystery. But in my experience, that's not what happens. I'm an opera lover, and I've seen certain operas a dozen times—I can hum them. Why do I go? All the power and pleasure is still available, even in something you understand well. The idea that the best sex life comes from surrender to the unknown—like in the movies, being swept away by the waves—it's a myth. It's an image. When you talk to people about their sex lives, it's not the surrendering ones who seem to have the best time. Like with everything in life, the more you know about it, the more you enjoy it.

So I want to open up people's minds. Explode those myths. Instead of just talking about an erection or orgasm, let's talk about pleasure. You want pleasure? A lot of pleasure is conditioned. It's anticipation. It's not in the skin. It's not in the genitalia. It's what it means that imbues it with that sense of joy. Otherwise, it's just like eating a peach in the summer. I mean, it's really nice, but it's not ecstatic—well, it depends on the peach, but it's usually not that ecstatic. It's the symbolic investment that makes sex ecstatic.

That's why the best approach is to educate ourselves about the symbolism. Sex is always changing. I don't know exactly what sex used to be like, and I don't know exactly what sex will look like in the year 2150. I don't mind that I don't know. It's not a problem. The idea is to prepare people to deal with the messages they are getting now. I can't stop Pfizer from plowing ahead with Viagra. I can't stop the efforts of the Right. And even if I could, we know from history that something else would pop right up in its place. The point is to educate people to be prepared to deal with these messages in ways that don't infringe on their enjoyment of sex, to keep an open mind and, if possible, to keep a sense of humor about it all.

chapter 5

THE MCDONALDIZATION OF SEX

Food has been a lot in the news. Perhaps, like me, some of you have gobbled up a recent eye-opening and horrifying exposé, Eric Schlosser's *Fast Food Nation*, about the creation of the fast food industry and its sad consequences for workers, animals, consumers, and the environment. Being of a historical bent, I followed that with the 1975 book that Schlosser said inspired him, *Eat Your Heart Out: How Food Profiteers Victimize the Consumer*, by Jim Hightower, the left-wing politician and commentator from Texas.

And then, just when I thought I had heard enough bad news about American food, Marion Nestle, head of Nutrition and Food Studies at New York University, published *Food Politics: How the Food Industry Influences Nutrition and Health*, and I learned how the very people who the public trusts as experts on food and health—nutritionists, journalists, and scientists—are deeply in the pockets of the mega-billion-dollar food industry.

It seems that to fully understand a subject requires a lot of background, and background isn't often what we get in mass media stories about obesity and epidemic weight problems. You don't learn much about how the industry and then the public got so big. You'll have to read Schlosser or Hightower or Nestle to get the full story.

Hightower used the term "The McDonaldization of America" (p. 237) to refer to the standardization that is the hallmark of fast food. But it took a sociologist named George Ritzer to really explore the idea of McDonaldization. His 1993 book, *The McDonaldization of Society*, has ironically become a bestseller on many of the same college campuses where McDonald's have replaced college cafeterias. The "McDonaldization" of society, according to Ritzer, is a process by which four principles of the fast food restaurant are coming to dominate American and world society:

First, EFFICIENCY. Ritzer argues that the success of the fast food restaurant is based on streamlining and simplifying every possible aspect of work and food preparation in order to save money and increase profits.

Second, CALCULABILITY or an emphasis on *numbers*. Calculation is everywhere in fast food from the optimum size of a french fry to the right amount of worker turnover to save money on employee benefits to promoting a bargain mentality so the consumer keeps wanting more for less.

Third, PREDICTABILITY. Each McDonald's replicates the same standardized menu, pricing, decor, architecture, employee training, kitchen equipment, food preparation, etc. There are no surprises at McDonald's.

The fourth and last principle is the quest for CONTROL over workers and customers, especially by using machinery. The food arrives at McDonald's precut, preformed, presliced, and pre-prepared by machines. Soft drinks are dispensed in exact quantities while cashiers ring up totals using preset buttons with pictures of foods.

Ritzer describes these four pillars of McDonaldization as they were first developed in assembly-line factories and then perfected in the postwar fast food industry.

Let's see how this four-part McDonaldization model applies to sex in contemporary America.

Contemporary America is dominated by mass media and mass media are dominated by sex. Every day in every way media culture is a hothouse of sensational sexual stories and images. If it isn't priests, it's presidents, if it isn't sexy celebrities falling in and out of love at warp speed, it's terrifying all-news-all-the-time-cable-TV stories about abducted children and incurable pedophiles.

Every aspect of sex, gender, and reproduction is being transformed by globalization, technology, and longer life. Just look at how the new reproductive technologies are breaking down traditional ideas of father and mother and bringing babies into the world in completely new ways.

But these social changes in sex, gender, and reproduction produce a lot of stress, as each of us, raised with one set of values, has to adjust to new ideas and life choices. Adjustment to such big changes in emotional subjects would be hard enough, even with help, background, information, a calm approach, and tincture of time. But too often adjustment and understanding about sexual topics are made practically impossible because they are approached in the spirit of sensationalism and polarization.

I saw a flyer in midtown Manhattan, for example, protesting the *New York Post*'s reaction to the decision of the *New York Times* to publish photos and announcements of same-sex commitment ceremonies in the previously marriage-only "Wedding" pages. The first such announcement appears in the *New York Times* on August 1, 2002. Two nice Jewish men, Daniel Gross and Steven Goldstein, one a Yale graduate and one from—yes—Harvard, are pleased to announce, and their parents are pleased to announce, that they are having their ceremony today in Vermont.

The politically conservative *New York Post* ridiculed this decision in a cartoon showing a man and a chicken, holding hands(!), with valentine hearts flying around their heads. The man was saying to the editor of the *New York Times*, "I hope you're progressive enough to publish our domestic commitment ceremony." This cartoon is the kind of sensationalism that creates polarization without giving the public useful background about new ideas.

The *New York Post*'s anti-gay chicken joke brings me back to sex. Recall to mind the McDonaldization model: efficiency, numbers, predictability, and control. How is this happening to sexual life?

Sexuality, which could be a life-affirming source of intimacy, pleasure, and renewal, seems too often to have become an opportunity for personal and interpersonal anxiety. A competitive performance mentality is taking over sexual life, with people feeling they must measure up to ever-higher standards of sexual attractiveness and sexual adequacy. People feel disqualified from a "good sex life" if they don't have a perfect body, hair, teeth, or skin, can't perform suave and athletic maneuvers, or, worst of all, if they don't have the proper sexual responses.

When I first studied sex therapy twenty-five years ago, the main problem I learned about was "performance anxiety"—the fear people had that they wouldn't be able to perform sexual activities properly. People literally avoided relationships or sexual encounters because they felt ashamed that their bodies didn't perform the proper way.

"Performance anxiety" continues to be extremely common. But now I also see lots of people with "response anxiety"—the fear that they don't *feel*

enough, that their inner experience isn't properly passionate. This is especially true for young people just starting out their sexual lives, people in
new relationships, and people in midlife who find their sexual experience
changing along with their bodies, and overreact to these perfectly predictable developments with panic or shame. This is a very sad situation.

I don't mean to romanticize the past, by the way, not at all. It used to be
that sex was so secret, so hidden, and so private that people felt completely
unprepared and anxious that they wouldn't know what to do and would
somehow do it wrong. Now, sex is so not-secret, so not-hidden, and so not-
private that people feel anxious that they can't possibly measure up to
what they think is the "normal" standard of sexual life.

It doesn't help at all when people are told that sex is all about the birds
and the bees and that "normal" function is built-in and preprogrammed. I
am not kidding when I tell you that I stopped believing in the built-in and
pre-programmed theory when I realized that animals never wear lingerie or
light candles.

Where do people get their ideas of what the "normal" standard of sexual life is supposed to be? Standards come partly from the mass media, e.g.,
from TV shows that show passion around every water cooler and hospital
emergency room, from pop songs with lyrics that are more explicit than sex
advice columns, from articles in men's and women's magazines about the
10 top tips to drive him/her wild in bed, from celebrity lifestyles all about
youthful looks and lots of money, and from advertisements for clothes and
perfumes and deodorants and hair gels that sell by threatening that you'll
be a sexual and social loser if you don't buy them. Messages and images
make it seem that a highly active sex life is necessary for anyone to be
happy or normal—the kind of standardization I relate to McDonaldization.

But there's another source of the new standards that you may be less
aware of. It's the medical profession, with its new men's sexual health clinics and even newer women's sexual health clinics. These things are popping up all over, almost as fast as new McDonald's. And they really are
fast-food franchises that specialize in efficiency, predictability, numbers,
and control. Everyone who comes in with a sexual complaint gets an expensive workup of genital measurements that seems superscientific. But
nine times out of ten, the customer walks out with a prescription for Viagra, and since in the future there will be a dozen or two dozen such sex

drugs—for both men and women—if the first one doesn't work the patient—or is it now merely a customer—will be encouraged to try another and another and another.

The message of the new sexual health centers really comes from the global pharmaceutical industry that bankrolls them: the proper sexual life consists in perfect, routine, regular desire for "normal" sexual performance, i.e., intercourse and orgasm. Anything else is a dysfunction, and you probably should take something to correct your problem. Preferably something expensive that you'll have to keep taking for your whole life.

Nothing is said in the drug promotional material about how some perfectly normal people or couples might like to do without much intercourse, or without sex altogether, and don't need to be told on ads every day on the 6 o'clock news that they are dysfunctional. These ads never connect cultural diversity to sex, or validate sexual changes over a person's life as their body and feelings about their partner changes—no, that's not part of the universal, one-size-fits-all new model that stresses routine, standardized performance.

I think the medical model of sex, the mass media model of sex, the McDonald's model of sex, is popular because it seems to soothe a public made anxious by being exposed to sexual hype day and night. It seems to provide simple answers and solutions to people anxious about sexuality in fast-changing times. But the medical model doesn't really soothe, it actually exploits because it sets up a high and inflexible standard of sexual normalcy—and offers no coaching, training, or teaching to help people prepare for it.

Think about it. Unlike many parts of the industrialized world, there's no systematic, comprehensive sex education in the United States. The U.S. government only funds sex education that promotes sexual abstinence. Comprehensive sex education is considered a danger to moral development. No wonder sex drugs like Viagra sell so much better in the United States than Europe—it's not that there's more dysfunction, there's just more anxiety and far more ignorance.

The Unitarian Universalist Association, by the way, has been a pioneer in developing sex education materials, a bright candle in this otherwise bleak landscape. The "About Your Sexuality" curricula in the 1970s won many awards, and the new "Our Whole Lives" curricula are not only for children and youth, but even for adults.[1]

The Clinton impeachment hearings taught me some things about the strange picture of media and sexuality in the United States. As a sex educator and therapist I was hopeful that the impeachment news coverage might educate about why people get sexually excited by power and danger or why a married fifty-year-old leader of a superpower and a single twenty-one-year-old intern from Los Angeles would be erotically drawn together. I was asked by the *Los Angeles Times* to write an op-ed column about the Clinton-Lewinsky affair from the perspective of a sex therapist. So I wrote a little essay about the realities of erotic life, and they wouldn't publish it. They paid me but they wouldn't run it because, they said, I didn't moralize. I said I'm a sex therapist, not a minister. No, they said, they wouldn't print anything that didn't talk about right and wrong. So much for media sex education. We see the same results as with how hamburgers are made—gullibility, unhealthy behaviors, and confusion.

When people think about buying a car nowadays they know that the choices they have are related to large global stories. They've heard about oil and the Middle East and the environment and mergers and job losses and Korea—a car is no longer just a commodity but it's part of a bigger picture of politics and social values. You can still choose whatever car you want, but at least you know the background story.

That's what's happened to fast food with the publication of *Fast Food Nation*. A hamburger is part of larger stories about workers and justice and the environment and people now can choose their food more knowingly.

Maybe someone should write a book called *Fast Sex Nation* to show people how a standardized model of sexual relations is being promoted by commercial interests and may be endangering—well, maybe not workers and justice and the environment—but what we might call the spiritual potential of physical relations for intimacy, pleasure, and renewal.

Aldous Huxley wrote, in his great 1932 science fiction novel, *Brave New World*, about a future totalitarian time when people are taught from early childhood to have as much sex as possible with as many people as possible, and to take several pleasure pills every day. But in *Brave New World*, sex has ceased to express individuality in any way, and the sex looks routine, standardized, and bleak.

We are all embodied spiritual beings, all sexually different, and we need to affirm that our physical expression of love and intimacy, our capacities for pleasure and sensuality, are not for sale, and, like our other spiritual capacities, must not be standardized.

Each of us needs background to fully understand sexuality. The media are going to throw sexual images at us twenty-four hours a day, including ads for more and more alleged wonder drugs. Our job is to avoid being gullible and uninformed. If "Our Whole Lives" isn't your cup of tea, check out the library, the internet, or the bookstore. You'll be amazed by how many fascinating new books about sex there are. With sex, as with hamburgers, reading is fundamental, and you'll be surprised how much you can learn about *all* your sensual pleasures.

Notes

1. http://www.uua.org/owl/main.html

chapter 6

DOING THE VIAGRA TANGO: SEX PILL AS SYMBOL AND SUBSTANCE

A four-page full-color advertisement for Viagra tablets has appeared in the latest issues of the *American Psychologist,* the flagship scientific journal of the American Psychological Association (APA). The ad shows a healthy, well-dressed couple dancing and smiling into each other's eyes. They seem to be in a public location, maybe a hotel or train station, since they are dancing in front of a curved marble staircase with several blurry figures holding suitcases. The couple are happily absorbed with each other, and the words read, "Success is one simple step away. . . . Introducing new Viagra, the simple new step to improve erectile function." There has never before, to my knowledge, been an ad for a drug, an ad in color, or a four-page supplement for anything in the *American Psychologist.* The APA is doing the Viagra tango.

Viagra was approved by the U.S. Food and Drug Administration for prescription to men with "erectile dysfunction" on March 27, 1998. In the short time since then, it has become a player and symbol in many ongoing sociocultural and socioeconomic debates, including but not limited to ones focused on sexuality. For example, a front-page article in the August 2, 1998 *New York Times* began, "Seizing upon the celebrity of the male impotency pill Viagra, family planning groups are pressing lawmakers in Congress and the states on a long-ignored demand that employers cover the costs of contraception as a health benefit." What does Viagra have to do with contraception? Gender politics! If insurance will pay for men's sexuality, so the argument goes, it should pay for women's sexuality. Viagra's sudden symbolic value as God-sent gift for men may allow American women finally to achieve their long-frustrated demand that health insurance cover the cost of contraceptives.

Viagra, though officially marketed as a treatment for a medical condition, erectile dysfunction, has been seized on by the hyperactive, hypersexual media industry much like that other perfect story, the American president's sex life. The media do the Viagra tango in news and features, highbrow and lowbrow. As metaphor, Viagra is coming to signify positive, energetic, strong, and solving of all difficulties, as in "Viagra politician" (contrasted with "Prozac politician") and "Viagrafied old age." The word-clever are having a field day.

There are many stories to tell about doing the Viagra tango, but let me limit myself to four. The first is about how Viagra the pill, but more importantly, Viagra the symbol, may affect the sexual conduct and experience of women and men in many parts of the world. The second is about how the arrival of Viagra has already changed the practice of scientific sex research and policy in substantial ways. The third is about how Viagra, as shown by the story on contraceptive insurance, will play a role in contemporary political disputes involving gender, sexuality, health care, and aging. And the fourth is about how the celebrity and sexiness of Viagra can enable progressives to get people's attention for important, but often dry, political and economic discussions. People, it seems, will read anything about Viagra; so, read on.

Sexual Conduct and Experience

There are scant data so far to let us know what impact Viagra has on the sexual lives of individuals. In terms of anecdotes, we are swamped in media and industry-sponsored research hallelujahs, but they are highly selective and untrustworthy. Several months before Viagra was released, I asked a group of sex therapist colleagues to suggest its likely impact. Their fairly predictable speculations focused on who would benefit ("older men in good relationships," "anxious widowers returning to dating"), and who would not ("couples with long-standing erotic avoidance and lack of affectionate touching," "men whose lack of erection expresses unconscious hostility," "men whose experience with Viagra will only decrease their own self-esteem"). One sex therapist suggested that this last group would suffer the terrors of "the padded-bra syndrome," with fear of disrobing (either admitting use of the drug or having sex without it) maintaining the very insecurity the bra/pill was supposed to eliminate.

Will Viagra, the sexual security blanket, further postpone the emotional maturity allegedly lacking in the baby-boomer generation (or is it old-fashioned to think that some narcissistic wounds are important to maturation)? Will Viagra be most popular in patriarchal cultures where women's sexual bargaining is reduced, men are entitled to use family resources for their sexual pleasure, and potency is the major measure of masculinity? News stories about black markets for Viagra in Kuwait, Egypt, Vietnam, Japan, and China support such global speculations.

Some have argued that, like the contraceptive pill, Viagra will simply eliminate a major anxiety associated with heterosexual intercourse, and will free couples to engage in spontaneous, worry-free lovemaking. But will the sexual script of Viagra lovemaking actually be flexible and worry-free, or will Viagra-sex be all about worshipping the penis, since no one spending upwards of $10 to have an erection will ignore it? Will men feel relaxed or worry about fraudulence? In the worst-case scenario, Viagra could cause both men and women to feel resentful and less erotic—women, because the drug eliminates their sense of desirability and sexual efficacy; men, because the pill is just further proof that they are less potent and less masculine than they used to be.

Journalists have applauded Viagra (together with the Clinton-Lewinsky sex scandal) for normalizing discussions of sexuality and sexual problems, but I am not so sure. The extent of public discussion seems limited to the same old repertoire of jokes and bragging, and while the language may be more technical ("oral sex" and "erection" instead of "doing the nasty"), it seems that ancient jokes about "dirty old men" and "Is that a gun in your pocket or are you just glad to see me?" are just being recirculated. The one exception seems to be that men being treated for prostate cancer, such as former senator and presidential candidate Bob Dole, can publicly admit that they need and use Viagra.

Sex Research and Policy

Sexuality has been a marginal academic topic throughout the twentieth century, and the USA still lacks any departments of sexuality studies in colleges and universities.[1] Sex researchers are often one of a kind in their institutions. Sex research is chronically underfunded, and sexuality scholars find their publications and congresses ridiculed by colleagues and the media. Following the conservative political shift in the 1980s, sex research became even more unpopular and unfundable since it was associated with "permissive values."

In this climate, the recent interest of the pharmaceutical industry in funding sex research has understandably been thrilling to many sexologists. It represents security for a research program (space, graduate students, technical assistance) and reduces nagging from one's university administration (since American academics, especially those in medical schools, are expected nowadays to contribute generously to their departmental budgets).

However, the involvement of the pharmaceutical industry has created substantial conflicts of interest for sex researchers. Under the influence of inter-company competitiveness, collegial relations are severely threatened. "Proprietary secrecy" has suddenly gagged scientists from speaking about industry-"owned" data because of nondisclosure agreements they have signed in order to obtain funding. I know of one researcher studying the effects of Viagra on women who completed data collection in February 1997 but, as of August 1998, is not yet permitted to discuss the data publicly. The danger of such nondisclosure agreements goes beyond the frustration of researchers to possible harm to the public, since despite Viagra being tested only on men, many doctors are writing prescriptions for women, and the media are irresponsibly speculating about effects on women and publishing unsubstantiated anecdotes.

But Viagra's challenges to sex research go beyond ethical conflicts. Pharmaceutical industry funding endorses an essentialist, biomedical model of sexuality that ignores relationality, the social construction of sex, and most sociocultural factors. While no one prevents researchers from pursuing broader sex research or even broader sex research on erection treatments, industry money is only available to those following industry protocols, and that means comparing dysfunction treatments using limited outcome definitions. Mandatory questionnaires ask whether taking the pill affected the hardness of the erection, the frequency of intercourse, and the satisfactoriness of intercourse. Such quantitative research assumes that all men mean the same thing by "erection," "intercourse," and even "satisfaction," though much sexological research has shown that terms in questionnaires are interpreted quite diversely. Furthermore, industry-sponsored research won't examine how use of Viagra affects couple power dynamics or the subtle effects on sexual techniques and communication.

In addition to gender politics in contraceptives' insurance coverage, let me indicate a few other current political stories which have seen new life because of Viagra.

1. Government pharmaceutical regulation. As of summer 1998, a few dozen well-publicized deaths have been attributed to use of Viagra. The manufacturer claimed coincidence given the drug's vast popularity, but consumer health organizations seized the opportunity to publicize their demands for increased government regulation of drug testing, for expanded warnings to consumers about drug side effects, and for elimination of computer on-line drug dispensing.

2. Insurance coverage for pharmaceuticals. Quite aside from the issue of contraceptives for women, there has been enormous debate over whether and to what extent Viagra itself should be paid for by health insurance. This controversy has offered oceans of publicity to players in health insurance disputes. When Kaiser Permanente, the USA's largest health maintenance organization (9.1 million subscribers) announced its refusal to cover Viagra because of cost worries (the pill is wholesaling at about $7 per 100 mg pill), consumer advocates and progressive politicians argued that insurers were like "camels sticking their noses under the tent" to see if the public would go along with drug exclusions based on cost.

   Additionally, the language used in disputes over Viagra coverage has been examined for its policy implications. For example, when insurance companies rejected Viagra because it is used not only for "medical necessity" but also for "lifestyle enhancement," disability-rights groups publicized the threat such language poses to their situation, such as the elimination of insurance reimbursement for wheelchairs.

3. Government regulation of "danger." Viagra has made it possible to discuss publicly what a terrible thing the threat of impotence is. So, for example, in the fight over regulation of cigarette smoking, advocates for raising the legal age for cigarette purchase have recently added "threat of impotency" to the dangers of smoking from which young people must be protected.

4. Right-wing sexual agenda. No topic related to sexuality could possibly escape some connection with homosexuality or other biblical sexual transgressions in the current U.S. atmosphere. An Alabama state representative named Sims recently called a press conference to announce his plan to introduce legislation "banning doctors from prescribing the impotence drug for anyone known to have a sexually transmitted disease." This coded threat allowed Representative Sims to remind voters that he is opposed to anything that might increase the predatory capacities of HIV-positive homosexuals (or unfaithful heterosexuals).

Viagra's sexiness and celebrity can be used to hold the public's attention for education about global economics. The public is interested, for example, in the cost of the miracle drug, and might learn how inflated drug costs are connected to huge advertising and marketing budgets. A French marketing and communications organization was recently hired "to accelerate market acceptance of [Viagra] and sustain marketability . . . [through] advertising and promotion, contact sales, publishing, medical education, public relations, interactive multimedia," and so on. Such a story illuminates the interlocking worlds of science, government, and commerce.

Newspaper business pages are full of stories showing how Viagra-influenced "market dynamics" have triggered shifts throughout the entire "erectile dysfunction industry." The manufacturer of Muse, an older erection treatment drug administered intra-urethrally instead of orally, changed its international sales strategy because Viagra's popularity suddenly brought primary-care physicians into the forefront of sexual medicine. Like the contraceptive pill, Viagra will have intended effects, and many unintended effects. Because of commercial media, the Internet, and the reach of global capital, Viagra has suddenly appeared to participate in the construction of gender, sexuality, aging, and medicine, just to name a few. Everyone can use this latest fantasy symbol to their own ends. Everyone will dance.

Notes

1. Since this talk was given, San Francisco State University has inaugurated a Human Sexuality Studies Program. One . . . and counting.

part three

FEMINISM AND SEXUALITY

I can't imagine what I would have been thinking about for the past thirty years if there had not been a women's liberation movement. Would I have just plugged along, using my training in physiological psychology to continue studying hormone and rat copulatory behavior as I had done in graduate school? Many people do continue academic careers in just such a way, and I have been friends with some of them for half my life! Not me, though. As the essays in this section demonstrate, I became a critic and analyst within sexology. I had no sooner gotten a lab of my own than the women's movement hit me, and I began to question the very purpose of lab research within sexology. In the words of Betty Friedan, "it changed my life" (Friedan, 1976). Once I realized that sex was a social construction, I was a changed person.

It has been feminist scholarship that showed me the incompleteness of the traditional sexology perspective on sexuality. Maybe you know that something is up when you're in the middle of a revolution, but you certainly don't see the full scope of the thing. The same irreversible processes of social change that created intellectual feminism—which so affected the content of my professional work—gave me the independence to go to graduate school (and, though divorced, to finish), to pursue a career in teaching and research, and to follow my own ideas. When I arrived at my first academic job in 1969, I became the first woman in a psychology department of twenty-seven. Back then, without the language of sexism and sex discrimination and with no feminist theory to help me, it took me quite some time to realize the trouble I was in! I just knew it was hard to make friends among many of my new colleagues because for some reason we weren't seeing psychology, gender, and so many other subjects in the same way!

It is no wonder that feminist theory has come such a long way in thirty years—we started from scratch to figure everything out. Once you put women at the center of scholarship, it really changes the questions you ask, what you notice, and the conclusions you reach. I'm enjoying a history of vacations at the moment (Aron, 1999), and a book about the politics of the food industry (Nestle, 2002). Neither of them is "about" women, but women's lives and gender politics inform the scholarship in a thousand little ways that never would have happened thirty years ago.

One thing that has helped my scholarship immensely is having *sitzfleisch*. The German language has some great words for things. This one means a sort of sitting-patience that I take in my case to be an intellectual curiosity about how everything works and a willingness to put in the time to figure things out. I'm actually not very patient with people (myself or others), but I can attend lectures and seminars on pretty much anything and find some connection to gender and sexuality. Feminist scholarship has showed me that there is a gendered aspect to every subject, whether it is the history of art, environmental politics, holiday planning, or restaurant operation, and that has remained fascinating.

Sexologists, however, have typically taken a narrow view of gender. Whether the method is survey, clinical, or lab studies, sex research has used the two categories, male and female, as a way to divide subjects (animal or human) into groups for comparison. As Bem (1993, 1981) says, we are a gender-schematic society that is overprepared to focus on gender differences. I have worked hard over the years to reveal how this focus obscures situational factors, ignores issues of class and culture, over-emphasizes genetic and biological causes with implied unchangeability, and obsesses about genital components of sexuality. I have repeatedly tried to get people to think of gender as a *dependent* variable in sex research, not just an independent variable, but hardly any sex research looks at how masculinity and femininity are constructed by sexual scripts.

Some of the articles in this section were originally written as speeches in the heat of the moment. Seeing my work as part of a struggle

with ideological opponents has characterized my professional outlook.
Maybe it started by trying to explain feminism to those twenty-seven
male colleagues. As a '70s feminist, a "second wave feminist" as we are
now called, even though I was a sexologist, I felt comfortable analyzing
social injustice and working for change.

It's not all that easy to keep on keeping on, though, as the civil rights
slogan has it. I have learned to my dismay that there are too few political
people in the world. As I kept trying to bring a feminist message to sexology, I have often needed the support of the Association for Women in Psychology (AWP), a feminist group with a definite political slant that was
founded in 1969 (and that I found in 1977). Some readers of this book
might like to check out the website and attend an AWP conference—they
are very student-friendly: http://www.awpsych.org.

chapter 1

AN ACTIVIST IN SEXOLOGY

The award I am receiving today recognizes not only me, but my ideas, a notion that terrifies me a little, since my ideas are fundamentally iconoclastic. What does it mean when a critic, an outsider, gets recognition?

I've received considerable criticism over the years for being *political and ideological* about sexuality when I should have been *professional*, for somehow confusing what should be separate life departments, and I would like to take the opportunity of receiving this Kinsey award to ruminate a little about these issues.

Becoming an Activist

I have discovered that I have the soul of an activist, a person committed to social change and the amelioration of social problems. The eldest child of leftist Jewish New Yorkers, it should have been obvious that I would grow up expecting to be involved in the struggle against injustice and oppression. The locale of struggle, the particular issues, these would depend on the social and personal vicissitudes of my life and times, but my background inescapably oriented me toward involvement in progressive issues.

I was on the University of California campus at Berkeley from 1963 to 1969 throughout the Free Speech Movement and the various antiwar campaigns, and I must tell you that then I didn't lift a finger. I felt agitated a lot; I went to rallies; I watched. I wanted to get involved. But I was frightened and alienated by mass events, no one I knew was involved, and I really didn't understand the politics. Despite my background, political reality really only began for me when the women's movement came along in the 1970s. I became an activist in Fort Collins, Colorado, where I had gone to teach psychology at Colorado State University after getting my Ph.D. from Berkeley in 1969.

As I look back, I realize that these were the questions that concerned me in the early 1970s: How do you maintain your commitment when it becomes clear that the struggle will not soon be over? How do you deal with disappointment and victory? How do you choose which issues to engage? How do you balance the mixed feelings that come with coalitions? How do you deal with the social marginalization of activism? Especially marginalizing was the fact that it seemed that very few people in my profession were active in political change movements and my colleagues often criticized my activities.

For years my feminist activism was separate from my "career" as a sexology researcher and teacher. Although I spent endless hours working for equal access to sports facilities for women students, founding town and campus feminist organizations, advocating gender equity in faculty salaries and promotions, developing a course in the psychology of women, and writing letters to newspapers protesting sexism in news stories and advertisements, I was at the same time publishing my research on prenatal hormones and mating behavior in the golden hamster and the rat and going to conferences listening to other papers on prenatal hormones and mating behavior in the golden hamster and the rat. And in the 1970s, although I noticed the sexist behavior of colleagues at these conferences, and I noticed the paucity of women scientists, I did not see the sexism in the paradigm or in the methods. And I did not see the racism at all.

Beginning with a publication in 1978 (just forget everything before then—for example, my first publication, in 1969, entitled "Mating Behavior of Male *Rattus norvegicus* in a Multiple-Female Exhaustion Test"!), I gradually became aware of how sex research is shaped by social and political values. The single most helpful factor in raising my consciousness about my profession was reading the growing literature in women's, ethnic, and gay and lesbian studies.

In 1982 I joined a biweekly seminar at the New York Institute for the Humanities called "Sex, Gender and Consumer Culture." It was full of politically active New York journalists and humanities professors trained to look at meaning and to disdain universals. The seminar had no other psychologists or health-domain types at all. Here were people who relished the links they made between intellectual theories and political context, the complete opposite of the "neutral, objective" stance I had been taught in my profession. Although I admit I was often over my head in that seminar, and for years I couldn't figure out how understanding Picasso in Barcelona or turn-of-the-century French postcards could help me understand sexuality in people's lives today, I gradually underwent a sea change in my perception of how sexual lives are shaped by sociohistorical context.

I began to blend politics with my profession when I volunteered to give a talk on "Changing Conceptions of Sex Roles: Impact on Sex Research" for my graduate school mentor Frank Beach's sixty-fifth birthday celebration in 1976. The theme of the celebration was "Sex Research: Where Are We Now, Where Are We Going?" I volunteered for two reasons. First, I was under the spell of the women's movement, which said, "Speak out!" Since I had been giving countless speeches in Fort Collins about equal pay and equal athletics and equal graduate admissions, I guess I thought I could somehow easily segue into a speech on equal sexology.

Second, I was having a sabbatical year at Bellevue Hospital in New York to learn about human sexuality. At Colorado State I had been assigned the task of teaching human sexuality because I knew a lot about the sexuality of hamsters and rats, and I had learned pretty fast that a background in comparative psychology was not an adequate preparation for teaching human sexuality. New York has more bookstores than Fort Collins, and I was doing a lot of reading that year. I was terrifically excited by one book I read—the first-ever collection of essays on feminist social science. The editorial introduction began:

> Everyone knows the story about the Emperor and his fine clothes. Although the townspeople persuaded themselves that the Emperor was elegantly costumed, a child, possessing an unspoiled vision, showed the citizenry that the Emperor was really naked. The story instructs us about one of our basic sociological premises: that reality is subject to social definition. The story also reminds us that collective delusions *can be undone* by introducing fresh perspectives. Movements of social liberation are like the story in this respect: *they make it possible for people to see the world in an*

enlarged perspective. . . . In the last decade no social movement has had a more startling or consequential impact on the way people see and act in the world than the women's movement. (Millman and Kanter, 1975, p. vii, emphasis added)

In retrospect, I realize now that part of my motivation at Beach's sixty-fifth birthday party in giving a very provocative paper about feminism and sex research was anger—I wanted to show that the emperor birthday boy and all his buddies were naked, that is, intellectually. In this way, I now realize, I intended to get intellectual revenge for the sexist prejudice I had suffered during my years of graduate training. In addition, as any good clinician will point out, at the very same time I was attempting to win, through some sort of tour de force presentation, the intellectual recognition and approval denied to me by those sexist practices.

The paper criticized biological determinism and genital preoccupations in sex research, exposed the stereotyped assumptions about males and females that limited research designs, and called for more qualitative and subjective elements in sex research. Although my ability to make those arguments was pretty thin in 1976, it surprises me how well the general points have stood the test of time.

The paper was received with quite a lot of anger. People felt it was inappropriate to a birthday celebration to criticize the assumptions guiding the past fifty years of work of the guest of honor, and, of course, now I can see that they were right. Personal motives frequently incite social justice actions, and it neither justifies nor dismisses those actions to acknowledge the motives. People often look for motives of maladjustment in the work of social activists, and indeed, activists *are* maladjusted, "creatively maladjusted," Martin Luther King, Jr., said. Indeed, if activists weren't maladjusted, they would be adjusted—adjusted to the status quo—and that is the whole point. But there is a time and a place for everything, even social justice, although it's hard sometimes in the heat of the struggle to understand that.

After the party and ceremonies, as I was preparing the chapter based on my talk for publication in the celebration volume, I received several letters from male colleagues suggesting I tone down the feminism. One colleague wrote: "Do you think you can modify your chapter to meet these criticisms. You obviously had something on your mind and you got it said. . . . But I'm not sure that putting all your thoughts and speculations in the 'permanent record' is a good idea for you [or] for the point of view you champion" (Tiefer, 1992c). I opted not to change much of the speech for the published version (Tiefer, 1978), and in 1979 I received a Distinguished Publication Award from the Association for Women in Psychology for my chapter.

These two extremes have characterized reactions to my work ever since up to 1993. Until now, my sexologist colleagues have persistently told me that although I had some interesting observations, basically I was too strident, too political, too angry, and too repetitive. In contrast, feminist audiences persistently embraced me, encouraged me, and thanked me for bringing a message about sexuality that they found illuminating and liberating. In all honesty, it's hard to say which reaction has been the greater source of motivation. After all, I am the daughter of a Communist whose passion in life was playing the stock market. I'm used to having my feet in very different camps, to having a fragmented identity, to reading disparate literatures always looking for syntheses. I have kept going to sexological meetings, and I have kept going to feminist meetings.

A Midlife Crisis?

In 1991, I published a record seven papers, most of which were based on speeches I had been invited to give. Two things seemed to have happened. First, I found that I suddenly had a lot to say, and second, to my astonishment, I found that people in my field wanted to hear me. Why?

I had a lot to say partly because ethnic, gay and lesbian, and women's studies had provided fascinating material that I thought could be relevant to sexology and the study of human sexuality. I was particularly taken with the efforts of feminist writers to show how science constructs nature, rather than discovering it, and in particular how animal research is used to construct images of "human nature" that may not be in women's best interests (e.g., Haraway, 1991). The new *Journal of the History of Sexuality* (volume 1, 1990), dominated by gay, lesbian, and feminist scholars, has been making available dozens of fascinating examples of the varying construction of

sexualities in the past. And ethnic minority intellectuals have been expos-
ing the limitations of many academic concepts and categories that are
blind to factors of race and class (e.g., hooks, 1984, 1989).

I also had a lot to say because I could tell a narrative of social construction, the story of the medicalization of male sexuality, from the inside
(Tiefer, 1986a). This narrative gave my years of criticism of sexology's biological reductionism, phallocentrism, stereotyped gender assumptions, and
context-stripped research a credibility that overcame, for the moment, the
stigma of being an ideologue.

Also, sexologists have wanted to hear my kind of ideas recently because
it's become so obvious that sex research is inexorably political. AIDS,
abortion, pornography, homosexual rights, and child sexual abuse claims
and counterclaims have put sex and sex research continually on the front
page. Time has caught up with me in a funny way.

It seems quite possible, however, that my time in the sun may be brief.
A recent analysis argues that the radical critique of science has given birth
and given way to professionalized sociological treatments of scientific
knowledge in a newly reputable subspecialty in sociology (Martin, 1993).
Even if many of my suggestions for transformation and reform are heeded,
a similar fate may befall sexology if it continues to privilege its own survival rather than the improvement of people's sexual understanding and
sexual lives. The transformation of sexology into a tool to fight oppression
and injustice is still only a dim possibility far out on the horizon.

But, popular or not, I expect to continue to look for opportunities to
move the struggle forward. Let me conclude by describing two I have recently taken. This past year I was able to participate in the National Institutes of Health (NIH) Consensus Development Conference on Impotence.
This conference marked the first time the NIH chose a topic in sexuality
(Tiefer, 1992a). *Impotence,* I believe, is a term essential to maintaining phallocentrism in sexology and therefore a term I agitate against wherever I can.
Discussion of impotence converts problems of the penis into problems of
the man, converts problems with sexual performance into weakness and
lack of masculine control. Thus, a field devoted to the diagnosis and treatment of impotence supports the quest for phallic perfection—a quest that
ignores women and women's sexual interests—recruiting enormous economic resources for this purpose.

I was invited to speak at the NIH conference about ethnic and cultural influences on impotence, an important topic, but one about which there is no research. Instead, I insisted on discussing nomenclature and partner issues, topics that weren't even on the schedule. I was determined to bring women into this "all boys' toys" situation. And I did make a difference, albeit a small one, in the final report of the NIH consensus panel. Activism extends not only to such participation but also to telling the story of the consensus conference, as I have at several meetings this year, to show how the social constructions of sexuality and gender actually proceed daily in minute ways.

Conclusion

What can I abstract from this odyssey of an activist who happens to be a sexologist? It's important to view whatever subject you are interested in from many perspectives by reading, joining interdisciplinary seminars, and participating in out-of-venue activities. It's important to understand political reality and to see how the subject you are interested in fits into politics. Professions exist to perpetuate themselves, and any good they do must be effortfully worked into their mission. You need another place to stand in addition to just being a competent professional. If you are committed to social betterment, you must take action; analysis alone is insufficient. Unfortunately, it's never clear that a particular moment is the right one or that a particular action will make a difference, so you will have to take action without certain knowledge of its impact. Since challenging the status quo is likely to make you unpopular, make sure you have a political base of some sort to provide moral support when the going gets rough.

I said I would mention two opportunities I've recently taken to move the struggle forward. The second one is to put these ideas into speeches such as these. Is this again the manifestation of maladjusted motives? I feel that any venue is the right one to say that feminism is a struggle to eradicate the ideology of domination—the cultural basis of group oppression (hooks, 1984, p. 25)—and to remind anyone within the sound of my voice to extend their feminist thinking to contend with racism as well as sexism.

We live in a time of intensely competing sexual discourses, and sexuality is one of the arenas for struggle against oppression and injustice. There is really no way to be apolitical as a sexologist—every action supports some interests and opposes others. My message as I thank you for honoring me with this award is a call for you to choose your work with intentionality and to incorporate race and class analyses into your research and clinical efforts.

chapter 2

BIOLOGICAL POLITICS (READ: PROPAGANDA) IS ALIVE AND WELL IN SEXOLOGY

In 1982 Janet Sayers called for "an adequate feminist account of the effect of biology on women's social situation . . . a valid analysis of the relationship between biology and women's destiny, if only to counter the biologically phrased arguments of antifeminism" (Sayers, 1982, pp. 1–2). Sounds straightforward, no? Let's set down some biological facts about women's social situation and straighten those patriarchs out.

Perhaps it seemed straightforward twenty years ago, but the terms of debate have shifted and those goals no longer seem appropriate. Many excellent scientists work around the clock to offer "an adequate feminist account of the effect(s) of biology on women's social situation." But contemporary scientists think less about connecting "Biology" writ large to "Women's Social Situation" writ large, and more about connecting particular biological variables to particular social variables in certain groups of women. We don't think in terms of a unitary category of "women" the way we did in 1982. Moreover, we learned that "Biologically phrased arguments of antifeminism" were political arguments where science was used as a smokescreen. I don't think we quite realized then how little impact good science would have on gender arguments. Now we are more savvy about politics and smokescreens, more cynical about the intentions of those with grand theories, and doubtful that good research can solve political dilemmas.

Or are we? It's difficult to inhibit the impulse to slay the antifeminist dragon with just one more good study or just one more meta-analysis.

Biological Politics

There are as many current biological explanations for why men and women live different lives as there ever were, although contemporary theories of difference do not immediately segue into claims of inequality (psychological, intellectual, artistic, athletic, political, etc.) the way they did before 1970.

Nowadays, gender inequality is supposedly a thing of the past (or only happens in "other" cultures), and arguments for male superiority are a cliché, a joke, or an opportunity for a lawsuit. We live in postfeminist times; the oppression of women has been defeated (though not everywhere). But men and women are (everywhere) still living different lives, and research about why this should be is still very popular. Scientific investigation of the sources of sex/gender differences remains totally acceptable, and biological discourse (which is so beloved precisely because it seems so "neutral and objective") is alive and well.

Much of that discourse continues to be biological reductionism, that is, the so-called explanation of differences between men and women by biological variables. Such biological explanations ("biobunk," according to Carol Tavris, 2001) survive because they get repackaged in whatever biology is popular at the moment—regional brain anatomy, brain lateralization, evolutionary theory, gene effects, hormones, etc. The biological methods only become more sophisticated and expensive. Mass media get wildly excited every time a new technology uncovers some measurable physical sex difference and use each technonews opportunity to trot out familiar generalizations, exaggerations, unreplicated findings, and selective measurements—the whole two thousand years' worth, it sometimes seems. Headlines and cover stories proclaiming the latest "breakthrough" in biological "bases" of sex differences must sell really well.

Although I became highly suspicious of biological research on sex differences after years of observing the repackaging dance, I wasn't suspicious twenty years ago when Janet Sayers wrote her book. And so it is helpful to revisit Sayers' arguments and think about why I have rejected the open-mindedness of those earlier years.

My own particular angle of observation on biological politics comes from being a sexologist over the last twenty years—a time which has not only seen the survival of Sayers' target of sociobiology (now repackaged as evolutionary psychology), but also the ascendance in the field I know best, clinical sexology, of a biomedical model of sexual experience. That this occurred despite the best political, empirical, and theoretical efforts of feminist scholars is strong evidence that evidence has nothing to do with the matter. This has been deeply disappointing.

Even now, as medical sexology embraces the alleged purity of "evidence-based medicine," it is not evidence that determines the direction of research and theory, but rather politics, propaganda, and, inevitably in the era of globalization, the vicissitudes of cold, hard cash. I am not being cynical, if cynicism is attitude without justification. My bias is born of experience and disappointment.

Sex and Biological Politics

Sex (not gender, but the part of life and behavior we think of as erotic) has been bound to sexual politics (the politics and meanings of masculinity and femininity) by historic linkages between sex and reproductive biology. According to this line of thinking, the "normal" conduct of sexual life involves a man and woman engaged in coitus, and this central iconic image continues to resonate deeply, though not universally, through all cultures into the twenty-first century. The contraceptive revolution, especially the oral contraceptive pill of the 1960s, was supposed to separate sexuality from reproduction, but even among enthusiastic contraceptors, heterosexual erotic scripts remain coitus-centered. Heterodominant thinking itself (the "normality" of the man-woman union) is a legacy of the reproductive model of sexuality. Ironically, actual reproduction of the human species is increasingly separated from coitus not only by cultural shifts privileging contraceptives and sex-for-pleasure, but by new assisted reproductive technologies whereby many human lives are beginning in petri dishes and test tubes. Nevertheless, these developments have not affected coitocentric models of sexuality.

The coitus-centered model of sex ("real sex") is justified by evolutionist biological thinking, i.e., sex evolved to perpetuate species, desire for sex inevitably involves desire for the reproductive act, biological factors (genes, brain, hormones, whatever) dictate that sexual activity is focused on vaginal penetration and intravaginal male ejaculation, etc. The fact that lots of people find primary erotic satisfaction in non-coital activity or activity with a non-reproductively-appropriate partner is ignored or labeled as deviance. Likewise, the prevalence of autoerotic activities (using sexual fantasy, video, television, or the Internet with or without masturbation) seems not to give pause to the narrow thinking that equates erotic life with genes-driven reproduction.

Diverse erotic lives and new methods of reproduction are possible because of psychological processes such as symbolization and conditioning that are connected to ever-changing cultural formations. This, it has long seemed to me, is what evolution contributes to sexuality in human beings—higher neocortical capabilities. But the centrality of culture and conditioning to sexual life is ignored by most media commentators and, sadly, often dismissed or ignored in academic and professional sexology. A simplistic, universalized, biomedical model of coital sex and the survival of species remains ascendant.

Sayers suggests at the outset that her book will be partly concerned "with the way in which those opposed to changes in women's social role have sought to appropriate biology for their cause" (p. 1). I have observed that arguments about sexuality emphasizing biological *differences* between men and women's sexual lives as well as those emphasizing biological *similarities* have been used to ignore the sociocultural components. For example, Masters and Johnson's (1966) physiological research showing similar sexual physiology between men and women in arousal and orgasm has been used to create identical sexual "dysfunction" categories for men and women, ignoring the social inequalities that are so crucial for understanding women's sexual problems (Kaschak and Tiefer, 2001). Similarly, differences between men and women's sexual behavior patterns (e.g., masturbation frequency, sexual script flexibility, and definitions of satisfaction) are called "reproductive strategies" and are linked directly to evolutionary biology, bypassing sociocultural issues (Buss, 1994; Diamond, 1997). Whenever biology enters the picture, it seems that cultural issues fly out the window.

Interests Keeping Sexual Life Tied to Reproductive Biology

Over the last thirty years, at the same time as the women's and gay and lesbian studies movements have generated new knowledge about sexual variations, biomedical sex experts continued to dominate the health and science media and much public thinking. For every one story on sex in *Newsweek* or the *New York Times* that comes from social science, it seems that ten come from medical and biological science.

There have been numerous opportunities for a discourse of sex that is not focused on biology and not focused on normal/abnormal divides to gain ground, but they have failed. Here are a few examples:

1. Non-coital "outercourse" eroticism was never widely promoted as a model of safe sex in the HIV/AIDS pandemic. Is this because covert anti-gay politics subtly dominate the media and reject any pro-sexual solutions to HIV transmission?
2. Following the approval in 1998 of Viagra, the first erection-enhancing drug, media accepted a mechanical and reductionist narrative of erectile dysfunction instead of pursuing broader questions about the impact of drugs on sexual life, identity, and relationships. Might this be due to the influence of the global pharmaceutical industry?
3. We are currently in the middle of a similar promotion ("creation," cf. Moynihan, 2003) of "female sexual dysfunction" that reduces women's sexual satisfaction to arousal and orgasm associated with genital function. Why are journalists uninterested in the multitude of socio-political factors that affect women's sexual lives?
4. There have been many political and religious debates in the U.S. over sexual values (Freedman & D'Emilio, 1988; McLaren, 1999). Hot issues at the moment include abortion, comprehensive sex education in public schools, public funding of sex research, and proper prosecution of child sexual abuse. Why are the media afraid to use local battles

around these issues as opportunities to look at the diverse sexualities of real children and real adults?

Janet Sayers focuses her 1982 sociobiology chapter on how "parental investment theory" is used to promote biological-evolutionist explanations for persisting sexual inequalities in workplace and childcare arrangements. In the subsequent decades, public conflicts over whether women with children should work and use daycare have largely subsided because of global economic shifts that require two people's income to sustain the average family. However, the same sociobiological language is now used to "explain" gender differences in sexual desire, attraction and partner choice (courtship behaviors), promiscuity, interest in masturbation, etc. (LeVay & Valente, 2002). The same kinds of animal illustrations Sayers decried (is there really any similarity between "promiscuity" in anglerfishes and humans?) are still popular.

It seems like a shell game—the specific targets change, but the attacks against feminist theories go on. Let's call this continuing biologization politics, not science. Ignoring or minimizing cultural and social constructions of human sexual life is antifeminist propaganda, subtle though it may be, and we are in a stronger position in 2003 than 1982 to understand how it works and why it persists.

chapter 3

GENDER AND MEANING
IN THE NOMENCLATURE OF
SEXUAL DYSFUNCTIONS

Michel Foucault ([1976] 1978) argued that sexuality has been constructed over the past 150 years as "a domain susceptible to pathological processes and hence calling for therapeutic or normalizing interventions" (p. 68). How best can we understand today's constructions? One clue comes from Foucault, who suggested, "The history of sexuality must first be written from the viewpoint of *a history of discourses*" (p. 69, emphasis added). A fundamental task for feminists interested in sexuality is to read texts so as to *reveal and decode* their *gender meanings* and significances.

APA's Diagnostic
Manual as a Text of Gender Politics

The first edition of the *Diagnostic and Statistical Manual of Mental Disorders* was published by the American Psychiatric Association in 1952 (*DSM-I*); the second in 1968 (*DSM-II*); the third in 1980 (*DSM-III*), the revised third (*DSM-III-R*) in 1987, and the fourth in 1994. Remember "The Great Misdiagnosis Debate of 1985–1986" wherein feminists successfully agitated to keep new psychiatric inventions such as "self-defeating personality disorder" and "premenstrual phase dysphoria" out of the *DSM-III-R*? Why did we care so much? Simply because the *DSM* is the standard naming text of mental health and mental disorders used throughout the world. It has been translated into dozens of languages and is used everywhere as the authoritative reference to current psychiatric conceptualizations. As the *New York Times* said in covering the misdiagnosis debate, "The *Diagnostic and Statistical Manual of Mental Disorders* is the official standard by which psychiatric diagnoses are made. Diagnoses listed in the manual are generally recognized in the courts in making legal decisions, by hospitals and psychotherapists in keeping records and by insurance companies in reimbursing for treatment" (New Psychiatric Syndromes Spur Protest, 1985).

Add to that list researchers who want a standard language for classifying subjects and behaviors, and teachers, who often teach classification language uncritically as a straightforward description of reality, and you have extraordinary opportunities for social influence. Classification of behavior offers fertile terrain for social control at both the material and imaginative levels (Schneider and Gould, 1987). Classification is about *creating differences*, which seem inexorably, in our culture, to entail inequality and hierarchy (Rhode, 1990). Thus, classification sets into motion processes that often include intimidating and stigmatizing certain groups (Kitzinger, 1987), setting and enforcing norms, creating culturally dominant language and imagery, and not least, creating and shaping individual desires and needs. As revolutionaries have repeatedly pointed out, *naming is power*.

In an era in which gender meanings and relations are being examined, destabilized, and renegotiated on every social and personal front, feminists must analyze any text on health, sexuality, bodies, children, domestic life, work life, emotion, laws, power—on *any* domain or metaphor of social life—as being at least in part *about gender*, and therefore as a location to be scrutinized. Eternal vigilance is the price of feminism.

The *DSM*, because of its powerful social location and its relations to most of the elements identified above, can be read as a work *about gender*. The task of feminist psychologists, as Michelle Fine and Susan Gordon (1989) suggested, is first to "interrupt the discipline," that is, to demystify ideology; to disrupt and problematize the seeming neutrality of theory and practice, to open ideological choices.

DSM Listings of Sexual Dysfunctions

The sexual dysfunction nomenclature has changed dramatically over the different editions of the *DSM*. In the first edition (1952), there is no list of sexual dysfunctions, only the statement that "Sex impotence, psychogenic, [appeared in previous taxonomies, along with other specific conditions, but] since these are symptomatic diagnoses, they will be classified under any of several diagnoses dependent upon the clinician's opinion as to the basis" (APA, 1952, p. 107). That is, sexual difficulties (and note that only one is included) were considered *symptoms* of psychiatric disorders, not disorders themselves.

The second edition (1968) mentions sexual problems under "Psychophysiologic Disorders," in a subcategory of "Psychophysiologic Genitourinary Disorders." The text states: "This diagnosis applies to genito-urinary disorders such as disturbances in menstruation and micturition, dyspareunia [pain during intercourse] and impotence in which emotional factors play a causative role" (APA, 1968, p. 47). Here we have two sexual problems mentioned, and again both relate to the performance of intercourse, but now they are a type of psychophysiologic disorder, that is, psychiatric disorders that express themselves through physical dysfunction.

By the third and revised third editions (APA, 1980 and 1987), the list and description of sexual dysfunctions occupied six entire pages. This expansion indicates both the dramatic changes that had occurred in conceptualizations of psychiatric disorders and the importance of sexual function in the contemporary period. The list of dysfunctions in the *DSM-III* and *DSM-III-R* editions is similar. By *DSM-IV* the sexual dysfunction section is nineteen pages, but the basic outline remains the same.

Sexual Disorders, subcategory Sexual Dysfunctions:

DSM-III (APA, 1980)	*DSM-III-R* (APA, 1987)	*DSM-IV* (1994)
Desire disorders:		
Inhibited sexual desire	Hypoactive sexual desire disorder	Hypoactive sexual desire disorder
	Sexual Aversion Disorder	Sexual Aversion Disorder
Sexual excitement disorders:		
Inhibited sexual excitement	Female sexual arousal disorder	Female sexual arousal disorder
	Male Erectile Disorder	Male Erectile Disorder

(continued on next page)

(continued from previous page)

Orgasm disorders:

Inhibited female orgasm	Inhibited female orgasm	Female orgasmic disorder
Inhibited male orgasm	Inhibited male orgasm	Male orgasmic disorder
Premature ejaculation	Premature ejaculation	Premature ejaculation

Pain disorders:

Functional dyspareunia	Dyspareunia	Dyspareunia
Functional vaginismus	Vaginismus	Vaginismus
		Sexual dysfunctions due to a medical condition
		Substance-induced sexual dysfunction

Parameters of Sexuality in the DSM

In all editions, the description of each dysfunction is lengthy and technical, but the details disclose the subtext of sexuality as viewed by the psychiatric establishment. The definition of a dysfunction implies that sexuality is *universal and innate*. Since 1980 the definition of a sexual dysfunction has been as follows: "The essential feature of this subclass is inhibition in the appetitive or psychophysiologic changes that characterize the complete sexual response cycle" (APA, 1980, p. 290). Notice that it is "the" changes that characterize "the" complete cycle. Sexual abnormality is deviation from a fixed sequence (essentially desire, arousal, and orgasm). Although nothing is specifically mentioned about instinct, sections of the text clearly imply that sexuality is a sequence of universally encoded biological reactions of male or female body parts that are set into motion by "adequate" stimulation (e.g., "female arousal disorder" is defined as "failure to attain or maintain the lubrication-swelling response").

Second, sexuality consists of reactions of *body parts*. Despite the bodily emphasis throughout the terminology, the body as a whole has no meaning but instead has become a collection of disconnected physical parts. This compartmentalization lends itself to mechanistic images, to framing sexuality as the smooth operation of complex components, and to seeing sexual problems as calling for high-technology evaluation and repair. Much of the mystification of the *DSM* conceptualization of sexuality derives from this segmented physiologizing, and the implication is that only those who know a lot about tissues and organs can understand sexuality. In descriptions of the sexual dysfunctions, body parts and functions are either self-evidently gendered, as in "outer third of vagina," or the terms *male* and *female* are prominently included, as in the definition of dyspareunia as "genital pain in either a male or a female." Through this language the *DSM* affirms the centrality of gender even amidst the fragmented body parts.

Third, sexuality in the *DSM* is obsessively *genitally focused*. Every one of the dysfunction categories except for sexual desire mentions genital organs in one way or another. When the genitals perform correctly, there is no sexual problem; when they don't, there is always a sexual problem. Genitals, of course, remind us of generation, that is, procreation, and allusions to procreation inevitably connect sexuality to gender, reminding us of the necessary roles of biological male and female.

Fourth, the *DSM* validates *heterosexual intercourse* as the normative sexual activity, repeatedly describing dysfunctions as performance failures in coitus. *Sexuality, in the DSM, is heterosexual genital intercourse.* For example, DSM-III-R specifically points out that inhibited male orgasm "is restricted to an inability to reach orgasm in the [*sic*] vagina" (APA, 1987).

Gayle Rubin (1984) has argued that privileging heterosexual intercourse over other sexual activities establishes a scale in which "individuals whose behavior stands high in this hierarchy are rewarded with certified mental health" (p. 279). In addition, defining sexuality in terms of coitus associates sexuality with gender, since coitus is defined as an act occurring between a man and woman.

Thus, in at least four ways, the language of the DSM overtly and covertly speaks the language of gender and of the most biologically reductionist version. By using only the terms *males* and *females*, never *men* and *women*, the gender language fixes people in the world of animals and locates whatever governs sexuality in "the animal kingdom."

Although the changes are small, the 1987 revised version of the DSM is even more insistent than its 1980 predecessor in making sure the reader gets the gender message. There are five more mentions of *male* and *female* in 1987 than in 1980, for a total of fifteen rather than ten. No *women* appear in 1987 (there was one in 1980), but one additional *vagina* and a new term, *penetration*.

DSM sexual dysfunction classification is laid out in a scrupulously gender-equal way. Men and women each have three dysfunctions. There is identical emphasis on difficulties with desire, arousal, orgasm, and pain. Yet, I would argue that the subtext of the *DSM* nomenclature rejects gender equality. The scrupulous insistence on males being males and females being females is of course the giveaway that we are not in the land of self-determination. But I am ahead of myself here.

What's Omitted
from the Classification?

By "reading back from the narrative to its excluded possibilities [in order to] comprehend its ideological operations" (Jeffords, 1989, p. 49), the *DSM* model of sexuality makes fundamental omissions that reveal it to be a deeply conservative document.

First, despite the scrupulous listing of women's sexual responses, which, by itself, could imply that women's sexuality is as important a concern to the *DSM* as is men's, *women's actual sexual voices are absent* from this conceptualization. The sexual concerns that women talk about, as we know these from popular surveys, questionnaire studies, political writings, and fiction, are absent here (Tiefer, 1988a).

There's nothing in the *DSM* about emotion or communication, whole-body experience, danger and taboo, commitment, attraction, sexual knowledge, safety, respect, feelings about bodies, breast cycles, pregnancy, contraception, or getting old. The only tiny reference to age is under "Inhibited *male* orgasm," where the clinician is reminded to take age into account. Pleasure is mentioned: A person has an arousal disorder if they don't have pleasure during sexual activity, but it's hardly highlighted. By making the choice to bypass the issues women have raised since anyone has been asking women to speak about sex, the *DSM* insults and dismisses women.

Second, the *DSM*, with its superficial gender equity based on sexual biology, denies women's social reality; that is, *gender inequality*. Women, lacking equal opportunity for sexual freedom, lacking equal encouragement to experiment, burdened with a poorer physical self-image and a weakened bargaining position in their intimate relationships, more often traumatized by past sexual exploitation, and far more often harassed by insecure reproductive rights and a limited window of sexual attractiveness, come to sexual opportunities severely disadvantaged compared to men. To speak of "a normal sexual excitement phase" as being determined by "activity that the clinician judges to be adequate in focus, intensity and duration" trivializes women's sociosexual reality and, by omission, perpetuates sexual patriarchy. The biological emphasis in the *DSM* that strips sexuality of its social context is a trick played on women, who need to understand social context as much as organs and tissues in order to steer a course for their sexual lives.

Conclusion

On careful examination, we see that the *DSM-III* and even more the *DSM-III-R* are hardly neutral in the contemporary struggle over the construction of sexuality. Men's interests thrive in this discourse, and women's are secondary. John Gagnon has argued for the past twenty years that gender training and experiences during development result in fundamental gender differences in adult sexual scripts and responses (see Gagnon, 1979). Men's experiences in adolescence with genital arousal and orgasm, in conjunction with homosocial competitiveness and identification, create expectations and conditioning that bias men toward a goal-oriented, genital, self-focused sexual style. Masculinity depends on sexuality for its enactment (Jeffords, 1989). Put it all together and you get the heterosexualized and male-defined sexuality represented in "the" human sexual response cycle model of the *DSM*. Looking closely at this text reveals that nomenclature is a subtle agent of patriarchy.

This insight is not new. Some feminists have argued that throughout the twentieth century sexologists have played a consistent and significant role in indoctrinating women to adjust to men's sexuality. In "Sexology and the Universalization of Male Sexuality (from Ellis to Kinsey and Masters and Johnson)," Margaret Jackson (1984) argued that the role of sexology all along has been to normalize and universalize "the coital imperative" and the "primacy of penetration" in order to undermine women's resistance to compulsory heterosexuality. Similarly, Mariana Valverde (1987) argued that sexologists' role as marriage reformers in the twentieth century led them to insist that women, like men, have sexual needs and desires and that, conveniently, women's sexual needs and desires were just like men's, albeit a bit slower. Janice Irvine (1990), in her extended analysis of the history of sexology in the United States, likewise argued that sexologists' primary concern has been for their own professional status and legitimacy and that this emphasis has required strategies and alliances that have time and again co-opted any interests they may have had in women's self-determination.

So, it seems that the DSM's choice to argue that anatomy is destiny once again limits women. Just because orgasm is in there doesn't mean this is a prowoman document. The construction of gender in the official psychiatric sexuality nomenclature is easily summarized: Men and women are the same, and they're all men.

chapter 4

SOME HARMS TO WOMEN OF RESTRICTIONS ON SEXUALLY RELATED EXPRESSION

As a feminist and a psychologist specializing in research and clinical work on sexuality, I have concluded that *women are in more danger from the repression of sexually explicit materials than from their free expression*. If the vast range of items considered pornographic have anything in common, it is that they can be described as "sexually transgressive material." But because women's sexuality has been repressed, suppressed, and oppressed, what's needed is more transgressive opportunity, not less.

I want to justify this claim with five arguments and try to bring in some ideas about the current state of women's sexuality as I've learned about it through my experience in psychotherapy practice and work in several different medical centers. I have to begin with the usual disclaimers—that the people whose sexuality I know the best all come to me because they have complaints and dissatisfactions, and thus they probably do not reflect a cross-section of the culture. However, I have worked with a wide variety of patients, and although many of them have been Western, white, and middle class, I have also worked with many people of color, immigrants from Burma to Barbados, couples in their twenties and their seventies, and people raised in many different religions and ethnic groups.

The fundamental context of women's sexuality in our time is *ignorance and shame*. More than even fear, I would argue, women's experience is constructed and colored by ignorance and shame. And yet sexuality is given tremendous importance in terms of social norms. The societal message is that you *have* to be sexual, you have to *want* to be sexual, you have to be *good* at being sexual, and you have to be *normally* sexual. Yet there's no tradition of sexual coaching or intercourse training or masturbation training or honest feedback or places to go to get all your questions answered by a friendly expert. I and clinicians like me have become the friendly expert—which is ridiculous when you think about it in terms of cost, availability, and the medical model context of therapy.

I suspect that under managed care friendly sex therapy is not going to be included in the basic benefits package. That would be all right if there were better sex education or less social pressure to be sexual. So much of sex therapy is remedial sex education that should have occurred during childhood and adolescence. Too much of it is the untwisting of inhibitions that never should have gotten established in the first place.

In fact, a great deal of sex therapy focuses on expressing and undoing feelings of undesirableness, badness, and dirtiness. Many people are raised with the religious or cultural message that the feelings and pleasures of the body and mind are dangerous and dirty. Most women are ambivalent at best about their bodies throughout their lives. It's easy for politicians or the media to prey on the large variety of early negative feelings. And although antipornography arguments seem to rely on scientific research or moral principles, I often see just the projection of these internal feelings of shame and dirt that were taught at an early age.

Women Need Power, Not Protection

Empowerment, not protection, is the route to women's sexual development. In May 1993 I read in the newspaper that on Mother's Day the Rev. Calvin Butts, pastor of the Abyssinian Baptist Church in New York, was going to show his respect for women by taking dozens of compact discs of rap songs that insult women into the street and running them over with a truck.

I think this is a silly and empty gesture, but unfortunately, it's a common gesture toward women. If Rev. Butts wants to increase the respect shown toward women, he needs to help increase the power held by women, not try to "protect" women from disrespect by riding in on a big truck (do I hear echoes of the knight in shining armor?) and whisking away the danger. He should preach that respecting women means giving women and men information and skill about safer sex practices to prevent HIV transmission. Better yet, he should go on a hunger strike to demand that the federal government research a female-controlled method of HIV virus-killing so women can protect themselves from AIDS. Women need to be able to protect themselves with information, power, and skill if they are to gain respect.

Encourage Women's Tentative New Sexual Visions

If we accept that women's sexuality has been shaped by ignorance and shame and is just beginning to find new opportunities and voices for expression, then now is exactly the wrong time to even think about campaigns of suppression. Suppressing pornography will harm women struggling to develop their own sexualities: History teaches us that any crackdown on sexually explicit material always falls the hardest on experimental presses, alternative artists, small theaters, and the like. Little bookstores and individual galleries do not have the money for lawyers or the time to spend in endless legal disputes. Magazines will fold; performers will go hungry; sex educators, if any are left, will be too intimidated to teach more than the blandest facts of genital plumbing.

Criminalizing explicit sexual expressions will force erotic experimentation in art, video, books, and performances underground and deprive most women of access to unconventional inputs to their erotic imagination. Women will feel that old familiar shame when confronting anything but the most mainstream sexual concepts, and they will not be able to break out of their historic repression.

Now is the time for more sexual experimentation, not shame-soaked restraint. This experimentation should include freedom for new sexual science and art, new ideas about desire and pleasure, and new practices that will lead individuals, families, and couples away from the ruts worn by centuries of religious inhibition, fear of pregnancy and disease, and compulsory heterosexuality.

What is clear to the sex therapist and sex educator is that there will be no new options for sexual behavior or experience for women at all without open talk about sexual possibilities. And there will be no open sexual talk if every seedling effort is met by religious disapproval, talk-show or media ridicule, scientific neglect, or criticism from activist women.

Accusations that pornography harms women amount to a powerful form of backlash against new sexual forms. The consequence is a blanket of inhibition. I have often heard that inhibition in the form of defensive, reactionary voices almost whining, "Why do they need to do that? My husband and I have been getting along just fine for thirty-five years, and we would never do that!" This type of comment is a form of social control that prevents more experimental women from breaking out of historical limitations. Without freely available information, ideas, and images, women's sexual liberty is just a joke.

Respect Sexual Imagination

A third harm to women from suppressing pornography is that it deprives people of learning more about the human imagination. The antiporn feminists argue that pornography is to be interpreted in a literal way—if it's a picture of a woman being fucked while lying across three tall stools in a coffee shop, it's a picture of an embarrassed, uncomfortable, and unhappy woman. But this isn't the way sexual fantasy actually works.

For example, I have a patient who came to me because she did not enjoy sex with her husband of six years. Every story is complicated, but to boil this down, some of the contributions to this state of affairs had to do with her strict religious upbringing of sexual shame and conflict, her compulsive and perfectionistic mental functioning learned from her immaculately clean hausfrau mother, her aversion toward her tyrannical father, and her obsession with her weight. Although she had chosen her husband for various good reasons, she did not find him sexually appealing. Most people who hear this description may think, "Good grief, this is truly hopeless," but in fact this combination of circumstances is not at all uncommon in women's lives given families, religion, and patterns of socialization for girls.

This woman had some sexual pleasure when she masturbated; however, this pleasure was diminished by her shame about the sexual fantasy she had developed. In the main part of this repetitious fantasy, she was the unhappy provider of sexual excitement to a group of seedy men in a seedy living room. She danced naked, encouraged them to undress, fondled them, and provided fellatio around the room. Although in the fantasy she was never excited, in real life she would get excited and masturbate to orgasm. This gave her a sense of pleasure and mastery but also feelings of shame and confusion.

This kind of story is more common than I can tell you and illustrates the paradoxes women often find themselves in today. Is it correct to interpret this woman's fantasy as the straightforward story of a degraded and humiliated and subjugated woman? No. Such a simplistic assessment does not accurately characterize the "meanings" of her fantasy. This woman felt aroused by the sexual power of her dancing and her power to arouse the seedy men. They were turned on; they wanted her. She felt desired and irresistible, and this feeling aroused her. Hers was a pretty sexually empowered fantasy, in its own way. The vicissitudes of her upbringing and this misogynist culture produced the more negative elements—the undesirable setting and partners and the lack of her own arousal in the fantasy. She couldn't feel entitled to openly enjoy sexual arousal, which was exactly what was going on with her husband.

Ellen Willis has pointed out that "women have learned, as a matter of survival, to be adept at shaping men's fantasies to their own purposes," and I think this patient's fantasy is a good example of this idea (Willis, 1988, p. 55). In another place and time, this woman and the vicissitudes of her life would have come up with a different way to deal with her sexual conflicts. Anyway, the point is that pornography is about fantasy and identification with characters in stories as symbols. It cannot really be understood just on a literal level. And if pornography is suppressed, women will not learn things about themselves and their imaginations that they can learn through experimenting with and reflecting upon their reactions to pornography.

Don't Reject Women in Pornography

Opponents of pornography often argue that women in pornography are seriously harmed while doing the work and that eliminating pornography would help these women escape from abominable conditions. But the same argument has been made over and over again that eliminating prostitution would allow women to escape abominable conditions, when in fact prostitutes themselves repeatedly argue that what they want are safe and healthy working conditions, not further stigmatization.

Suppressing pornography and the production of sexual images will directly harm women who make their living in many sex industries, including models and sexual performers of various sorts. These women have appealed to feminists for support, not rejection. The more sex industry work is made antisocial and illegal, the more it goes underground and the more the women who work there are subject to abuse and oppression. Improved working conditions for these women will come from decriminalization, destigmatization, feminist support, and public pressure, not from being pushed underground and out of public sight. Sex industry workers, like all women, are striving for economic survival and a decent life, and if feminism means anything it means sisterhood and solidarity with these women who are also striving for self-determination.

Masturbation, the Subtext of the Pornography Debate

Finally, and perhaps most important, suppressing explicit sexual materials will harm women by strengthening the power of the conservative religious lobbies. And since the goals of the religious right are incompatible with women's economic, spiritual, and reproductive freedoms, such influence must be resisted at all costs. Conservative religious groups have historically rejected pornography not because of "harm to women" but because of its connection to masturbation. In fact, the debate about pornography is in large part a debate about masturbation. I think the reason no one talks about *women's* use of pornography and *women's* interest in pornography has to do with discomfort with the idea of women masturbating. The "harm to women" argument arose from feminist theorizing and has been adopted as rhetoric by the religious right, but I do not believe that is where their real antipathy lies.

Another disclaimer is called for here. Whenever sexologists talk about sexual specifics it is assumed that we are talking in a normative way—this is good, this is bad, this is healthy, this is sick. So, in talking about masturbation, am I saying it is good or bad? Neither. Both. I really don't care! By talking about pornography and masturbation, I'm talking about sexual practices and what they are useful or not useful for.

Sexuality is an option in life, although one wouldn't think so to listen to many "experts" talk. If someone wants to have a long and lively sexual life—and believe me *I don't care* whether anyone does or does not want to, and I am making no recommendations—but a person who does want to needs to learn about sexuality and take time to practice. Masturbation is a form of learning and practice that is known in every culture. It's also a hobby, and like many hobbies it can be practiced frequently or rarely.

What always amazes me is people who want to have exciting and gratifying sex but who think it just comes "naturally" without practice or knowledge. I'm sorry, but no one can play Rachmaninoff without putting in a lot of piano practice! If someone just wants to have a little bit of sex in his or her life, or if the experience itself is not very important, then masturbation is of much less relevance or importance for that person. As a sexologist my goal is to discuss sexuality without choosing values, without endorsing particular acts or patterns.

For the religious right, however, sexuality is always a moral issue. Conservative religious organizations oppose women's autonomous sexuality and believe that sexuality is for procreation, for families, not for individual pleasure, identity, and exploration. Masturbation or individual sexuality is a threat to the vision of sexuality as the tie that binds a family. Ideally, the right wants to return to the years before the women's movement demanded and won the right to abortion, contraception, mandatory sex education, accessible day care, women's health centers, and so on. Picking on pornography to "protect" women attacks women's independence, and I propose that masturbation is an important subtext. Supporting women's sexuality requires supporting (though not mandating) women's masturbation and the availability of explicit sexual materials of all sorts.

Conclusion

Shame and ignorance make cowards of us all, but now is no time for cowardice about women's sexual practices or imaginings. Censorship harms women because women need sexual empowerment, not sexual protection.

Antiporn campaigns say that porn gives men power. But in fact, men already have power. Explicit sexual materials and performances can contribute to women's sexual power. People who do not like certain types of pornography can avoid them. Or better yet, they can create something completely new.

chapter 5

TOWARDS A
FEMINIST SEX THERAPY

Sex therapists often think of themselves as social liberators, helping people move beyond restrictions and inhibitions created by the Judeo-Christian body/mind split, deprecation of women's sexuality, and pre-occupation with procreation. Feminists also view themselves as social liberators, helping people move beyond restrictions and inhibitions embedded in gender roles and stereotypes and institutionalized in all parts of society. One might have expected that such compatibility of aims would have long ago produced a feminist sex therapy, yet no such program has emerged. Much of the reason lies in the many sexual subcommunities within feminism, each with its own ideas about sexual motives, choreographies, and norms.

Recent decades have seen enormous social changes from both feminist and sexual perspectives, but there has been no single vision within feminism as to the meaning, priority, or ideal nature of sexual activity, feelings, or relationships (McCormick, 1994). It seems appropriate to try, without universalizing, to imagine how the insights of feminism might help design an array of ameliorative practices for sex therapy.

Sex Therapy Now

Sex therapy is a form of psychotherapy developed to treat couples in stable, usually long-term relationships who are not happy with their sexual experiences together. It has also been applied to work with individuals and occasionally to groups. Current texts and casebooks make it clear that there is no single method of sex therapy, and no one appropriate training background (Leiblum & Rosen, 1989; O'Donohue & Geer, 1993; Rosen & Leiblum, 1995). However, amongst all the technical and theoretical eclecticism, a few commonalities persist.

First, sex therapists are committed to homework. There may be different kinds (diaries, reading, communication exercises, etc.), but homework always includes quite a bit of bodywork involving looking at and touching oneself and one's partner. Even in LoPiccolo's (1992) "postmodern sex therapy," where all sorts of theory cohabit, all roads still lead to the bed and bath, i.e., to assignments of looking and touching. Everything in my experience supports this tradition. Talk in the office is all well and good, in fact it is essential, but sexual activities and feelings in our confused society require the kind of demystification and desensitization that only hands-on practice combined with office debriefing can provide.

Second, sex therapists are almost all wedded to the diagnostic framework of "sexual dysfunctions" as articulated in the American Psychiatric Association's (1994) manual of mental disorders (DSM-IV). This document describes problems individuals may have with sexual arousal and orgasm, especially in relation to heterosexual coitus. I have written lengthy criticisms of the APA nomenclature which I will not repeat here, except to say that this framework is very poorly suited to women's sexual reality on this planet (Tiefer, 1991c, 1992b, 1995). In fact, I believe the DSM framework, based on Masters and Johnson's physiological research, exemplifies a significant part of women's oppression, despite its supposed gender equality and encouragement of women's sexuality. By ignoring the social context of sexuality, the DSM nomenclature perpetuates a dangerously naive and false vision of how sex really works.

It gives me great pleasure to jettison that conceptual framework and to think about alternatives, not an easy task. Making any list of sexual "problems" assumes that the author knows what kind of sexual life is good and where to "draw the line." At all costs I want to avoid the enduring nineteenth-century "sex hierarchy" described by Gayle Rubin as "the charmed circle" of "good, normal, natural, blessed sexuality" and "the outer limits" of "bad, abnormal, unnatural, damned sexuality" (1984, p. 281). There must be a better way to conceptualize problems.

The new field of "relational diagnoses" offers some ideas, but its relevance to sexuality has not yet emerged (Kaslow, 1996). This is not the right place to propose a diagnostic scheme. On the other hand, it is never the wrong place to recommend ignoring the DSM.

Components of Feminist Sex Therapy

My clinical work as a sex therapist is informed by both psychodynamic and systems ideas, whereas my personal strengths have always been as a teacher and a leader. It is no surprise, then, that I particularly favor the role of sex therapist as psychoeducator-coach. In that spirit, I envision two tracks running through feminist sex therapy. The first is remedial and compensatory, and includes a focus on skills and attitudes women need in order to cope with the sexual world as it is now. The second track is visionary and transformative, and focuses on reframing sexuality (idealistically, perhaps, for a world of greater equality of opportunity). For both tracks a little body-prologue is an important option.

Although I eagerly participated in that early-1970s, women's-health-movement era of show-and-tell with plastic speculums, I do not have experience touching or physically examining patients. Yet I know that many, many women have unanswered questions and concerns about their physical status. I most definitely do not subscribe to "the body is the fundamental bedrock" school of sexuality—far from it. But nagging questions about one's body can easily get in the way of exploring and expanding psychosocial meanings. Thus, I strongly recommend that a feminist sex therapist work in partnership with a feminist physician or nurse-clinician who can conduct a thorough, educational medical history, physical exam, and conversation focusing on sexual experience. Such a consultation may constitute the whole feminist sex therapy experience (which I have seen happen many times), or it can precede or accompany psychotherapeutic work.

Part I: Remedial and Compensatory Coping (Something for Everybody)

Over the years I worked with many women in sex therapy and came to know their sexual lives very well. Sometimes they wanted therapy because of their own sexual problems, and sometimes because their partner was identified as having sexual problems. I also have many friends, lesbian and heterosexual, of diverse cultural backgrounds, whose sexual lives I have learned a lot about. And, of course, I know about my own life. All these women, living in the real world, could use at least some of the five remedial-coping components.

Feminism 101

Feminist sex therapy begins with feminism, up close and personal. In discussion, in self-exploratory written homework and in reading, reading, reading, the issues include: What is gender? How are individuals shaped into gendered beings? What does it mean to be a woman? How is sexuality related to femininity? What does it mean to be a woman within the various subcultural categories relevant to the woman receiving the sex therapy? What is sexuality all about for such a woman?

Many women find the study of feminism to be immensely and immediately liberating, as they realize the connection between their personal problems and burdens and the larger structures of gender. In reviewing their own life histories in light of feminist readings, women examine, for the first time or with a new framework, their mother's and other influential women's sexual lives and attitudes, their own earliest sexual learnings, how their expectations about sexual life were shaped, and their past sexual experiences and opportunities.

A small group of women reading and talking together would be ideal for this type of exploration. The group experience may be the same as it was in the 1970s consciousness-raising groups of early second-wave feminism. Today, however, there is more to read and more to grasp about how sexuality is a discourse of disease and morality, of pleasure and vulnerability, of fear and victimization, of bodies and products, of performances and standards.

Corrective Physiology Education

Harriet Lerner (1976) pointed out that the ubiquitous parental mislabeling of female genitals as "vagina" (and little else) can lead to lifelong confusion and inhibition for many women (also see Gartrell & Mosbacher, 1984). Every sex therapist I know can say "Amen" to that. I have talked with dozens of women whose uncertainty about their own body persisted through decades of marriage and babies and surgeries. It is not just that the genitalia are important to sexual pleasure; it is more that uncertainty about one's genitalia seems to create an inhibiting insecurity. No wonder that the homework assignment of drawing one's vulva, as Barbach (1975) recommended therapeutic eons ago, becomes a milestone.

Fifteen years ago a group of feminist health activists published *A New View of a Woman's Body*, which contained a revolutionary chapter: "The Clitoris: A Feminist Perspective" (Federation of Feminist Women's Health Centers, 1981). Feminist self-examination revealed a vast clitoral system of erectile tissue, far more important but far less well-known than the [*sic*] G-Spot, which the authors called "the perineal sponge of the clitoris" and "the urethral sponge of the clitoris" (p. 43–44). They wrote:

> This redefinition of the clitoris is no mere semantic quibble . . . if the perineum is part of our sex organ, an episiotomy . . . becomes a mutilation of the clitoris. Also, thinking of the clitoris as a functional unit is very different from thinking of it as a collection of structures and areas as described by Masters and Johnson. . . . After self-examination of the clitoris, discussions of our sexual experiences became much more concrete and specific. We finally had a vocabulary and conceptual framework with which to communicate. (p. 47)

Women do not suffer from penis envy, but many of us suffer from vulva insecurity. Affirmative genital education is essential to reverse the ignorance and discomfort engendered by patriarchal messages.

Assertiveness Training

An early component of feminist therapy, assertiveness training has not been talked about too much lately. It may have been absorbed into the psychotherapy bag of tricks. It even seems a little dated, belonging to an era less obsessed with sexual violence, and fitting best with a feminist therapy that focused on independence and autonomy.

Nevertheless, "communication" is extensively discussed in every sex therapy book, and in our field it is widely agreed that difficulties in communication lie at the heart of many couples' sexual difficulties. The trouble is that most sex therapists seem oblivious to the fact that heterosexual marriage is an unequal playing field. As a result, they continue to discuss couples' failures in communication in strictly psychological terms (e.g., Schnarch, 1991) rather than acknowledging how communication is linked to sex roles and power dynamics. Only in feminist family therapy is women's subordinate position connected to issues of communication, for example, to the silence and indirectness typical of many women. Some feminist therapists have even observed that increasing women's assertiveness in families may result in negative labeling and increased aggressiveness from their partners (Burck & Daniel, 1990).

Thus, in recommending sexual assertiveness training as part of the new feminist sex therapy, we cannot be overly idealistic or naive (Hurlburt, 1991). Many of the verbal and interactional exercises developed in women's groups twenty years ago could be updated to deal with contemporary issues and women's diversity (Carlson & Johnson, 1975). In addition to group work, extensive couple work on communication must occur to allow women's assertiveness to be assimilated and integrated.

Body Image Reclamation

A forest of trees has been cut down for books on women's feelings about their bodily appearance, and related causes and consequences thereto pertaining (e.g., Chapkis, 1986; Wolf, 1991). Women have suffered immensely on account of their looks, and there seems no end in sight to "looksism." A large part of Feminism 101 is devoted to discussion of how women are valued for their physical appearance and how that attitude is reflected in social institutions. Feminism 101 also teaches women how the worlds of marketing and advertisement perpetuate their insecurities. The intellectual insight from such subjects has great therapeutic benefit.

However, in order to achieve a lasting therapeutic transformation, women need to move from experiencing their bodies as primarily the focus of comparison-based appearance appraisal to experiencing their bodies as ever-changing individualized sources of sensations and competencies. This requires a massive reframing, which we might call "affirmative bodywork" in line with the affirmative genital education discussed earlier.

Components of this work are already part of many diverse therapeutic and non-therapeutic situations: eating-disorders treatment, self-defense training, exercise physiology education, disability rights education, physical rehabilitation, childbirth preparation, and cancer support groups. A compilation of strategies in these areas would be very interesting and useful to all of us—providers and consumers alike.

Although pernicious attention to women's looks appears to be a worldwide phenomenon, there are numerous differences in the ways the attitude is manifested in various sociocultural groups (differing in age, race, ethnicity, able-bodiedness, etc.). After all, "difference" is usually defined with respect to some aspect of the body. Because women's pain around issues of their looks is so deep, at least part of this remedial work should have the safety and protection of like-bodied segregation.

Masturbation Education

Masturbation education has been a centerpiece of women's sex therapy ever since Betty Dodson's 1974 pamphlet, *Liberating Masturbation*, and Lonnie Barbach's (1975) description of women's group work. Dodson's pamphlet of inspiration and technical advice continues to live in expanded form under a new title (Dodson, 1987). She has also produced videos illustrating the body-image, breathing, and vibrator techniques of the amazingly transformative nude weekend workshops she conducted over the past decades (Dodson, 1991) (see www.bettydodson.com).

Interestingly, a recent critique of the use of masturbation in sex therapy argued that the self-focus of masturbation is detrimental to intimacy, "bypasses" issues of emotional connection, prevents important collaborative sexual learning, and may even lead to sexual "addiction" (Christensen, 1995)! To no one's surprise, this article made no reference whatsoever to gender, as if the use of masturbation education in sex therapy were irrelevant to gender realities and politics.

Masturbation education remains central to the remedial component of feminist sex therapy. As a metaphor for empowerment, as a technique for teaching about orgasm, as a reframing of the purposes of sexuality, as an opportunity to learn about oneself from fantasy, and as a site of emotional sexual experience, masturbation remains the premier in vivo therapeutic opportunity for both bodywork and mind work (Davidson & Darling, 1993; Sarnoff & Sarnoff, 1979).

Part II: Reconceiving

Feminist sex therapy must not only offer remedial interventions or opportunities to learn coping strategies to resist ongoing oppression. Just as feminist scholarship is not only about correcting the omissions and distortions of the past, feminist scholarship on the social construction of sexuality must be used to expand our metaphors and our theories. A million ideas are waiting to be born here. What is sexuality, and what could it be? Here are four thoughts.

Contact Comfort

Lesbian scholarship has begun to discuss the sexuality of loving, committed relationships between women that have a small or nonexistent genital sexual component (e.g., Rothblum & Brehony, 1993). Such relationships may have been more common during certain periods in history, but they are not uncommon in lesbian communities even today. These relationships often involve a great deal of emotional and physical intimacy, including talking (in person, by telephone), hugging, holding hands, and other physical contact. Genital sexual acts either are not desired or play an occasional role. Hall (1993) has called this form of female pleasure and intimacy "genital incidentalism."

Many studies of nonlesbian women also support the wish for and pleasure in nongenital physical affection, touching, and holding, often called "cuddling" (e.g., Cline, 1993; Hollander & Mercer, 1976; McCormick, 1994). It may be that such forms of intimacy provide satisfaction equivalent to genital sexuality, that is, they satisfy the "same" psychological needs. It may be that the "sex drive" as related to a coital imperative represents a social imperative. Research that does not privilege coitus or orgasm is needed to better understand the role of genital sexuality and other forms of physical intimacy in the lives of women and of couples. Feminist sex therapy could incorporate such information to challenge the accepted norms of sex drive.

Mental Masturbation

Recent literary and historical studies of autoeroticism have discussed the connection between daydreaming, novels, and poetry, and the type of self-absorption and fantasy present in masturbation (Bennett & Rosario, 1995). The "onanist," which Eve Kosofsky-Sedgwick (1995) suggests is the earliest example of a category of sexual identity, was characterized not only by an addiction to genital masturbation, but also by a dreamy preference for creative thinking. This may be a rich and rewarding form of sexual experience.

For much of this Freudian century, cultural, political, and spiritual interests have been considered to be manifestations of sublimated sexuality—sort of sexual, but in a distorted way. The endogenous sex drive, it is said, is shunted in such situations into substitute activity because of anxieties developed in early life. If, however, we do not consider the sex drive as primitive and elementary, but rather view sex as the elaboration of life-affirming potentials which can be developed in other ways to provide life satisfaction, the idea of "mental masturbation" takes on another meaning.

Mental masturbation is closely connected to "sexual fantasy." This concept, widely used, has never been well defined, and the area is desperately underresearched. Women's sexual fantasies have been studied by literature scholars analyzing soap operas and sentimental and romance novels (e.g., Modleski, 1984), with their less coital/bodily/naked eroticism contrasted endlessly with "pornography," which is still held to constitute men's favored sexual fantasies. As more and more books and visuals with bodily eroticism clearly meant for women become available, however, the gender differences seem to be diminishing. Nevertheless, we still do not know enough about the meanings and pleasures of sexual imagination to know what they will have to offer in feminist sex therapy. Future feminist sex therapy may be able to teach women to use sex fantasies to instruct, enhance, substitute, relieve, assuage, modify, retrain, clarify, implement. . . .

Sex and Gender

Sexual activity and feelings frequently serve to affirm gender identity (Person, 1980). Gender identity, however, ain't what it used to be in these postmodern times, as we move from a simple "essentialist" two-category model to a view of gender as impersonation, role, and social construct (Butler, 1990). As our ideas about gender become more complex, people (and their families) do not necessarily have quantitatively more worries about gender, but will have more diverse ways to feel insecure about assigned, chosen, and evolving gender identities. Gender experiments with clothes, tattoos, and jewelry, or even with hormones or cosmetic surgeries, are likely to increase in frequency and trigger reactions and anxieties. A feminist sex therapy, eager to assist society's move beyond our historic rigid gender system, must evolve a range of strategies and concepts to help individuals, couples, and families cope with more fluid gender conceptualizations and expressions.

Sexual Talent

It is my definite impression that some people are good at sexuality, take to it easily and confidently, and seem to have talent for it. Others feel perpetually awkward, ill-at-ease, and uncomfortable. This difference may have little to do with capability for arousal and orgasm. This is not to say that people who feel awkward don't often enjoy sexual relations, or that people with talent have nothing but enjoyment. But, the pleasure in sexual activity seems clearly related in part to the ease with which a person adopts a sensual mode of being and feels spontaneous and at ease with bodies, movements, secretions, and intimate performances. In some clinical discussions, the implication is that anyone not spontaneous and sensual must be suffering the aftereffects of physical or sexual abuse. Unless those terms are defined so broadly as to be practically tautological, I doubt if that is the complete answer.

I fail to see why there can't be such a thing as "sex talent," akin to talents for music, athletics, dance, mathematics, humor, or maze-learning directionality—the various other special psychomotor or cognitive gifts we already recognize and celebrate. Sexual talent might be related to tactile or kinesthetic capabilities or concentrational/trance abilities. It might result from certain early sensual or pleasurable or intense experiences. To insist that everyone is equally talented at sex seems fraudulently democratic and related to simplistic ideas of evolution.

A feminist sex therapy with a notion of sex talent would not, of course, dismiss or condemn the untalented, but would take extra concern that they receive explicit teaching and coaching if sexual activity were an important goal, and would make sure that their struggle was normalized as representing a common part of the human range.

Conclusion

Viewing sexuality as a social construction, a way of labeling certain psychological and bodily potentials, opens up a new world for feminist sex therapy beyond the sexual response cycle, beyond the coital imperative, beyond the norms of patriarchal culture, even beyond the norms of diverse feminist groups (Tiefer, 1995). Such a point of view will allow sex therapists to continue to liberate women (and their sexual partners) as society continues to evolve. Feminist therapy offers us more than twenty years of theory and practice (Brown, 1994), and there's certainly plenty of fascinating sex theory. It's way time to begin.

chapter 6

THE CAPACITY FOR OUTRAGE: FEMINISM, HUMOR, AND SEX

Prologue: Confessions—and a Warning

Three of the things most important to me are sexuality, feminism, and humor. I have written, taught, researched, and lectured for many years about the first two, and the third has been my lifelong companion. I've often felt that I could handle almost anything except waking up one day no longer funny. Who would I be; how would I stand myself? As a person to whom being funny always came easily, I have sometimes wondered just exactly what I was doing. Is it about being angry a lot? Raised to have an outsider's view of things? Speaking before you think?

Being invited to write this essay led me to historical, cultural, psychological, and sociological theories of humor, and now I see that humor is every bit as complicated as sexuality. Clearly, it would take another lifetime to really know what I am doing when I'm being funny. Well, I never did figure out what I am doing when I have sex, either. Perhaps, on both subjects, remaining ignorant has its benefits—in which case the reader might be well advised to take a look at the cartoons and skip the rest.

Introduction: Feminist Humor Is Political Humor

Political humor takes many forms but has one clear purpose—social change. Through satire, jokes, cartoons, sarcasm, parody, standup, burlesque, camp,

wisecracks, gags, puns, lampoons, mockery, ridicule, and wit of every written, verbal, and visual sort, political humor comments critically on social
injustice and challenges the social order. Political humor can stand alone or
be part of speeches, columns (Lydia Sargent's monthly column, "Hotel
Satire," in Z magazine), legislation, court cases, rallies (protest signs about
chads at George W. Bush's inaugural), petitions, investigative journalism,
diaries, essays, folk songs (Tom Lehrer), electronic organizing, speakouts,
documentaries, etc.

Feminist humor subverts sexism and patriarchy by legitimizing women's
concerns and deflating anti-women positions. "Women belong in the
house, and the Senate" is on thousands of bumper stickers and speeches,
and it still makes me smile. Feminist humor can be soft or loud, obvious or
subtle, a lengthy tome or a one-liner, or even just a fleeting facial expression. It qualifies as feminist if it expresses alienation from normative gender
and sex roles, and it qualifies as humor if it uses some form of incongruity to
make the point. "I'm drowning in the typing pool." "Rock the boat, not the
cradle." "A woman who tries to be equal to a man lacks ambition."

Feminist humor serves the women's liberation movement as both attack weapon and in-group cohesive. There's nothing as bonding to movement partisans as sharing the laughter of recognition and outrage with
one's comrades, and I've been to many feminist events that opened with a
comedian. "We use our humor as a cure for burnout," wrote Gloria Kaufman in the introduction to one of the most important books on feminist
humor, *Pulling Our Own Strings* (Kaufman and Blakely, 1980, p. 12). I remember when Rep. Pat Schroeder of Colorado spoke at an Association for
Women in Psychology conference in 1987. "One of the best jobs for a
pregnant woman," she said, "would be a position on the Supreme Court.
The work is sedentary, and the clothing is loose-fitting." Perfect.

Feminist Humor vs. Women's Humor

It's important to distinguish feminist (political) humor from humor by or
about women that lacks social awareness or social purpose. For example,
these two jokes sit next to each other in a "treasury" of humor about
women (Myers, 1999, p. 155):

1. "I think, therefore I'm single."

2. "Husband: Dearie, don't you think our son gets his brains from me? Wife: I suppose so, dear. I still have all of mine."

The first joke could easily fit in a feminist volume, with its ironic comment on the complexities of women's relation to self and marriage that produces humor by unexpectedly altering a familiar quotation. The second joke seems no more than a traditional wifely put-down, a gotcha wisecrack that is formally funny (it pivots on two meanings for the word "get," a common pun strategy), but lacks social significance. In fact, this type of humor, while formally pro-woman (the woman "wins" the verbal joust) is in fact anti-feminist, in the sense that it reinforces the stereotype of wife as ball-buster. But, one might argue that, by inappropriately taking credit for their offspring's intelligence, he asked for it, so maybe her refusal to chime in, "Oh, sweetie, your side of the family has all the brains" is a bit of feminist assertion. Well, who said it was a clear distinction? Continue discussing this among yourselves while I return to the theory of feminist humor.

> The persistent attitude that underlies feminist humor is the attitude of social revolution—that is, we are ridiculing a social system that can be, that must be changed. . . . The *nonacceptance* of oppression characterizes feminist humor and satire. (Kaufman, 1980, p. 13)

As Regina Barreca (1996) suggests, "Much women's humor, while not *explicitly* political, nevertheless raises questions concerning the accepted wisdom of the system" (p. 1). Her example of this is a joke by actress and comedian Pam Stone:

> I had a girlfriend who told me she was in the hospital for female problems. I said, "Get real! What does that mean?" She says, "You know, female problems." I said, "What? You can't parallel park? You can't get credit?" (ibid.)

Humor theorists would explain that this joke is funny because of the irrational, illogical incongruity between hospital problems and parking and credit problems. Murray Davis (1993) would call this an example of "descending incongruity" because the second topic is clearly of lesser significance than the first. The comedian goes for an even bigger laugh by pairing the sexist stereotype of women not being able to park with a political observation, women's difficulties obtaining credit, offering a twist that makes this joke half-feminist, at least. Are you with me?

Barreca continues, "When it *is* explicitly political, women's humor often satirizes the social forces designed to keep women in 'their place,' a phrase that has become synonymous with keeping women quietly bound by cultural stereotypes" (ibid., pp. 1–2). For humor to be political to Barreca, the subject matter has to focus on some specific area of oppression such as public life, employment, the family, or sexuality. But feminists have shown that, dispiriting though this is, no aspect of life or culture is free from sexism, and thus any content will work. As with manslaughter vs. murder, the essential element in deciding whether something is political or not is intention. Is the comedian, cartoonist, or satirist identifying with a movement or struggle, or just out to get a laugh? Oh, gee, I didn't mean to upset you by mentioning manslaughter.

Why Is Women's Humor Revolutionary?

Naomi Weisstein, a feminist psychologist best known for an influential 1969 critique of sexism in clinical psychology, explained in her introduction to a book of Ellen Levine's feminist cartoons why women's use of humor was a revolutionary tactic (Weisstein, 1973). Weisstein began by observing that women's capacity for humor had too often been held captive by female socialization. Most women's "livelihood depended on charming some man, having a provider," she wrote, and

> the definition of what was charm depended primarily on our being beautiful, passive, accepting, and mute. . . . We had an obligation to laugh endlessly at men's jokes . . . to be witty and pleasing. But to be able *to mock the requirement that we be all these things* is quite a different thing . . . laughing at all and only those things which we are expected to laugh at is part of maintaining our charm. . . . When people tell us we've lost our sense of humor . . . [it] means that we may actually be changing our social roles, that we have stopped trying to please." (ibid., pp. 6–7, emphasis added)

Weisstein points out that the first level of women's consciousness-raising about humor is becoming aware of how women are trained to be appreciative audiences for men's humor (e.g., responding to the husband's taking credit for their offspring's intelligence with a giggle and a smile). The next step is to take a long, serious look at traditional men's humor and recognize how much of it actually targets women, rationalizing their social inferiority and oppression as "natural" and just (of course, the kid would get his brains from his father, and his penchant for stalling the car on steep hills and losing his credit cards from his mother).

This consciousness raising, so painful in the early 1970s, may seem to some like ancient history, so effectively has the women's movement changed social norms. A *Playboy* cartoon drawn by Cliff Roberts that I saved from the 1970s, for example, shows a man at a desk with a framed painting of a screw behind him, saying to a woman job applicant, "The painting behind me represents many things, my dear. It's my product, my philosophy, and what I expect twice a week from my secretary." In the present climate, this cartoon just seems stupid. By denaturalizing traditional gender rules and sex roles, feminist humor helped bring about these momentous changes.

> One of the paths of coming into consciousness, [Weisstein continues], into politics, for an oppressed group is the realization that their misery is not due to some innate inferiority, to their own flawed characters, but that there is something going on outside that is keeping them down, and that it is *not fair*. . . . [Feminist cartoons] represent . . . part of the effort to build a tradition which defines our oppression, fights it, and *mocks the roles we are forced into and the roles others take in relation to us*. . . . There have been extraordinary obstacles to the development of a woman's fighting humor . . . we must try out forms which throw off the shackles of self-ridicule, self-abnegation; we must tap that capacity for outrage. (Weisstein, 1973, pp. 8–9)

With feminist humor, Weisstein concludes,

> we are reclaiming our autonomy and our history. . . . The propitiating laughter, the fixed and charming smiles are over. When we laugh, things are going to be funny. And when we don't laugh, it's because . . . we know what's not funny." (ibid., p. 10)

Humor is a form of power, of resistance against oppression, sometimes public, sometimes private. "Making fun of our inferior position raises us above it" (Mindess, 1971, p. 48). The effectiveness of this form of resistance is shown by laws in Nazi Germany and Soviet Russia making political humor a direct attack on the government and joke-tellers subject to arrest, deportation, or worse (Lipman, 1991). Yet, these settings produced a huge underground of spirit-saving, irreverent, savage humor. Although, humor has a different role in a democracy or a family than in a totalitarian state, feminists, often living in situations where direct expression of their oppression would be punished, express resistance and hope through humor.

This chapter offers a convenience sample of some feminist humor, some of it about sex. I pulled these examples conveniently (or not so conveniently, since I fell off a chair once, but you don't care about that) from my mostly professional, technical, nonfunny library. It would be overwhelming to sample all of popular culture for what it can tell us about feminist humor—television sitcoms, newspaper funnies, comedy clubs, film comedies—I'm hyperventilating just at the thought. I did find one reference to just such an encyclopedic overview (Rowe, 1995). If someone gets a chance to read it, would you drop me a note and let me know what you learn?

Pictures With
(Or, Occasionally, Without) Words

The earliest feminist humor material I have is visual, so let's start with that domain.

Early Political Cartoons

I bought Alice Shepard's (1994) history of cartoons in the American suffrage movement because I thought they'd inspire me and make me laugh. Surprisingly, I didn't "get" many of them because conventions in cartooning have changed, and political humor refers to events and people who are soon forgotten. "The role of political cartoonist was judged masculine because it wielded power and served as a privileged vantage point from which to expose and ridicule social structures and political leaders" (Shepard, 1994, p. 25). Shepard introduces us to numerous unheralded suffrage artists. Their cartoons were published in some mainstream outlets, but mostly they drew, unpaid, for movement publications now crumbling in obscure archives.

In the first illustration, from 1915, cartoonist Katherine Milhous uses straightforward satire to ridicule the claims of those who argued that voting would make women less feminine, would "unsex" them. This cartoon uses a vocabulary and form of humor still appropriate almost a century later.

Cartoon by Katherine Milhous, "Votes for Women," postcard dated 1915. Reproduced by permission of the Alice Marshall Women's History Collection, Penn State Harrisburg Library, Middletown, Penn.

A second example, however, seems quaint, rather than funny.

In this 1914 magazine cartoon, Annie ("Lou") Rogers, probably the most prolific and best-known suffrage cartoonist, has Abraham Lincoln welcoming womanhood into full citizenship. This kind of cartoon, more symbolic and inspirational than transgressive in its challenge to the status quo, drew from the repertoire of authority symbols—patriotic, biblical, regal, literary—to advocate for women's rights.

Cartoon by Lou Rogers, "If Lincoln Were Alive," reprinted from *The Judge,* June 20, 1914, New York, N.Y.

IF LINCOLN WERE ALIVE

"I go for all sharing the privileges of government who assist in bearing its burdens, not excepting women."—*Abraham Lincoln.*

Rogers offered a more humorous image in the next example, published in 1913, that ridiculed anti-suffragists as outmoded and ignorant.

Cartoon by Lou Rogers, "The Latest Addition to the Junk-Heap," reprinted from *Woman's Journal and Suffrage News,* October 18, 1913, Boston.

LAST LAUGHS

The Latest Addition to the Junk-Heap

Do we relate more to the older cartoons that criticize rather than the ones drawing on inspiring symbols because our sources of inspiration have changed? Or because an inspiring image might work nowadays as an illustration, but a contemporary cartoon needs some sort of punch? Or does it have to do with the fact that women have had the vote for so long that the subject is too tame to give a twenty-first century reader any sort of frisson?

Early Second Wave Political Cartoons

Fast forward to so-called second wave feminism to see more recent cartooning tactics at work. Ellen Levine's 1973 book *"All She Needs . . . "* is full of drawings that reveal women's frustration and anger with the status quo. Sexual pleasure and sexual violence, major themes of women's liberation, are favorite subjects, as in the next two examples:

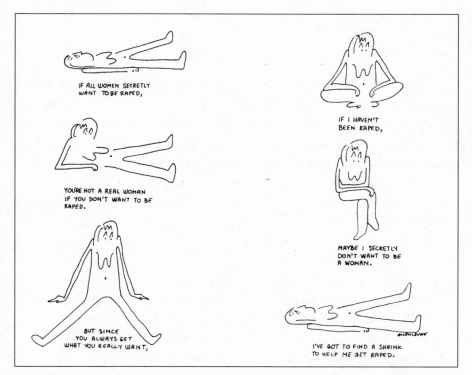

Cartoon by Ellen Levine, reprinted from Levine, *"All She Needs . . . "* (New York: Quadrangle/The New York Times Book Co., 1973).

SEVEN YEARS IN ANALYSIS
AND NOW THEY TELL ME
ABOUT THE MYTH OF THE
VAGINAL ORGASM

Cartoon by Ellen Levine, reprinted from Levine, "All She Needs . . . " (New York: Quadrangle/The New York Times Book Co., 1973).

The barebones style of drawing a woman—naked but unsexy—is itself a feminist statement, and the captions repeat hotly contested 1960s and 1970s arguments about sexual issues. Will these cartoons speak to a contemporary twenty-something woman who has always lived in a culture where the clitoris is known and violence against women is taken seriously? Will she see these cartoons as quaint the way I see some of the suffrage ones?

Another cartoonist of the early second wave was a woman who signed her cartoons Bülbül. At the beginning of her book, *I'm not for women's lib . . . but*, she explains her philosophy:

> I have tried in this cartoon collection to draw what I think and feel about a few aspects of the male culture. Some of the cartoons show the social mechanisms by which women are kept under control and, "in their places" by men. Some cartoons show that the deep male prejudice against women covers the entire political spectrum from white male money bags to hip counter-culture. . . . My hope is that these cartoons in their small way will help women, with a chuckle, in their struggle for dignity and self-determination. (pages unnumbered)

So earnest, so uncomplicated! In Bülbül's world, women usually have little power or voice. Two tiny men fight on top of a huge woman's body, and one says, "Get off! This is MY territory." A bearded guitar player strums an instrument made of a woman's body, singing "Love me baby! Me! Me! Me!" In successive panels, a woman says to a man, "I feel thoroughly put down," "It's a constant struggle for simple dignity," "For personhood," and in the final panel, the man replies, "You need a good lay, chick." But, in one cartoon, a woman goes into the office of "Doctor Tut-Tut Shrink." He first says, "You are suffering from your inability to handle your proper female role," and then, "My dear, you are suffering from the delusions of an over-emotional female." Finally, she sits up on the couch and says, "Doctor, what I'm suffering from is reality" and, leaping off the couch in the final panel, she shouts, "AND YOU!"

Bülbül's captions, especially as presented without the drawings, seem so overstated as to provoke a backlash of embarrassment. "Oh, come on. Men/psychiatrists don't really talk like that." It's a variant of "where's your sense of humor, honey, getting angry over every little thing?!" But, exaggeration is a hallmark of certain kinds of American humor (think of Paul Bunyan). "The easiest way to make things laughable is to exaggerate to the point of absurdity their salient traits" (Max Eastman quoted in Davis, 1993, p. 86). If, in other settings, this kind of humor is accepted, complaints against it when used by feminists is a form of backlash. It reveals how uncomfortable we are with overt hostility, and how precariously feminist humor must be balanced to work. Sigh. I always get depressed by backlash, you'll have to excuse me. Sisyphus was just not my favorite Greek.

Grrlz Comics: Are We Getting More Than We Bargained For?

Fast forward to the current world of comics, which, like the larger world of popular culture, is complicated, segmented, and a little overwhelming. A recent lavishly illustrated text provides an overview history of comics about girls and women, which, not coincidentally, are only recently drawn by girls and women themselves (Robbins, 1999). Comics, stories told through pictures, are always funny, as in incongruity or transgression. However, at the point in the 1970s when feminist cartoonists like Bülbül and Ellen Levine emerged, a new genre of "womyn's" or "wimmen's" "comix" emerged in the new underground comics scene with titles like *It Ain't Me, Babe, Tits 'n' Clits, Wet Satin*, and *Pudge, Girl Blimp*. Sometimes labeled as pornography, these cartoon novels, occasionally funny but always provocative, took on issues important to women's lives—menstruation, contraception, lesbianism, abortion, sex, family, nuclear war, tampons. These books continue to the present time, but, as with feminist culture in general, the number of woman-drawn woman-topic-oriented comics is minuscule within the overall genre.

The Best Feminist
Sex Cartoon in the World

I have gotten huge laughs of recognition and appreciation in the past couple of years when I show this feminist Viagra (or is it anti-Viagra) cartoon as part of my lectures on the medicalization of sexuality.

The idea of Viagra "supplements," in the first instance, directly attacks the idea that Viagra, with its limited peripheral hemodynamic effects, is sufficient to make a man into an adequate lover. Many women are apoplectic over the utopian messages in Viagra marketing that imply romance, love, and tender

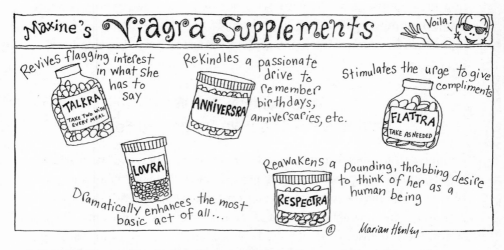

A "Maxine" cartoon by Marian Henley. Reprinted by permission of the artist.

passion are likely side effects of the little blue pill rather than the nausea and headaches listed in the insert pamphlet's small print. Moreover, cartoonist Marian Henley has pinpointed five of the areas feminist sex researchers like Shere Hite (1981, 1987) repeatedly emphasize are central to many women's sexual satisfaction. The humor of this cartoon raises consciousness about what many women want and how we continue to wait in vain.

Words With
(or, Occasionally, Without) Pictures

How has feminist humor told its story in words? There are one-liner jokes, of course. They are the icing on the cake. But real, doughy, feminist humor requires an extended opportunity to lay out an argument. It's hard, after all, to stuff into a one-liner: a statement of a social problem, a few illustrations to show it's not just a little-bitty problem, a dozen more illustrations to show we are really talking global, a hundred more examples to show this problem has been with us since people lived in caves, and then wind up with some feminist solutions. Here are a few favorite examples.

The Bloody Body
Gloria Steinem's 1978 essay in *Ms.* magazine, "If men could menstruate" (reprinted in Kaufman & Blakely, 1980) is a skyscraper in the landmarks of feminist humor (have I got your attention, Mrs. Bunyan?). Incorporating exaggeration, punning, parody, and an escalating string of zingers, this satirical essay is a premiere example of how feminist humor can take a subject of central importance to women's everyday lives and show how contemporary culture, dominated by topics important to men, trivializes, ignores, and treats it with contempt. I'll give you only a brief taste of this amazing satire:

> What would happen, for instance, if suddenly, magically, men could menstruate and women could not? . . . Men would brag about how long and how much. Boys would mark the onset of menses, that longed-for proof of manhood with religious ritual. . . . Congress would fund a National Institute of Dysmenorrhea. . . . Sanitary supplies would be federally funded and free [although] some men would still pay for . . . prestige . . . brands. . . .

Military men . . . would cite menstruation . . . as proof that only men could serve in the Army ("you have to give blood to take blood"). . . . Men would convince women that intercourse was *more* pleasurable at "that time of the month." . . . (Steinem, 1980, pp. 25–26)

Why is this so funny? First of all, it is about how menstruation, a topic not easily discussed in public and often regarded with paralyzing embarrassment, shame, and disgust by women in many cultures, could overnight become a topic of extreme pride if cultural rules were changed. In a brilliant trick of reversal, Steinem shows how there is nothing *intrinsically* bad about menstruation, it's stigmatized by sexism and patriarchy. The relief from embarrassment and shame that women experience on hearing this satire (as with the popular *Vagina Monologues* by Eve Ensler) is a measure of the subject's offensiveness and contemptuousness, exactly the feminist point. Steinem's satire specifically pinpoints ways that women are generally oppressed that the feminist reader experiences relief, release, and sheer triumphant pleasure. Perfect.

Margot Sims and the Tradition of Antifeminist Sociobiology

Feminism is about destroying ideologies and practices of female subordination. One of the most enduring antifeminist ideologies says female inferiority is dictated by nature, biology, hormones, genes—by whatever is most unchangeable in current scientific thinking. No wonder some of the most pointed feminist satires take on the so-called evolutionary origins of gender inequality.

Margot Sims (1982), claiming to be the founder of The Center for the Study of Human Types (on the site of a former seminary for the Order of the Most Precious Bleeding Heart in central Nebraska!!), argues that, no matter what measure you use, men and women cannot possibly be members of the same species. Whether the measure is anatomy, reproductive physiology, puberty, fertility, sexual response, sexual conditionability, courtship patterns, or masturbatory habits, Sims argues in 140 illustrated pages that male humans are closer to primates and other animals than are women, i.e., that women are a more evolved species. The only solution to human harmony, she concludes, tongue planted firmly in cheek, is not segregation of the two sexes, not humanization of the male gender, but "female bestialization." I'll get to that in a moment.

Sims's satire, as with Steinem and other feminists, allows her to comment indirectly on many feminist issues. I'll quote first from the chapter on courtship:

> Members of the same species are innately interested in identifying and co-operating with other members of their species for the purpose of mating. . . . Since beast humans [men] and true humans [women] are not very closely related species, it is no surprise that they employ courtship behaviors which are anti-complementary. This is an obvious clue that human beings could not possibly all be one species. The male beast human . . . favors the quick and overt; the [female true human favors] the slow and subtle. . . . Without the ability to fantasize, women would certainly be more insane than they normally are. With their fantasy of "let's pretend men are true human beings," many can go for long periods of time. (Sims, 1982, pp. 77–78)

Or consider this, from the chapter on sex physiology.

> The relative complexity of a species' sex response appears to be correlated with evolutionary ranking. Sex research pioneers Masters and Johnson found the true human's sex response cycle to be extremely varied and complex, the beast human predictable and simple . . . the beast human travels the same, well-worn unswerving path every time he ascends Mt. Orgasm . . . the true human by contrast, rarely travels the same path twice. (ibid., p. 37)

Sims goes on to equate these differences with more elaborate brain development in the "true" human, and the superiority of cognitive processes like thought and emotion over reflex functions. When, in her conclusion, then, Sims gets to the necessity of "bestializing" women to make them more equal to men, she focuses on the surgery that women will need:

> The problem, of course, lies in determining exactly where in the female anatomy the emotional nugget is located so surgeons can pluck it out. I predict that someday bestialization of newborn girls will be as routine as circumcision of newborn boys is today. (ibid., pp. 130–131)

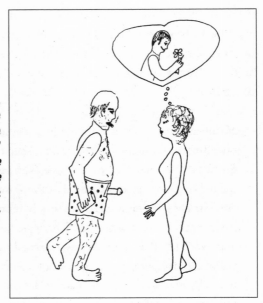

Cartoon by Margot Sims, "Fantasies Enable Many True Human Females to Cope More Satisfactorily with Their Lives," reprinted from Sims, *On the Necessity of Bestializing the Human Female* (Boston: South End Press, 1982).

Margot Sims lampoons the endless efforts to pinpoint the physiology of complex sex differences and sociobiology's quest to reduce human behaviors to evolutionary and biological origins. Her book is a refreshing lozenge for the feminist scientist with laryngitis from decades of preaching against pseudoscientific misogyny.

So Many Ways to Be Crazy, So Little Time

Extensive feminist research has identified how social oppression against women has been disguised and reframed as individual women's pathologies. Instead of focusing on the lack of child care and good education, experts say children are at risk because of incompetent mothering. Instead of attacking oppressive fashion and film images, women learn to believe they are fat and ugly. Instead of identifying how sexual harassment, low pay, poor benefits, and other working conditions are stressful and exploitative, overworked women label themselves as having depression and other psychological problems.

There have been many satirical contributions on this theme. *Our Syndromes, Ourselves* (Hamilton, 2000) is an outstanding recent effort to ridicule the endless production of new sicknesses with which to label women. By calling "bad perms," "blind dates from hell" and "road trips with the kids" causes of "post-traumatic stress disorder," for example, Hamilton marries an Erma Bombeck-like attention to the minutiae of women's everyday life to the feminist *Our Bodies, Ourselves* tradition of naming our own problems rather than letting the medical establishment have the power.

Feminist psychologists have written about the harmful multiplication of psychiatric mental disorders like "premenstrual syndrome (PMS)" and "self-defeating personality disorder" (Caplan, 1995). One of my favorite examples of feminist humor on this theme is the slim satire *Are Children Neglecting Their Mothers?* by the pseudonymous "famous psychoanalyst" Hadley V. Baxendale, M.D., Ph.D. (1974). In Chapter Three, Dr. B. explains that if children do not pay enough attention to their moms, if they play too often with their friends or go to summer camp too enthusiastically, that there will be trouble down the road.

> If a child never makes his mother feel that she is the focal figure in his life, if
> he insists on leaving her every day in pursuit of selfish interests of his own, . . .
> the mother may go through an unusually trying climacteric, have a nervous
> breakdown, or grow addicted to prescription drugs. (Baxendale, 1974, p. 30)

This book begins with a disclaimer, "A warning to the literal minded reader. All interviews in this book are, of course, fictitious" (ibid., p. 11). Unfortunately, when *Psychology Today* magazine offered some of Dr. B's ideas in a short 1975 piece titled, "Why a Person Who Menstruates Is Unfit to Be a Mother," it neglected to indicate that this was satire, and the magazine was flooded with complaints (Tavris, 1992).

The failure of readers to recognize Baxendale as a feminist humorist is revealing. Humor inverts reality, offers something incongruous. If the humor is not recognized, then reality has not been inverted. Some feminist readers of *Psychology Today* were appalled that Dr. Baxendale would call for mothers to mistreat their children for their own selfish purposes. They felt Dr. Baxendale was anti-woman! It's as if a feminist humorist called for women to walk naked back and forth past construction sites so workers could get a proper eyeful without endangering themselves, and readers complained, saying that such women might catch cold. Lack of humor about certain topics is a sign of how important they are, but excessive political correctness (nothing bad about women can ever be said or drawn) can also be oppressive.

Feminist Humor About Sex

Are you ready for the quiz? What would feminist humor about sex focus on most? (a) men's genital organs, those that work and those that don't, (b) hot lusty women wanting lots of sex in lots of ways, (c) lesbian meeting and mating habits, (d) men's ideas of pleasure and romance, (e) what women think about during sexual activities, (f) rape, incest, and sexual harassment? If you answered, "all of the above," you have got the point of this chapter. It's not one subject, it's one spin. The feminist wit will spin genital physiology, lust, men's foibles, and anything else in order to raise consciousness and resist sexism.

And what form will the feminist humor take? Any and every form. Mae West camped her answer. Sophie Tucker sang. Cynthia Heimel's sarcastic magazine essays, collected in half a dozen collections, have drop-dead titles like *If You Can't Live With Me, Why Aren't You Dead Yet?* (Heimel, 1991). There's standup comedian Kate Clinton and cartoonist Nicole Hollander. Feminist cartoonists and comedians have even taken on sexual abuse through ridiculing the ways police and psychiatrists trivialize these subjects.

In a famous 1948 parody, Ruth Herschberger interviewed Josie, a chimpanzee in the lab of primatologist Robert M. Yerkes, about the conclusions the scientist drew about her sexual behavior. Yerkes seemed unable to see Josie's sexuality as anything but subordinate to her mate, Jack. Josie complained. "Receptive? I'm about as receptive as a lion waiting to be fed."

> Jack and I can go through almost the same motions, but by the time it gets down on paper, it has one name when Jack does it, and another when it was me. For instance, when Jack was at the food chute and I gestured in sexual invitation to him, . . . this was put down as "favor-currying" on my part. . . . The reason people are so sure that I traded sexual accommodation

for food . . . is because nobody thinks women enjoy . . . sex. . . . Maybe human females don't enjoy sex, but we chimps resent any forced analogy with humans. (Herschberger, 1948, pp. 10–12)

Feminist Humor and
the "War" Between the Sexes

If feminist humor is a weapon, are men the target? Is feminist humor just a form of man-hating? In her 1992 analysis of gender relations and gender ideologies, *My Enemy, My Love: Man-Hating and Ambivalence in Women's Lives*, journalist Judith Levine argues that "Man-hating is a collective, cultural problem. . . . Man-hating isn't a function of feminism; it's a function of the *reasons* for feminism" (p. 4). She sees man-hating as an inevitable result of the feminist insight, "The personal is political,"

which means figuring out how the big hand of Oppression feels when it comes sharply into contact with one's own person. To recognize oppression is to be infuriated, and to recognize it right here at home is to be infuriated at *someone*, someone you know [a brother, boyfriend, coworker, husband, or father, for example]—sometimes, in fact to hate him. (ibid.)

In our fast-changing society, Levine argues, relations between men and women are uncertain, awkward, improvisational, and, frequently, full of tension. The changes, of course, are more often celebrated and promoted by feminist women than the men in their lives, producing the myriad forms of hostility ("taxonomy of manhating") Levine documents. Man-hating is disguised in most women's lives, in part from fear, women's continuing emotional and financial dependency, and women's own often unacknowledged ambivalence about contemporary sex roles and sexual changes. And humor plays a big part in this overall picture.

Gloria Steinem tried, unsuccessfully, to draw a clear line between good dirty pictures, erotica, and bad dirty pictures, pornography. Trying to do that with humor about gender is equally ill-fated. There is no clear line between good "feminist" humor (constructive, political, reformist) and bad "nonfeminist" humor (hostile, women-are-good-men-are-bad, simpleminded) although we can make some meaningful distinctions, as I indicated in the introduction. The struggle against misogyny (woman-hating), sexism, and patriarchy is a huge revolution, and every one of us is involved, like it or not. During the interview tour after her book was published, journalist Levine found that the word "man-hating" in her subtitle was so inflammatory that many people couldn't get past it to read the book. So, in the paperback version, she changed it to *Women, Men and the Dilemmas of Gender*. But she left all the jokes in, like this description of sex by the British comic Jenny Lecoat. It's pure revenge, and most probably not good feminist humor, but it says a lot in a small space.

> He, laboring away, pauses to ask, "Are you nearly there?" "It's hard to say," says she. He plunges on. "If you imagine it as a journey from here to China, where would you be?" She considers. "The kitchen." (Levine, 1992, p. 59)

Epilogue

Writing this essay reminded me of many painful things about women's lives and struggles for change. I couldn't stand dealing with it all in silence, so I looked for some music to keep me company. Over and over I played the original cast recording of the 1997 Broadway musical (not to be confused with the movie of the same name) *Titanic* on the CD-player next to my desk. And each time I heard the overture, the finale, and some of the passionate songs about aspirations and innocence destroyed, I cried. Builder, owner, captain, crew, rich first-class passengers, poor immigrant passengers—all sing to an engineering miracle that will bring their hearts' desire—and bang, they're dead. I'm writing about feminist resistance and triumph through satire and cartoons, and I'm weeping, sniffling, and wiping my eyes over a tragedy brought about by pride, greed, and bad luck. Feminist political humor exists at the edge of tragic hopelessness, and you need to feel that edge to get it.

part four

THE MEDICALIZATION
OF SEXUALITY

My arch-enemy, the medical model of sex, seems to gain ground every day. Today's *Philadelphia Inquirer* (July 17, 2003) announces that a new drug for erection problems will be advertised at National Football League games. Soon, it seems, everyone will be taking pills, not for treatment, not even for enhancement, but just in order to be as good as they assume everyone else is. This may be a perversion of the old-fashioned medical model that says treatments are for diseases, but it fits right into the way consumer culture and the pharmaceutical industry have developed a new medical model that says it's OK to take drugs for "lifestyle" problems.

I have had a lot of trouble seeing how sex fits into the old medical model, and I'm not doing any better with the new one. For me, medicine is the proper framework when a definable disease condition with a physical basis requires someone expert about the body. This is not very often what is wrong, however, when people are unhappy with their sexual lives. Unfortunately, doctors are poorly prepared to know what to do when the lab numbers are normal, as they almost always are. I teach in two New York City medical schools, and I can tell you that doctors get precious little training in sexual culture.

Although current interdisciplinary work emphasizes the cultural and psychological aspects of medicine (e.g., Aronowitz, 1998), most doctors don't learn about this, certainly not in sexual medicine. The pressures of managed care and the biological reductionism of medical training mean psychosocial issues are usually left out of the equation. It is really weird that doctors should be the reigning experts on sex. Even though I have made my living as a clinical psychologist for the past twenty or so years and done a lot of sex therapy, I don't focus much on what is or isn't normal. That typically is something couples fight over and accuse each other about. "You're not normal." "No, you're not normal." I don't want to be a normality referee; normal shifts too much in response to political winds. I focus more on helping couples negotiate a consensual arrangement for their sex life than in curing "disorders."

But, as with other things, I am probably fighting a losing battle. Sex has become medicalized in the way that pregnancy, old age, drinking alcohol, menstruation, and so many other areas of life and conduct have become medicalized. Medicalization is a major social and intellectual trend whereby the concepts and practices of medicine come to exercise authority over particular areas of life. Sociologists have traced the way various interest groups promote medical research, publicize their views and findings, and call for medical labels. The public comes to view particular behaviors or bodily expressions as symptoms rather than cultural alternatives or normal ups and downs. People feel their general health and well-being will suffer without certain behaviors, rather than seeing them as optional. And they feel the people who can best help are medical experts, rather than educators or coaches.

A lot of the success of medicalization has to do with how a medical label allows people to avoid blame. It also seems to offer hope and a team of helpers. But there is a high price to be paid for medicalization. You have to see yourself as a patient, focus on getting your condition improved, take pills and other treatments regularly, and monitor your progress. If you don't, you're blamed again. Medicalization can make you more obsessed and unhappy than before, especially when medicine doesn't really have much to offer. When a medical perspective is applied to sex, I believe it narrows the potential for individuality and diversity, and changes a spiritual domain of self-expression, intimacy, and transcendence into something like car mechanics with a universal check-off list. Do this, then do that, and above all make sure you get the right score at the end.

I go back to the metaphor from Part One of this book, the one I got from my mother, the musician. I think of sex as a psychophysiological potential that can be developed a lot, a little, or not at all, depending on circumstances, talent, opportunity, interests, etc. I think of sexual life as more like a hobby than a medical function. Many people have a background that makes it hard for them to relax, enjoy their body in an unself-conscious way, or enjoy physical intimacy. They're not going to be great lovers and why should they be? Others have no particular disadvantage, but they just don't develop themselves sexually. Are these people disordered? Do they need medical treatments? Does everyone have to be hot hot hot?

The irony is that many factors actually make it hard to really enjoy sex in current U.S. society. Not only do we lack comprehensive sex education, but the same advertising companies that promote Viagra also make you feel that you smell bad, have rotten hair and skin, and are way too fat for anyone to love you. Much contemporary culture causes people to distrust their partners and be ambivalent about emotional commitment. The intimacy of the sexual encounter brings out emotional vulnerabilities that make honest conversation difficult and sexual satisfaction often suffers as a consequence. Are these all to be solved with pills and doctors?

The more important sex gets in the society, the more everyone needs independent advice and preparation. Since the U.S. lacks comprehensive sex education or coaching, doctors and other health providers are becoming important resources. But doctors are not well-educated about sex and often don't have time to help people get over the embarrassment of talking honestly. So they label things disorders and recommend pills. And that's where medicalization has gotten us.

"Premature ejaculation (PE)" might be a great example to end with. When I first learned about sex therapy I learned how to teach men to orgasm more quickly or more slowly through masturbation exercises, learning to pay attention to physical sensations, and reducing shame and anxiety over being "inadequate." Now, however, there are many prescription drugs under development to treat PE or "rapid ejaculation (RE)," as it will probably be renamed. Perhaps by the time this book is published there will be an RE ad campaign as big as that for Viagra. But most men who orgasm or ejaculate before they want to can learn to delay their orgasm or ejaculation with exercises that are available in many how-to books (e.g., Zilbergeld, 1994). Why isn't this preferable to taking drugs? Does it really make sense that men should take drugs *for the rest of their lives* just to delay orgasm? Won't these drugs have side-effects? Won't labeling PE or RE as defined by a certain number of seconds to orgasm make people more anxious and obsessed about their performance? Has everyone lost their mind?

chapter 1

SEXISM IN SEX THERAPY:
WHOSE IDEA IS "SENSATE FOCUS"?

A feminist analysis of the patriarchal bias in sexology could do worse than begin with one of the fundamental elements of the new sex therapy: "sensate focus." In Human Sexual Inadequacy, Masters and Johnson (1970) introduced "sensate focus" as an important educational device:

> Sensate focus . . . was chosen to provide the sensory experience most easily and appropriately available to marital partners as a medium for physical exchange in reconstituting natural responsivity to sexual stimuli. . . . These "exercises" are designed to free sexual dysfunctional individuals from inhibitions that deprive them of an opportunity to respond naturally to sensory experience. . . . Sensory awareness and its communication to another person can be extremely difficult for those who have not had the opportunity to develop sensate orientation gradually, under circumstances in which the experience was valued and encouraged, or at least not negated. . . . This educational process, as initiated in therapy by the sensate "exercises," permits gradual modification of negative reactions to sensory stimuli so that learning occurs. (Masters and Johnson, 1970, pp. 76, 77)

This argument for the importance of focusing on sensations during sexual relations sounds persuasive and even self-evident, and indeed "sensate focus" has continued to be a cardinal element of sex therapy while other aspects of Masters and Johnson's original design and rationale have been discarded.

But just why should sensory experience be the normative centerpiece of sexuality? Consider contrasting points of view expressed by participants in Shere Hite's research:

> Sex is important because during sex you can be as close as possible with another person.
>
> Sex is beautiful because such a complete contact with another person makes me feel my being is not solely confined to my own body.
>
> Sex plays a very important part in my life because it is a symbol of the love I am sharing with my man. I know it is his way of showing that he loves me.
>
> I become very emotionally involved in my sexual relations. I think I have sex almost always to consummate a bond, to develop and perpetuate closeness. (Hite, 1976, pp. 283–284)

These are quotes from people for whom emotional and not sensory focus is the centerpiece of sexual experience; it is no surprise that the quotes are from women. An emotional focus for sexual relations offers a dramatically contrasting point of view.

Ellen Frank, Carol Anderson, and Debra Rubinstein's (1978) study of 100 white couples with self-defined "successful marriages" found that 77 percent of the women reported sexual difficulties like "partner chooses inconvenient time, inability to relax, too little foreplay; too little tenderness." Their responses in this area correlated with overall ratings of sexual satisfaction. Hite's (1976) entire volume is dedicated to a "redefinition" of sexual relations wherein routine scripts of foreplay-to-intercourse-to-orgasm would be replaced or at least enhanced by more spontaneity, variety, verbal communication, fun, and tenderness. Such a redefinition requires appreciating the deep gender differences in sexual socialization in our society and rejecting the notion that sex-as-usual represents the interests of all men and women.

But the fact that *sex therapy* has remained sensate-focused shows that many women's interests are being bypassed. It would, it seems to me, take only a little imagination to design an alternate sex therapy stressing emotional homework assignments (heavy on loving communication, eye contact, expression of feelings, and the like). Alternate assessment instruments could be designed to evaluate a couple's emotional knowledge, comfort, and connectedness during sex instead of their satisfaction with the performance of various sexual acts.

Therapists' commitment to a sensate view of sexuality not only represents a choice about what sort of sexual experience is "real" or "best" but also assumes that all partners are already sensually adept or would be able to learn how to focus on sensation. This is part of the claim (I would say "myth") of universality and "naturalness" that is such a central element in the Masters and Johnson approach. Can such assumptions be made?

A minimum requirement for a sensate focus would seem to be a lack of competing or distracting thoughts. A person would have to feel comfortable, safe, and entitled in order to focus wholly on his or her tactile experience. Can we assume that most women can be thoroughly relaxed in sexual situations given the inequality of so many relationships, given women's concern with their appearance, given women's worries about safety and contraception? The fact that this question is ignored in *Human Sexual Inadequacy* and other sex therapy texts indicates how unimportant the social reality of women's lives is for most sex therapists. In the eyes of sex therapy, men's and women's interests are the same and they are focused "by nature" on sensory and physical experience and performance. This biological reductionism suggests that sex therapy is likely to be a patriarchal tool unless feminists intervene.

chapter 2

WOMEN'S SEXUALITY:
NOT A MATTER OF HEALTH

The Power of Naming

What are the advantages and disadvantages of locating women's sexuality under the rubric of health? Designating sexuality a matter of "health" has important ramifications in terms of appropriate authorities, institutional control, language and imagery, methods for study, and, most important, people's views of its place in their own lives (Featherstone, Hepworth, and Turner, 1991; Conrad and Kern, 1981). In this context, it is important to note that "health" is not dictated by biology any more than "sexuality" is dictated by biology (Scott and Morgan, 1993); they are both matters of language and culture, sets of biological potentials expressed and constructed very differently in different sociohistorical situations. Diseases and illnesses are matters of classification, and they change as social values about "normal" aspects of age, fitness, and gender change. Yes, we all are born and die, and in that sense, biology dominates, but how we use and experience our bodily potentials in between those bookends is no more dictated by biology than is the style of our hats.

Thinking about the consequences of assigning categories, I am reminded that language does not name reality, it organizes reality (Potter and Wetherell, 1987). Topics within areas of health, mental health, and sexuality have been subject to repeated renaming and redefinition as social values have changed. Because sexuality is contested political terrain where various ideological forces struggle for legitimacy and cultural authority, all discourse about sexuality, including scientific and clinical discourses, represents some worldview and political agenda. The informed discussant accepts that there is no neutral ground, no apolitical ground of technical expertise where one can coolly and objectively discuss the facts and leave politics at the door.

Appeals of the Health Model

Feminists are attracted to a health model for sexuality in large part because they want the "legitimacy" and "moral neutrality" for their claims about women's rights and needs offered by what purports to be reliance on the "objective" facts of biological "nature." Many feminists celebrated the publication of Masters and Johnson's (1966) physiological measures of people engaged in masturbation and coitus, for example, because the study seemed to provide objective proof that women's sexual capacities not only existed but equaled those of men (e.g., Ehrenreich, Hess, and Jacobs, 1986). Feminists felt they finally had ammunition against the tyranny of the Freudian vaginal orgasm, not to mention against the earlier claims of women's passionlessness and frigidity. As Masters and Johnson (1966) themselves boasted, "With orgasmic physiology established, the human female now has an undeniable opportunity to develop realistically her own sexual response levels" (p. 138).

The legitimacy offered by the medical/health model of sex extends beyond descriptions of women's sexual capacities to the implicit assumption that sexuality, at least of the medically approved "normal" sort, is actually a component of health, that is, that sexuality itself is healthy. Because *healthy* has become the premier adjective meaning *goodness,* it can be used to endorse everything from behaviors to products and services (Barsky, 1988). The importance of such an imprimatur for sexuality cannot be overestimated in a culture where sexuality has long been located in the moral domain and where allegations about a woman's sexuality could easily destroy her social reputation and standing (Freedman and D'Emilio, 1988).

The legitimacy and entitlement offered women's sexuality by the medical model appear to derive directly from "nature" without the intervention of culture or cultural standards of right and wrong. I have elsewhere discussed how the discourse of "naturalism" and reliance on "laws of nature" are rhetorically tempting not only for the public but for sex researchers and activists (Tiefer, 1990b). Once having opted for biological justification, supporters of women's sexuality can even recruit evolutionary theory, that replacer of (or, sometimes, competitor of) divine law, as the ultimate and inarguable source of authority (Caporael and Brewer, 1991).

Locating women's sexuality under the rubric of health appeared to give it a strong, secure, and eminently respectable home that feminists could use as a base to press for improved sex education, protection against sexual violence, reproductive rights, elimination of the sexual double standard, and all the other components of the sexuality plank in the contemporary women's rights platform.

Hidden Assumptions of the Health Model

But, alas, all is not so simple. There are hidden assumptions accompanying the health model that make it deeply worrisome when applied to women's sexuality: the four medical model assumptions of norms and deviance, universality, individualism, and biological reductionism (Mishler, 1981).

Norms and Deviance

First and most important is the fundamentally normative structure of the health and medicine model—the assumption that there is such a thing as healthy sexuality that can be distinguished from nonhealthy (diseased, abnormal, sick, disordered, pathological) sexuality. The normative basis of the health model is absolutely inescapable—the only way we can talk about "signs and symptoms" or "treatments and cures" or "diagnosis and classification" is with regard to norms and deviations from norms. But where shall we get the norms for women's sexuality? What are the legitimate and compelling sources and what do they say?

In fact, sexuality norms are far better understood by sociologists than by health specialists. That is, sociologists have analyzed sexual category-making as part of the social discourse of sexuality with regard to such subjects as promiscuity, prostitution, masturbation, nymphomania, and frigidity (Schur, 1984; Sahli, 1984). Can health specialists demonstrate that their "sexual health" norms derive from scientific sources and not simply cultural values (Tiefer, 1986b)?

In my opinion there are no valid clinical norms for sexuality. There are diverse cultural and legal standards, and they have been selectively appropriated by the health and medicine domain. But just as playing canasta ten hours a day *may be* a sign of emotional malfunction, that doesn't mean there is a disease of "hypercanasta." That is, without being facetious, there's just too much lifestyle, historical, and cultural variability in sexual behavior standards for us to be able to establish *clinical* norms of sexual activity performance, choices, frequencies, partners, and subjectivities. One of my biggest worries about locating sexuality discourse within the domain of health is the potential abuse of norms. Sociologists point out that norms are the principal mode of social control over sexual behavior because the norms become internalized and even unconscious to the point where they can "police" people twenty-four hours a day (DeLamater, 1981). What we don't need in a society with a history of women's sexual disenfranchisement are additional sources of repression.

Universality

The difference between clinical norms and cultural standards is, presumably, that health is based on pan-cultural standards of biological functioning and malfunctioning. The only such standards for sexual function currently derive from the physiological research of Masters and Johnson (1966), and I have written at length about how that research is based on a flawed and self-fulfilling design (Tiefer, 1991c). Masters and Johnson's finding of a universal "human sexual response cycle" of arousal and orgasm was not valid because they only took measurements on subjects who were able to exhibit masturbatory and coital arousal and orgasm in their laboratory. I do not doubt that many (most? all?) human bodies can produce genital vasocongestion and orgasm. But should those physical performance capacities constitute universal medical norms? In other words, is there any "health" consequence that merits the claim that absence of these features constitutes a disorder?

Individualism

Although family medicine comes close sometimes, I know of no medical specialty that does not consider as the appropriate unit of analysis the individual person (or something smaller, such as the individual organ or organ-system) (Stein, 1987). Should we follow the medical model and situate sexuality in the individual person's physiology/psychology? Is sexuality better understood as an enduring or even essential quality of the self or as a phenomenon that emerges in a social context? Given the usefulness of systems perspectives in sexual therapy, sexuality as a concept may turn out to have much in common with friendship (Verhulst and Heiman, 1988). One can take a history of a person's lifetime experiences with friendship (or sexuality), but each experience will only be understood when contextual issues such as scripting, expectations, and negotiations are analyzed.

Moreover, women's sexual lives are embedded in, we might say "constructed by," sociohistorical frameworks that feminists have identified as patriarchal. Focusing on women's sexuality in terms of individual capacity and expression, as occurs within the biomedical framework, not only ignores the relationship context but also ignores the larger political framework, with the subsequent danger of mistaking something socially constructed and then internalized for some transhistorical essence (e.g., MacKinnon, 1987).

Finally, the individual focus of the health model "privatizes" sexual worries and difficulties, making them the result of some malfunctioning of a "natural" and "normal" capacity. The individual is often blamed for causing or contributing to the problem, which perpetuates shame and contributes to further ignorance about the way sexuality is socially constructed (Crawford, 1977). Any sense of entitlement to sexuality given by the health model is negated, it seems to me, when the same model misleadingly implies that sexuality is some individual and private birthright rather than a learned and deeply socialized phenomenon.

Biological Reductionism

Finally, a health model of sexuality inevitably focuses on the biology of sexuality and on biological standards for normal and abnormal functioning. When sexuality is seen primarily as a matter of health, research on biology predominates and is considered more central and definitive than research on sociocultural influences. An emphasis on biological research contrasts with what feminist historians have seen as the more progressive trend—an ever-widening awareness of the sociocultural factors that determine women's sexual opportunities and experiences (Duggan, 1990).

"Social actors possess genitals rather than the other way around," as one feminist essay put it (Schneider and Gould, 1987, p. 123).

Biological reductionism is also antifeminist because it is far less likely to result in policies that limit or reverse negative social elements. Linda Caporael and Marilynn Brewer (1991), for example, noted, "In the current Western milieu, people tend to feel a lesser responsibility to redress inequities attributed to biology than inequities that arise from defects in policy, law or social structure" (p. 2). Research showing the influence of hormones or neurotransmitters on women's sexual responsiveness will have a different impact on policy than research on the influences of rape prevalence, body image obsessions, gender socialization, or contraceptive availability.

The Medicalization of Men's Sexuality: An Object Lesson

These hidden assumptions of the health model are not just abstract worries—they have had visible consequences in the medicalization of men's sexuality (see the chapters in Part 4). To make a long story short, sexual health for men has been reduced to the erectile functioning of the penis. Impotence research and treatment constitute a new and highly successful medical subspecialty for urologists, and diagnostic and treatment technologies are a growth industry. The field of men's sexuality focuses on a specific physical organ and dictates universalized standards of functioning and malfunctioning. There's no real interest in the sexuality of a person, not to mention that of a couple with a particular culture and relationship. There's just universalized biological organ norms—as for the heart or kidney.

This medical juggernaut has resulted from the collusion of men's interests in a face-saving explanation for poor "performance," the societal perpetuation of a phallocentric script for sexual relations, economic incentives for physicians and manufacturers, the media appeal of medicalized sexuality topics, and the absence of a strong alternative metaphor for sexuality that would affirm variability. These are powerful forces, and in the presence of continuing social pressure for sexual adequacy as defined by intercourse performance, they have created an explosive new medical development.

The clinical developments around "impotence" are supported by a tremendous quantity of basic cellular research on the penis, and the hunt for biological variables that might affect erectile functioning and become a source for new diagnostic or treatment interventions is assured a long life.

In 1992, the National Institutes of Health held its first Consensus Development Conference on a sexuality topic (there have been several Consensus Development Conferences annually since 1977). The topic of the conference, "Impotence," confirms these trends. The participants were overwhelmingly urologists. The outcome was a lengthy document essentially ignoring culture, partners, lifestyles, or lifetime differences; it was a document reifying "erection" as the essence of men's sexuality and asserting the medical model as the proper frame of reference for understanding and intervention.

I foresee the same outcome for women's sexuality, should some new physiological discovery about the genitalia emerge that could be developed into an industry and a clinical practice. For example, the New York Times, covering the 1993 American Urological Association, quoted one urologist as casually speculating that vascular abnormalities of the clitoris might play the same role in women's sexual problems as the extensively researched vascular penile abnormalities (Blakeslee, 1993). Discussing women's sexuality in terms of health leads directly, it seems to me, to a biologically reductionist, compartmentalized, economically driven system that ignores far more than it includes the real complexities of women's sexuality.

A Man-Centered Sexology

It is not difficult to demonstrate that sexology is and has been man-centered (Tiefer, 1988b, 1991a). Despite the incorrect impression that sexology is friendly to women's interests (sex therapy seems to include a lot about communication and whole-body pleasure, lesbianism is considered a normal sexual orientation alternative, and so on), there is actually active resistance to feminist analysis within the field.

The most dramatic example of this resistance comes from a careful examination of the nomenclature for sexual dysfunction (Tiefer, 1988a, 1990a, 1992b; Boyle, 1993). Although there appears to be scrupulous gender equality in the numbers of sexual dysfunctions, and remarkable similarity in the types of dysfunctions listed, women's complaints as they are reported in their own voices are absent (Hite, 1976; Frank, Anderson, and Rubinstein, 1978). Women's official dysfunctions are directly related to performing coitus—proper vaginal lubrication, orgasm, absence of vaginal constriction, desire, and absence of genital aversions. There's nothing about love, gentleness, kissing, passion, body freedom, freedom from fear, lack of coercion, communication, emotional involvement, manual skills, cooperative contraception, infection avoidance, and the like. Although I have sent numerous letters to the authors of the 1994 edition of the nomenclature, there will be no changes.

Thus, sexology, in its current phase of tunnel vision, continues to neglect many variables important to women. Popular authors and feminist activists fill bookstores addressing women's issues and presenting diverse women's voices, but these voices are not represented in the professional texts, training programs, and licensing requirements or in insurance-reimbursable complaints, sex education curricula, or government conferences. Until the schism between the feminist literature and sexology is closed, the male-centered paradigm of sexology is dangerous for women.

Women-Centered Sex Research

My experiences with men's medicalized sexuality and with the unyielding male-centered sexology paradigm frighten me about the future of women's "sexual health." Ordinary people are especially vulnerable to mystification and exploitation. As feminists, our efforts on behalf of women's sexuality should be in terms of providing and financially supporting education and consciousness raising rather than health care at the present time. Sex research should raise up women's diverse voices, not impose a preexisting paradigm through questionnaires or measurements. And, of course, the most beneficial effects of all will come from efforts to promote women's political and economic power.

chapter 3

THE MEDICALIZATION
OF IMPOTENCE: NORMALIZING
PHALLOCENTRISM

In our time, phallocentrism is perpetuated by a flourishing medical construction that focuses exclusively on penile erections as the essence of men's sexual function and satisfaction. In this chapter I shall describe how this medicalization is promoted by urologists, medical industries, mass media, and various entrepreneurs. Many men and women provide a ready audience for this construction because of masculine ideology and gender socialization. Women's sexual interests in anything other than phallocentric sexual scripting are denied. As one author has put it, "Taken by itself, the penis is a floppy appendage which rises and falls and is the source of a number of pleasures. The phallus is more than this. It is the physical organ represented as continuously erect; it is the inexhaustibility of male desire; it is a dominant element within our culture" (Bradbury, 1985, p. 134).

Much successful effort in the past two decades has been devoted to defining, describing, and analyzing the circumstances and forces affecting women's sexual socialization and the construction of female sexuality (Tiefer, 1991a). Among the contributing factors has been that of medicalization, including medical ideology and practice regarding menstruation, menopause, pregnancy, childbirth, premenstrual syndrome (PMS), physical appearance, and fertility. Riessman argued that these areas have become medicalized as "physicians seek to medicalize experience because of their specific beliefs and economic interests. . . . Women collaborate in the medicalization process because of their own needs and motives. . . . In addition, other groups bring economic interests to which both physicians and women are responsive" (1983, pp. 3–4).

Men and their bodies can also be objects of systems of surveillance and control, however. Medicalization perpetuates a phallocentric construction of men's sexuality that literally and symbolically perpetuates women's sexual subordination through silencing and invisibility and thus operates to preserve men's power (Bem, 1993).

Method

This chapter is informed primarily by my impressions and observations working as a sexologist and psychologist in medical center urology departments for the past decade. My responsibilities have included conducting one-hour-long psychosocial interviews and preparing reports on men with sexual complaints who consult a well-known urologist (Melman, Tiefer, and Pedersen, 1988). At the time his appointment is made, each man is asked to bring his primary sexual partner to the interview, and I conduct a separate interview with any partner who comes (Tiefer and Melman, 1983).

To date (August 1993), I have interviewed and kept records on close to 1,600 men, approximately 60 percent of whom brought sexual partners. Only six of these patients said they were gay, and none of these brought a partner to the interview. Our patients are predominantly referrals from the biggest health maintenance organization in the New York metropolitan area. Their ages range from the twenties to the eighties, averaging late fifties; they are approximately two-thirds ethnic minorities; about half are high school graduates, with equal numbers having more or less education; and about half of them are blue-collar New York City government employees (transit, sanitation, corrections, etc.). In addition, my observations draw from sexology texts and conferences of the major U.S. and international sexology (and, occasionally, urology) organizations.

A True Story

In June 1989, a conversation took place during the annual meeting of the International Academy of Sex Research in Princeton, New Jersey, in front of a poster titled "Healthy Aging and Sexual Function" (Schiavi et al., 1990). One of the figures displayed depicted nocturnal penile tumescence[1] measures for a group of healthy male volunteers aged sixty-five to seventy-four. Referring to a particular subgroup of the volunteers, a urologist studying the figure said to the poster's author, a psychiatrist, "So, these men did not have rigid nocturnal erections, [so] they may actually have had disease." "No," the psychiatrist replied, "they were healthy, and in fact they were having sex, their wives confirmed that there was no dysfunction." "But," continued the urologist, "their wives may be satisfied, even they may be satisfied, but since *some* men in that age group *can* have rigid erections, *these* men must have had some impairment."

The urologist was promoting a model championing the authority of "objective facts" as revealed by technologies and the evaluation of body parts. The psychiatrist was defending the authority of human subjectivity and personal experience. In the urologist's model, women were invisible and irrelevant; sexuality yielded to "the erection" as the subject of professional interest and intervention. In this chapter I examine the recent expansion in cultural authority of the urologist and the constructions he (almost all urologists are men) advocates, as well as their consequences. By *phallocentrism* is meant this preoccupying interest and focus on the penis or phallus in sexuality discourse.

Medicalization

Medicalization is a major intellectual trend in the twentieth century, a gradual social transformation whereby medicine, with its distinctive modes of thought, its models, metaphors, and institutions, comes to exercise authority over areas of life not previously considered medical (Conrad and Schneider, 1980). For medicalization to work, the particular behavioral area must be divisible into good (i.e., "healthy") and bad (i.e., "sick") aspects and must somehow be relatable (albeit often distantly) to norms of biological functioning. It helps if medical technology can have some demonstrable impact on the behavior.

Two types of medicalization have been described. Type one occurs when a previously deviant behavior or event such as a sin, crime, or antisocial act (e.g., drunkenness, child molesting) comes to be redefined as a medical problem; type two occurs when a common life event (e.g., pregnancy, baldness, or memory problems) is redefined as a medical problem. This often focuses on the physical changes associated with aging. Medicalization transforms unacceptable erectile performance into a subject for medical analysis and management. Surprisingly, definitions and norms for erections are absent from the medical literature. The assumption that everyone knows what a normal erection is forms a central part of the universalization and reification that supports both medicalization and phallocentrism.

Medicalization occurs over a period of time. In the case of male sexual function, there are four groups identifiably active on behalf of medicalization (urologists, medical industries, mass media, and entrepreneurs), and many men and their sexual partners form a receptive audience. In addition, institutions with a stake in sexual restrictiveness may indirectly support medicalization because of its potential for social control through specifying norms, eliminating deviance, and enforcing conformity.

Advocates for the
Medicalization of Male Sexuality

Urologists
In the 1960s, in anticipation of an increased patient population to be generated by Medicare and Medicaid, the U.S. government stimulated the creation of additional medical schools and granted preferred immigration status to those holding an M.D. degree (Ansell, 1987). As a result, between 1970 and 1990 the number of physicians practicing in the United States jumped about 80 percent, from 325,000 to almost 600,000, and the number of surgeons increased from 58,000 to more than 110,000 (Rosen-

thal, 1989). This rapid expansion created competition within and between medical and surgical subspecialties, including urology.

Urologists began specializing in male sexual dysfunction in quest of new patients and research areas. Using the new nomenclature of sexual "dysfunctions" provided by clinical sexology and psychiatry (LoPiccolo, 1978), surveys began to show a significant prevalence of sexual complaints in the general population, in the medical population, and among patients taking prescription medications.

Urology-dominated treatments and technologies evolved in the 1970s. They currently consist of various penile surgeries, penile implants, injections of drugs into the penis to cause erection, and vacuum erection devices.[2] Besides its economic potential, sexual dysfunction is an attractive subspecialty because patients are not chronically sick or likely to die from their "disease"; there are also opportunities for diverse outpatient and inpatient services.

It is probably in the realm of diagnostics, however, that urology has advanced medicalization the most (Nelkin and Tancredi, 1989). By promoting sophisticated technologies for "differentiating" among various erection problem etiologies and by ensuring publicity of the claim that physical causes of erection problems are paramount, over the past decade urologists have come to dominate the "proper" diagnostic evaluation of men's sexual complaints (Spark, White, and Connolly, 1983; Rosen and Leiblum, 1992a).

The monthly American Urological Association newspaper contained a bordered box that read: "AUA Policy Statement/Male Sexual Dysfunction/Sexual dysfunction in the male is a disease entity, the diagnoses and treatments of which deserve equal attention to that given other diseases" (Poll shows, widespread use of three major impotence treatments, 1993, p. 6). This bold jurisdictional claim is an outgrowth of the prior decade's professional events. An informal 1978 meeting of urologists in New York had resulted in the 1982 formation of the International Society for Impotence Research (ISIR). The society began publishing its journal, *The International Journal of Impotence Research*, in 1989. The first "World Meeting on Impotence" was held in 1984, and a major overview of the new field of "impotence" was coauthored by three urologists a few years later (Krane, Goldstein, and deTejada, 1989).

Urologists have promoted their claims through consistent use of the words *impotence* and *impotent,* while sexologists' own language claims have been hesitant: "Although we strongly prefer the terms 'erectile disorder' or 'erectile dysfunction,' we have opted, after considerable discussion and debate, to grant each author editorial discretion and freedom of choice in this regard" (Rosen and Leiblum, 1992b, p. xviii).

In 1985, Mark Elliott reviewed the frequency of the terms *impotence* and *frigidity* (another term sexologists had rejected) in titles in the *Psychological Abstracts* from 1940–1981. Although initially, the terms were equally popular, the use of *frigidity* had almost disappeared in recent years while *impotence* was far more popular than ever before. In 1992, the National Institutes of Health (NIH) sponsored a Consensus Development Conference on Impotence.[3] I spoke on "Nomenclature" and suggested that the term *impotence* was pejorative and confusing (Tiefer, 1992a). The final conference statement begins:

> The term "impotence," as applied to the title of this conference, has traditionally been used to signify the inability of the male to attain and maintain erection of the penis sufficient to permit satisfactory sexual intercourse. However, this use has often led to confusing and uninterpretable results in both clinical and basic science investigations. This, together with its pejorative implications, suggests that the more precise term, "erectile dysfunction" be used instead. (NIH, 1992, p. 3)

Nevertheless, the final report (and all the media stories about it) was still titled "Impotence."

Medical Industries
Manufacturers and suppliers of medical devices, products, and services have obvious economic interests in expanding a new medical specialty. Individual pieces of diagnostic and treatment equipment can easily cost tens of thousands of dollars, and the field is very competitive. Interest has grown rapidly among pharmaceutical companies since the first effective injections of drugs into the penis to cause erections were developed in the mid-1980s (Wagner and Kaplan, 1992); clinical trials in my department currently test drugs that can be applied to the penis in cream or pellet form.

Medical industries provide resources to create the cultural authority essential to medicalization. The Mentor Corporation, for example, one of the five major implant manufacturers in the United States (Petrou and Barren, 1991), started an Impotence Foundation in 1986 as a "national information service" (Mentor Corporation, n.d.). It provides a toll-free information number, unlimited free patient education brochures and videos, and complete free information and materials for educational seminars (e.g., ad designs, slides, and script) for doctors.

Another contribution to medical hegemony comes from the U.S. health insurance industry's cutbacks in the area of multi-visit services, including mental health services (Kramon, 1989). For example, the majority of men with sexual problems whom I interview are New York City government employees with HMO-type insurance. The HMO will completely cover the cost of any surgical or pharmacological treatment for their sexual problems but will not pay one penny for psychological sex therapy treatment or education.

Mass Media

The mass media play a fundamental role in conferring cultural authority and legitimacy in the modern world (Nelkin, 1987). My belief is that the mass media favor medicalized information about sex because focusing on "scientific developments" or "health advice" allows publication of sexual subject matter with no taint of obscenity or pornography. Medicalized writing about sex is "clean" and "safe." New York Times readers will not see articles on techniques of fellatio, but they will see dozens of stories on penile injections. By quoting medical "experts," using medical terminology, and swiftly and enthusiastically publicizing new devices and pharmaceuticals, the mass media legitimize, instruct, and model the proper construction and discourse (Parlee, 1987). People underline and save "sex health" articles, and I have had patients bring in such materials even years following publication.

A two-part health column article on impotence in the New York Times illustrates the medicalized media approach to men's sexuality. The first part begins by publicizing the claim about medical etiologies: "Less than a decade ago, more than 90% of impotence cases were attributed to emotional inhibitions ... but ... experts say that more than half, and perhaps as many as three-fourths of impotency cases have a physical basis" (Brody, 1988, p. B4).

The article uses the term *impotence* and credits unnamed "experts" with generating a major shift in knowledge about the etiology of sex problems, though no new epidemiological studies are mentioned. A climate of conviction is created, which is reinforced when the reader sees the same claim in the *Wall Street Journal* under the title: "Research on Impotence Upsets the Idea That It Is Usually Psychological" (Stipp, 1987, p. 1).

Time magazine repeated the assertion: "Medical researchers have determined that up to 75% of all cases of impotence stem from physical problems, most of which can be treated" (Toufexis, 1988). This article, brought to me by several patients, quotes a seventy-six-year-old man with a penile prosthesis implanted after prostate cancer who says, "You'd think we were 26 years old again," and describes a forty-year-old former policeman with a fractured back whose wife is represented as "signalling her mood with the question, 'Have you had your shot [penile injection] today?'"

The title of the *Time* article, "It's Not 'All in Your Head,'" reveals the stigma associated with "mental" causes of sexual malfunction. Popular articles on men's sexual problems often begin, as had the 1980 *JAMA* lead article "Impotence Is Not Always Psychogenic" (Spark, White, and Connolly, 1980), with the mantra, "Until recently, medical literature attributed [fill in a high number] percent of impotence to psychological causes. But, now it is estimated that [fill in a high number] percent can be traced to organic disorders" (e.g., Blaun, 1987; Blakeslee, 1993).

Science and health journalism seems so superficial and uncritical as to be little more than advertising (Burnham, 1987). Emphasis is placed on new technologies, often with the disclaimer, as in the current case of penile injections, "not yet FDA approved." There is rarely any follow-up of initial reports. The articles are sprinkled with individual accounts of satisfied customers provided to the print or electronic journalist by hospital or manufacturer publicists. The last time my name appeared in a popular magazine article, my hospital public relations director called to ask if I would like to prepare some materials and provide some patients for a possible news release and press conference. Television and radio talk shows also publicize and promote the new medical technologies for men's sexual problems, and I have met with many retirees whose perspectives on sexual problems were largely informed by such shows.

Entrepreneurs

These advocates for medicalization include self-help group and newsletter promoters who have created a market by portraying themselves as something between consumers and professionals. The formation of Impotents Anonymous (IA), which is both a urologists' advocacy group and a self-help group, was announced in the *New York Times* in an article including cost and availability information on penile implants (Organization helps couples with impotence as problem, 1984). A story about the organization's founders, a married couple, was included. They had recently toured with their new book, *It's Not All in Your Head* (MacKenzie and MacKenzie, 1988; Naunton, 1989). Although the IA newsletter (*Impotence Worldwide*) features their organizational slogan, "Bringing a total care concept to overcoming impotence," it has only urologists on the advisory board.

The advocates for medicalization portray sexuality in a rational, technical, mechanical, cheerful way. Sexuality as an area for the imagination, for political struggle, or for the expression of diverse human motives or as a sensual, intimate, or spiritual rather than performative experience is absent.

Men as an Audience for the Medicalization of Sexuality

Men constitute a ready audience for the medicalization of sexuality because of male socialization and masculine ideology, both of which make erectile function central to masculine self-esteem (Pleck, Sonenstein, and Ku, 1993; Metcalf and Humphries, 1985). The chronic insecurity and intermittent desperation (Hall, 1991) that result from this situation render men vulnerable to offers of "magical" and permanent solutions such as those offered by the technological fixes of modern urology (Tiefer, 1986a).

In the past two decades, numerous texts have underscored the pressures experienced by heterosexual men as standards for masculine sexual performance escalate in response to the "sexual revolution" and women's "new" sexual expectations (Zilbergeld, 1992). Men themselves contribute to these insecurities by endorsing naturalizing belief systems about sexuality and women's sexual satisfaction. Patients I see often insist, despite my demurral, that women (a uniform class) cannot be sexually satisfied without intravaginal intercourse and claim that their motivation for the erectile dysfunction evaluation and treatment is to keep their wives from leaving them. Interviewed separately and asked if they thought their marriage could break up because of the erectile difficulties, the wives are often surprised and offended at the thought.

Phallocentric beliefs burden and pressure men, but at the same time they maintain sexual privilege for men. The "needs" of the naturalized erection dominate the sexual encounter script where phallocentric sexual activities generally ensure men's pleasure and satisfaction. Assumptions of universality free men from regarding themselves or their partners as sexual individuals.

In addition to maintaining the phallic focus, the medicalized construction of sexuality offers men an "objective" world of science and medicine to minimize anxieties provoked by public disclosures of sexual inadequacy. Although admitting any performance failure challenges masculinity as constructed within the ideology of "machismo" (Mosher, 1991), at least medicalized discourse keeps the sexuality focus on the physical and avoids inquiry into motives, values, wishes, feelings, or fantasies (Seidler, 1992). The mantra of sexual medicalization, "It's not all in your head," replaces the stigma of failed responsibility with the face-saving excuse of physical incapacity that men often learn in sports and the military.

Are all men equally attracted to a medicalized message? Schiavi et al. (1990) described a group of older men (not a clinical sample) who, because of inadequate erections, could not have vaginal intercourse with their wives on at least 50 percent of their attempts over a period of six months, yet who reported high levels of sexual and marital satisfaction. These men would seem to be have sexual activity scripts and masculinity constructions that do not require long-lasting, rigid erections. My urologist colleagues would say that these men (and their partners) are merely "adapting" to a second-best situation. They would say that such satisfaction is really "adjustment," and they would predict that offering such men the new penile technologies would get many of them to admit that more and better erections would really make them more satisfied.

Women as an Audience for the Medicalization of Men's Sexuality

The literature produced by the medicalization advocates often depicts women as supporting the medicalization of men's sexuality. For example, women offer testimonial to their preimplant unhappiness and postimplant sexual and relationship satisfaction in patient education videos available from penile implant manufacturers.

What about women's actual voices and self-representations? My interviews with the women sexual partners of the urology patients suggest that some do subscribe to a medicalized and phallocentric construction of sexuality. Sometimes they derive physical pleasure primarily or exclusively from coitus and, like urologists, talk about sexuality as requiring and centering around erections. Women who wish to become pregnant often focus on their man's erectile function as the centerpiece of sexuality.

Another subgroup is unhappily resigned to male privilege. They say men and women are sexually different and that men's phallocentrism is limiting, but they go along with the status quo. When asked how they would conduct sexual relations, they say, "I'm not sure, but there's got to be something better."

Other women I've spoken with strongly diverge from the medicalized and phallocentric construction. They often "cannot understand why he is so upset" because both partners enjoy nonintercourse activities. Some worry that their own sexual enjoyment (often increased since their partners' erection difficulties began) is endangered by penile injections and implants. "He'll want to use it all the time, and what will that do for me?" one wife angrily asked. Many women have asked me or asked me to ask the urologist to "talk sense" to their partners and make them less obsessed and unhappy.

Feminists have problematized coitus as the prime form of sexual activity if women's erotic pleasure is as important as conception or men's pleasure, yet coitus remains the prime component of the script of heterosexual relations (Clement, 1990). The feminist critique, for the men and women I interview, has merely added the clitoris to the standard phallocentric script; intercourse is still the main event and anything else is considered foreplay, afterplay, or "special needs."

Medicalization and Phallocentrism

I realized that medicalization was about phalluses rather than penises when I tried, at the NIH Consensus Development Conference on Impotence, to introduce the idea of multiple meanings of erections. Disputing the notion of the "standard normal erection," I argued that "different men and different couples expect and rely on different degrees and durations of penile rigidity to accomplish their sexual goals" (Tiefer, 1992a). Neither the audience nor the final report took any note of such an idea!

In the world of medicalization, erection is not a means to an end; there is a universal erection that is "normal," and deviations are abnormal and need treatment. The normal erection is implicitly defined as "hard enough for penetration" and lasting "until ejaculation"—informally that means a few minutes although I have never seen this in writing. Anything less is "impotence." Occasionally, men come in who have medically proper erections but who can't have two or three ejaculatory episodes. Like all our patients, they want their penis function to conform to their standards of masculinity. They request treatment, but nothing is available. Yet.

Medicalization reifies erections. Although no sexual encounter or relationship occurs in the examining room, within the medical context a man's sexuality is present when penile arteries or veins are technologically observed or when a history focusing on erections ("how hard?" "how often?") is taken. The message throughout the medical encounter is that the penis and the erection are what count—and are all that count. The patient takes home a machine to measure nocturnal erections (hardness and duration), but no instrument to assess his relationship, his knowledge of sexual techniques, his comfort with bodily expression, or anything about his partner.

Although the news reports make it sound like diagnosis and treatment of men's erectile problems follow well-established patterns, there is considerable disagreement within the field (NIH, 1992). The symbolic need for a universal phallus has prevented researchers from studying the range of real erections (not to mention variations in their subjectivity). Moreover, the available medical and surgical treatments for erectile problems can have worrisome psychological and interpersonal consequences, which are ignored by the media and the follow-up literature. John Kabalin and Robert Kessler (1989), for example, reported a 43 percent rate of malfunctioning and reoperation for 290 patients with penile prostheses operated on between 1975 and 1985. My own follow-up research documented that a variety of pervasive worries about health and safety may accompany the penile implant despite satisfactory function (Tiefer, Moss, and Melman, 1991).

An additional connection between medicalization and phallocentrism comes from classifications of mental disorders (APA, 1980; Tiefer, 1992b). The *Diagnostic and Statistical Manual of Mental Disorders* lists nine "sexual dysfunctions"; heterosexual coitus, requiring proper erectile function, is the sole focus. This nomenclature legitimates medicalization by relating sexuality to the (supposed) universal, biological norms of "the human sexual response cycle" (Masters and Johnson, 1966; but see Tiefer, 1991b). There is no place in the medical model of sexuality for the idea that erection and orgasm are social constructions given meaning by personality, relationship, values, expectations, life experience, or culture (Tiefer, 1987).

Conclusion

The new scholarship on men occasionally makes reference to the unbridgeable gap between the real and vulnerable penis and the mystical, all-powerful phallus (e.g., Metcalf and Humphries, 1985). Modern technology seems determined to bridge that gap or at least to keep hope alive that a perfectable biology is just around the corner. The complex ritual and devices attached to the penis in the examining room by white-coated technicians transform sexuality as they reduce it to neurology and blood flow. The spotlight directed on "the erection" within current medical practices isolates and diminishes the man even as it offers succor for his insecurity and loss of self-esteem.

Men may enter the system innocently looking to understand the cause of a change in their bodily and sexual experience; the options they are given for understanding and coping shape an ever more phallocentric experience. Their partners and any ideas or feelings these partners might have are usually irrelevant to the process (the protocol at the department where I work is unusual in this respect). Erections are presented as understandable and manipulable in and of themselves, unhooked from person or script or relationship. A discourse of vascular processes—blood flow, trapping mechanisms, venous outflow—takes over. Patient education literature teaches that organic factors account for erection problems, and patients may be led further and further into diagnostic tests to locate specific deficiencies. Since specific causes are usually not identifiable, some generalization ("your blood pressure medication," "some hardening of the arteries") is offered and a medical treatment recommended. Because the remedies do create rigid penile erections, the patient is understandably convinced that the biological rhetoric was correct.

Women occupy an essential place in the discourse (the need for vaginal "penetration" is the justification for the entire enterprise), but women are only present in terms of universalized vaginal needs; their actual desires and opinions are (conveniently) invisible, suppressed, neglected, denied.

It is not clear how one might slow or reverse this trend. Basic research continues to focus on the cellular and neurochemical operations of the penis, ensuring a future of more organic "defects." The new men's movement to the contrary notwithstanding, there is no end in sight to the medicalization of men's sexuality or to the phallocentrism it perpetuates.

Notes

1. "Nocturnal penile tumescenece" refers to the fact that men have erections (penile tumescence) throughout sleep. Measurement of these erections is a diagnostic test conducted with portable take-home measurement instruments worn during sleep. Men complaining of erectile dysfunction who display normal nocturnal erections are assumed not to have physical impairment.

2. This chapter was written before the approval of Viagra (1998), although the theoretical points are still valid. Viagra and the other new oral drugs are by far the most popular form of treatment, although implants and injections are still widely used.

3. The purpose of a Consensus Development Conference is to assess competing conceptualizations, assessments, and treatments in some medical domain and to arrive at a consensus of the current knowledge to serve as a guideline for practitioners.

chapter 4

PLEASURE, MEDICALIZATION, AND THE TYRANNY OF THE NATURAL

Don't forget that above everything else, sex is a natural
function . . . and whenever we engage in any natural function in a satisfying way, we experience pleasure. (Masters
and Johnson, 1976, p. 28)

Sex is popularly assumed to be all about pleasure, but, surprisingly, there's not much about pleasure in contemporary sexological writing.

There is nothing about pleasure dysfunction in the official medical sexual nomenclature, for example, and there's nothing in university-level or
medical sexuality texts about the physiological bases of pleasure, cultural
differences in pleasure, or the psychological development of pleasure.

In fact, even though most sexologists surely believe that pleasures are
absolutely central to the sexual experience, there is very little empirical or
theoretical research that focuses on pleasure at all.

An early '90s U.S. probability sample survey conducted in Chicago asked
one question about sexual problems experienced in the past 12 months, and
about twice as many women (27 to 17 percent, younger to older) as men (10
to six percent) reported that sex was not pleasurable (Laumann, Paik, and
Rosen, 1999). However, unlike the results about arousal and orgasm, these
provocative findings on pleasure were not further analyzed.

This gap would not be a problem if pleasure were a simple matter or automatically inherent in sexual activities, but as a clinician, I can support

the Chicago survey's belief that neither sensual nor emotional pleasure is simple or automatic.

As with sexual desire, orgasm, spontaneity, cooperation, and comfort the clinician's dirty little undemocratic secret is that the experience of pleasure, as with the other aspects of sexual experience, is distributed along a bell-shaped curve.

But the clinician's impressions remain unsupported by any interesting research into the permutations and vicissitudes of pleasure in sex. Why do we know so little?

I would like to address four reasons for the neglect of the study of pleasure in sexology: conceptual complexity, physiological complexity, political complexity, and the medical model myth of the naturalness of sex.

Conceptual Complexity

We use the term "pleasure" in many ways, to state the obvious (Tepper, 1999). Whereas simple sensory pleasures for infants (warm milk, light touching, googly sounds) may be universal, once a psychological and cultural history of conditioning and other learning develops, we no longer all agree as to what is even considered a sexual pleasure.

Only some use the term "pleasure" to describe experiences such as slipping into cool water on a hot day (not those who fear drowning) or tasting a spoonful of a perfect flan (not those who find puddings "yucky") or hearing a Mozart concerto (not those who dislike classical music) or dancing the samba (not those, alas, who are kinesthetically challenged).

As psychocultural history kicks in, experiences get hooked to meanings and pleasures and can move far beyond the sensory or sensorimotor. We speak of the pleasure of a good joke, of seeing an enemy defeated, of sharing a sunset, or of conversation, yet these pleasures are intellectual and emotional. Pleasure seems to be fundamentally evaluative, although we are usually unaware of the split-second processes involved in appraising an experience or situation before we produce our reaction.

All these processes arise, along with the added ambiguities of what is meant by "sexual," when we think of "sexual pleasure." For some, but not all, a genital component is required for an experience to be sexual. Others would say a kiss, a fantasy, a memory, or an embrace provide sexual pleasure even without genital arousal or awareness. And, of course, genital arousal can occur without pleasure. Sexual pleasures, then, are unique, varied, sensory, intellectual, emotional, and intimately involved with meaning. Research would need a qualitative dimension to capture such complexity.

Physiological Complexity

Periodic upsurges of interest in the physiology of pleasure are related to discoveries in neuroanatomy or neurochemistry, new methods of central nervous system study, or a renewal of research interest in particular (and usually socially disapproved) pleasures such as drug and alcohol use and abuse.

When I was in graduate school, implanting electrodes into animals' brains and observing them press a lever to receive a pulse of electrical current to their "pleasure centers" put the emphasis on the central role of limbic system brain structures. Later, the focus on "centers" gave way to tracing neuroanatomical circuits identified as "reward pathways." In turn the interest in neuroanatomical circuits shifted to neurochemistry and the role of synaptic transmitter substances, with dopamine identified as the crucial element in the reward circuits.

New noninvasive brain research methods are beginning to allow brain research on human beings in a way never before possible. However, the physiology of what happens when and where continues to be complicated, and when answers change every time new methods develop, the hope of definitive answers recedes.

At the same time as the research on the physiology of pleasure was evolving, a much greater quantity of research focused on the physiology of sexuality. Utilizing neuroanatomical and neurochemical methods to study nervous system components, and also analyzing the role of steroid hormones produced by the reproductive glands, this research has focused on behavior rather than subjective experiences like pleasure or desire. In animal research on many types of rodents, primates, birds, fish, etc., much has been discovered about how various physiological components are involved in species-appropriate mating behaviors. But, as to pleasure, animals are silent and researchers make interpretations.

Physiological sex research on people has necessarily used noninvasive methods and different endpoints, and some surprising results have emerged. This makes us skeptical about research that lacks inquiry into subjects' subjective experiences, and suggests that the connections between physiology and subjectivity will not necessarily be linear. For example, laboratory research on women has repeatedly demonstrated that, in response to looking at or hearing erotic videos, there is little correlation between (objective) measures of genital arousal and subjective ratings of sexual arousal (Laan and Everaerd, 1995).

Given the subjective nature of pleasure and its connections to cultural meanings and individual history, it seems plausible that research on the physiological bases or concomitants of sexual pleasure is going to be difficult. There will be no simple answers (for example, "It's endorphins! It's hormones! It's blood flow to the genitals!") because pleasures are so varied.

The possibilities for pleasure include, for example, the capacity for eroticizing nongenital parts of the body through conditioning and symbolism. As Jeffrey Weeks (1985) points out, "In S/M, . . . the whole body becomes a seat of pleasure, and the cultivation of roles and exotic practices the key to the attainment of pleasure. A degenitalization of sex and of pleasure is taking place in these practices . . ." (p. 241). Studying "the" physiology of sexual pleasure is thus bound to fail and should be replaced by smaller projects looking for smaller answers, always taking sexual history and attitudes into account. Again, a qualitative component seems essential.

Political Complexities

Conceptual and physiological complexities provide challenges, but there would have been more progress in theory and empirical research on sexual pleasure were it not for its perpetually ambiguous moral status.

The pursuit of pleasure, including sexual pleasure, is regarded in Western cultures as (a) dangerous, selfish, amoral, immature, short-sighted, and, at the same time, (b) a legitimate (perhaps *the* legitimate) aim of human endeavor on earth.

For every Greek myth celebrating the fall from grace of a pursuit of sexual pleasure without regard for honor, duty, or other virtues, there is clearly another myth (or even the underside of the first one) acknowledging the pursuit of sexual pleasure as inevitable and universal. The consequences of sex for pleasure are even shown in the kind of contemporary U.S. urban myths where the protagonist wakes up in a motel the morning after a night with a stranger with an STD or HIV as punishment for his or her hedonism (Whatley and Henken, 2001).

D'Emilio and Freedman, in their 1988 book *Intimate Matters: A History of Sexuality in America,* chronicle this ambivalence about pleasure through American history, with women consistently bearing the larger share of "tension, confusion, and guilt" (p. 176). They argue that "the dominant meaning of sexuality has changed during our history from a primary association with reproduction within families to a primary association with emotional intimacy and physical pleasure for individuals" (ibid., p. xv), but they also document in every generation the double standard between women and men who seek sexual pleasure.

In her important edited collection about contemporary feminism and sex, Carole Vance (1984) made clear how "the tension between sexual pleasure and sexual danger is a powerful one in women's lives" (p. 1). Women and girls attracted to pleasure must constantly resist charges that they are "bad" ("delinquent," "incorrigible") because pleasure is "selfish, antisocial, and dangerous." These charges are made by social purity groups "protecting" the family who support the exercise of social control over women's desire for pleasure.

Our enduring cultural ambivalence about sexual pleasure is vividly played out in the escalating moral panics about the sexuality of children and youth. Judith Levine's new book (2002) on this subject begins provocatively, "In America today, it is nearly impossible to publish a book that says children and teenagers can have sexual pleasure and be safe, too" (p. xix).

The Medical Model

Finally we come to the obstacle to research and theory on pleasure that concerns me the most—the pervasive influence exerted by the model that views sex through the lens of health and disease (the "medical model"), and the roots of this model in what can be called "the myth of sexual naturalism" (Tiefer, 1995, 1997, 1999a).

The medical model of sex rests on the idea of sex as a natural impulse (or drive) built into people, as it is into non-human animals, by evolutionary forces responsive to the survival- and reproduction-oriented pressures of natural selection. The sex impulse takes different forms depending on social custom and the vicissitudes of social repression, but at its root it is a biological universal. This perspective is known as "sexual essentialism" and has had a long history in writings about sex, from Darwinians like Havelock Ellis through Kinsey and Masters and Johnson up to the sociobiologists of the present time (Weeks, 1985).

Building on the idea of a natural sexual impulse comes the idea of a natural sexual function, as in Masters and Johnson's "human sexual response cycle." Their definition of sexual function was a built-in universal excitement-plateau-orgasm-resolution cycle expressed in the timely and proper operation of sexual (reproductive) organs such as vaginas and penises.

The idea of the cycle became the norm when the American Psychiatric Association (APA) in 1980 identified sexual "dysfunction" as "inhibition in the appetitive or psychophysiological changes that characterize the complete sexual response cycle" in its diagnostic manual. This language has remained in each subsequent edition and revision of the APA's list of disorders up to the present time.

I have written an extensive critique of the scientific basis of this "human sexual response cycle model" in the references already cited, but suffice it to say here that Masters and Johnson chose research subjects whose orgasmocentric sexual script produced the type of physical cycle they were looking for.

The "human sexual response cycle" was not discovered, in other words, but was scientific window-dressing for Masters and Johnson's political goal to create gender equality in sex by generalizing to women the male tumescence/detumescence process.

The Masters and Johnson model fit into traditional medical model themes summarized here:

- the idea of an objectively knowable, universal body governed by laws and processes that work independently of social life and culture (for example, penises are the same, whether attached to men in Siberia or Sumatra)
- a separation between mind and body (for example, normal sexual performance is defined as the proper arousal and orgasm behavior of the genital organs regardless of what is going on in the mind)
- the idea that sexuality is a quality or property of an individual
- a focus on biology rather than culture as the defining aspect of sexual experience
- objective lines of demarcation between normal and abnormal sexual function, drawn by scientific (read: politically and morally neutral) experts (Tiefer, 1996b)

Pleasure *per se* is nowhere to be found in this model or description of sexual (dys)function, since function was merely about the (im)proper performance of physical structures, as with digestion or respiration. The only subjective aspect of the experience mentioned was pain. "Meaning" was not relevant at all. Meaning had been too much emphasized in earlier psychiatric (read: psychoanalytic) literature, and the new nomenclature represented an effort to put psychiatric approaches to sexuality on a more scientific (read: physiological) basis.

Ironically, a recent modification of the APA's nomenclature for women's sexual dysfunctions, developed in a closed session sponsored by urologists and pharmaceutical companies, introduces the phrase "causing personal distress" into the definitions of the standard sexual disorders (of desire, arousal, and orgasm) (Basson et al., 2000). It does not appear, however, that this adds anything about pleasure. Rather, it seems that the reason for the addition of a "personal distress" requirement was to avoid diagnosing a woman as dysfunctional based on her sexual partner's opinion alone.

On the one hand, this seems to be a step away from the universalization of the previous nomenclature—one can have low desire or rare orgasms and not have a dysfunction. On the other hand, if the authors were truly interested in women's personal distress, they would have incorporated many other psychological and interpersonal items. As the purpose of the reworking seemed to be to provide "clearer specification of end points and outcomes . . . for clinical trials" of new pharmacological agents, it seems that considerations of pleasure would only introduce the kind of complexities discussed earlier.

The medical model is too close for comfort to sex as reproduction. The neglect of pleasure and the emphasis on function are tell-tale signs that a one-size-fits-all notion of sexual life and satisfaction is being promoted. This model, as with all sexual essentialism, seems fundamentally to misunderstand the psychocultural nature of sexual experience. In a misguided effort to support sexual health treatment, norms for sexual life have been created which are at best constricted and neglectful of political realities, and at worst, destructive to the human spirit.

As the global pharmaceutical industry seizes on sexual "problems" as a fertile new market, we must be ever more wary of the consequences of relying on any medical model of sex.

Women's Sexual Problems

In 2000, I convened a group of feminist social scientists and clinicians to develop a campaign to resist the medicalization of women's sexual problems being promoted by the pharmaceutical industry (Tiefer, 2001). (see www.fsd-alert.org). One of our first acts was to release a "manifesto" offering a critique of current trends as well as a new classification system (see www.fsd-alert.org/manifesto.html). Our manifesto redirected thinking about sexual problems away from a medical model toward a model based on human rights and women-centered research.

We explicitly endorsed the idea of pleasure as a sexual right as stated, for example, in the World Association of Sexology's 1999 *Declaration of Sexual Rights*, and listed "inhibition of sexual pleasure" as one of women's sexual problems. Our goal was not to develop a pleasure-centered model of sex but only to challenge the errors of the medical focus that arose without regard to women's sexual realities. It seems obvious that including pleasure is important to any classification system of sexual problems.

Conclusion

The neglect of pleasure as a subject in current sexological writing is the legacy of a puritanical and naturalistic sex-as-function, sex-for-reproduction model that is still popular in medicine. Although few sex researchers or educators would support such a narrow model, our research and educational approaches are still surprisingly silent on the subject of sexual pleasure. This is partly because pleasure, being subjective, is conceptually complex and difficult to study empirically. Mostly, however, it is because sex researchers and educators still find sexual pleasure a politically dangerous topic. You can unblinkingly apply for a grant to do research on sexual function—but sexual pleasure? You can offer a comprehensive sexuality education lecture on sexual function—but sexual pleasure?

Sexology may be inattentive to sexual pleasure, but the larger culture is busy 24/7 distributing overblown promises of sexual pleasure through consumerist films, popular music, advertising, and, in the latest twist on advertising—the promotion of sexuopharmaceutical drugs like Viagra.

Exaggerated and oversimplified expectations for sexual life must be met by a prepared public, and valid information about sexual pleasure must be an important ingredient in future sexuality education. Similarly, higher expectations produce greater disappointment, and future therapeutic systems will need a rich understanding of the operations of pleasure. If sex researchers and educators neglect the study of sexual pleasure, the public will continue to be vulnerable to shame and disappointment as well as gullible to every new Madison Avenue promise-pusher.

chapter 5

SEXOLOGY AND THE PHARMACEUTICAL INDUSTRY: THE THREAT OF CO-OPTATION

In recent years, the pharmaceutical industry has become very interested in sex as a focus for drug development and marketing. Many sexologists have embraced this new trend particularly because of greatly welcomed research funding and increased professional opportunities. However, this new relationship may be a Faustian bargain, and certainly raises serious ethical, political, theoretical, and research problems which must be openly discussed. This paper examines background elements which have led to this new science-industry rapprochement, discusses research and publication problems which have arisen, analyzes conflicts between the models of sexuality favored by industry and sexology, and offers advice for preventing further erosion of sexology's liberatory mission despite the threats of commercialization.

It's 1998. Turn on the television and you're sure to see a newsmagazine program about a new prescription medication named Viagra and its wonderful benefits for men's sexuality. Open a newspaper and you're sure to see a story about the promising effects of Viagra on women. Open the *Journal of Sex and Marital Therapy* and find an editorial announcing a "Pharmacological era in the treatment of sexual disorders" (Segraves, 1998).

It's 1999. Open the *Journal of the American Medical Association (JAMA)* to find an article reanalyzing old data to emphasize the high prevalence of sexual dysfunction in the United States (Laumann, Paik, & Rosen, 1999). Read the *New York Times* a few days later to find the *JAMA* article's sexologist authors identified as paid consultants to Pfizer, the manufacturer of Viagra (Grady, 1999). Receive your copy of the *Journal of Sex and Marital Therapy* and find the back cover has become a glossy multicolor ad for Viagra.

The search for aphrodisiacs to stimulate sexuality and potions to resist sexual decline is age-old, but it entered a new chapter at the end of the twentieth century with official federal Food and Drug Administration approval of sex-enhancing drugs. Sex researchers are playing a growing role in the development and distribution of the new sex drugs. Is sexology on its way to becoming a subsidiary of the pharmaceutical industry? I hope not, but the recent history of psychiatry shows how an entire field can be taken over by pro-pharmaceutical thinking and practice, and this example should make us very worried (Healy, 1998).

Is sexology in danger of being co-opted by the pharmaceutical industry? Co-optation is defined as appropriation or takeover of a previously independent group by a larger power in a kind of a bloodless conquest. For the smaller group the takeover offers certain benefits (e.g., increased recognition or protection) at the cost of intellectual or political independence. In this paper, I will argue that the creeping co-optation of sexology by the pharmaceutical industry represents a Faustian bargain, whereby in exchange for some new research and professional opportunities, sexology is in serious danger of selling out a unique and socially important sexual vision and role. Note that this paper is not about the co-optation of *sex* by the pharmaceutical industry. That's a somewhat different story. This story is about a possible takeover of sexology, a particular professional and academic family, by the pharmaceutical industry. You might say it's an essay on family values.

The paper begins with a wide-angle look at the background of this co-optation threat, which I see as the latest stage in the medicalization of sexuality, a subject I have been chronicling for over a decade (Tiefer, 1986a, 1994, 1995, 1996). Once we see how interest in this collaboration arises from a broad array of socioeconomic and political forces affecting both the pharmaceutical industry and sexology, we will be better able to identify its attractions and its dangers.

Coincidentally, or maybe not, a brand-new academic multidiscipline, *sexuality studies*, has developed within the humanities, social sciences, and cultural studies at just the present moment. Organizations, journals, conferences, and the other elements of academic infrastructure are emerging and participants in the new sexuality studies have proclaimed it to be resolutely antimedical in its approach to understanding sexuality (Gagnon & Parker, 1995).[1] If the new, intense pharmaceutical industry role heralds the sinking of independent biomedical sex research, it appears that an academic lifeboat may be at the ready for at least some scholars.

Why Is the Pharmaceutical Industry Interested in Sex?

This section will introduce themes in the larger social and economic culture which sex researchers typically ignore. It's important to notice that the pharmaceutical industry has only recently become interested in sex, and to discuss the reasons why: a favorable political environment, deregulation of the pharmaceutical industry, and favorable commercial opportunities.

Favorable Political Environment

Since 1980, enormous political and economic changes have occurred in both academia and business to bring the two closer together (Kennedy, 1997; Marsa 1997; Slaughter & Leslie, 1997; Teitelman, 1994). A new ideological climate (politically known as Thatcher-Reagan economic conservatism) came to prevail, which venerated competition and entrepreneurship in both public and private institutions. It resulted in important changes in tax and patent laws, laws governing nonprofit corporations, and federal funding of research and training. As public institutions and services from prisons to garbage collection have become privatized in the last two decades, universities and scientific communities have followed suit.

Sheila Slaughter, a sociologist of science, described a recent shift in science ideology from the "cornucopia" model of science to the "partnership in innovation" model of science (Slaughter, 1993, p. 284, p. 289). She recounts that, prior to the 1980s, academic biology was largely a basic science whose faculty were concerned with government-sponsored science and training grants. By the mid-1980s, however, most full professors of molecular biology served on the advisory boards of biotechnology corporations and owned stock in spinoff companies selling products based on the professors' academic research.

In Slaughter's cornucopia model, scientists pursued theoretical and empirical issues in an unfettered atmosphere, beholden only to the norms of science. Strong government funding encouraged knowledge accumulation that eventually would pay off in terms of theory, or application to health, defense, or industry. Klass (1975) called this the "gee whiz" model of science, although its total purity may have been largely mythical (e.g., Barnes, Bloor, & Henry, 1996). The cornucopia model held its own in academic science until the Reagan-Thatcher revolution introduced new sets of national priorities, identified commercial innovation as the key to prosperity, and earmarked science as the new partner of business (Slaughter, 1993; Slaughter & Leslie, 1997). Basic research became only the first step of a process which now included developing the original ideas and discoveries for the market. Adding application to the expectations of scientific work wasn't totally unknown, but making it a legitimate and expected part of academic science was new.

It is especially important to recognize that the overall ideological shift dictated that the new academic relationship with industry occurred alongside declining government support for research, students, and academic programs, and therefore that commercial funding for science became a university necessity in the 1980s (Kennedy, 1997). Repeated Congressional hearings during the 1980s, as the Democratic-controlled Congress struggled to resist the Reagan revolution, examined new conflicts of interest which arose as faculty energy was diverted into commercial pursuits. But those public examinations ended with the loss of the Democratic majority in both the Senate and the House in 1994.

Deregulation of
the Pharmaceutical Industry

The second background element to consider is pharmaceutical industry change. Payer (1992) argues that the pharmaceutical industry has become the most profitable industry in the United Satates (also see Pryor, 1997). Because there is so incredibly much money to be made, the industry is huge and hugely competitive, with thousands of intensely competitive employees working on new products, looking for new markets, and creating new ways to link the two. Challenges from managed care have been compensated for by increased marketing and speeded-up Food and Drug Administration (FDA) approval processes for new drugs (Balance, 1996; Eichenwald & Kolata, 1999). Most importantly, a cooperative Congress modified FDA regulations to allow television and print advertising directly to the public as of August, 1997 (Morrow, 1998), a change which pharmaceutical industry analysts predicted would multiply sales and increase companies' reliance on "blockbuster" drugs (Langreth, 1998). Currently, about one fifth of the revenue of leading companies results from sales of these "blockbuster" drugs (Balance, 1996). Drug ads to the public so far "are just the initial forays in what marketing experts believe will be a steady march toward the kind of aggressive, image-filled, and patently manipulative advertising that so successfully sells Americans everything from cars to cosmetics" (Morrow, 1998, p. 1). The internet has furthered the marketing of drugs into the home (Stolberg, 1999b).

The initial print ads for Viagra, popping up in publications from *Time* to *The American Psychologist* to the *Playbill* theater magazine given to every New York City playgoer, seem to be living up to this promise. They feature nothing but a large color image of a smiling couple in a dancing embrace and, in small print, the words "Viagra," "sildenafil citrate tablets," and either "let the dance begin" or "take the first step." Moreover, whereas drug ads have long been a staple in medical journals, for the first time a sex research journal features the same dancing couple Viagra ad on the 1999 back covers of *The Journal of Sex and Marital Therapy*. *The Code of Federal Regulations*, dealing with the FDA's rules for prescription drug advertising, describes a category of exceptions to the usual drug ad rules called *reminder advertisements* which are allowed to "call attention to the name of the drug product but do not include the indications or dosage recommendations" (Code of Federal Regulations [CFR], 1998, p. 60). Thus the dancing Viagra couple, sans any prescribing information, warnings, or indications, may become as ubiquitous as those globally recognizable golden arches.

Changes in FDA regulation are also relevant to the atmosphere and conduct of sexuopharmacology research (Healy, 1998; Liebenau, 1987). Regulations affecting drug approval, licensure, and advertisement invariably slow drug production and sale, and the industry has complained about

such limitations since the earliest regulatory acts of 1902 and 1906 first for-
bade unsubstantiated claims on medical labels. United States drug regulation has followed a pattern of expansion following a health disaster (e.g.,
thalidomide in 1962) and retraction once the immediate shock of the disaster is over (Merrill, 1997).

However, despite the simplified ad images permitted by the reminder
classification, drugs are powerful agents with serious physical consequences.
A 1985 General Accounting Office report showed that nearly half the new
drugs approved between 1976 and 1985 had fatal side effects not identified
during testing (Arno & Feiden, 1992), and the FDA is coming to recognize
that the rise in drug sales, combined with the aging of the population, is resulting in an increase in fatalities due to error and unanticipated effects of
mixing drugs (Stolberg, 1999a). It should come as no surprise to find a cover
story on Viagra in *U.S. News and World Report* less than 10 months after the
drug was approved reporting widespread side effects, with the sensational
title, "Dying for sex: The FDA approved Viagra quickly—perhaps too
quickly" (Brownlee & Schultz, 1999).

In addition, FDA deregulation has increasingly allowed off-label uses for
prescription medications. *Off-label* use was permitted by new regulations in
1982: "once a product has been approved for marketing, a physician may
prescribe it for use or in treatment regimens or patient populations that are
not included in approved labeling" (Ferenz, 1997, p. 41). Off-label uses
were never promoted, however, until recently, when manufacturers became
allowed to circulate off-label use information in exchange for promises that
off-label purposes for the drugs would be researched. This situation would
apply at the present time, for example, to prescribing Viagra for women. No
research on women was conducted prior to the initial approval, yet because
the manufacturer promises that such tests are underway, suggestive literature can be circulated.

Favorable Marketing Opportunities

Because a single blockbuster drug can lead to a significant realignment of
market share, companies are increasingly attracted to "lifestyle" drugs (e.g.,
for weight problems, hair loss, memory loss, skin improvement, mood alter-
ation) which appeal to large segments of the general public rather than
merely to people with particular illnesses (Weber & Barrett, 1998). As the

population ages, many more lifestyle drugs will focus on age-related issues. Almost every major pharmaceutical company has a fast-track program available for developing memory-enhancing drugs, for example (Hall, 1998). Although medical rhetoric surrounds all these drugs, company officials, when pressed, admit that they are fully aware of nonmedical uses of their drugs. As one such company representative acknowledged, "of all Prozac users—who buy about $1.8 billion of the drug each year—fully one-third have no medical need for it" (Hall, 1998, p. 56). A recent interview survey of over 2000 night-clubbers in northwest England showed that Viagra was already easily available for public nonprescription sale in clubs, and that people used it along with diverse other mood-altering and sex-enhancing substances (Aldridge & Measham, 1999). And, of course, there is the Internet as a marketing tool of inestimable proportions.

In sum, then, for a variety of converging reasons, recent political and economic developments favor the production and promotion of sexuality drugs by major pharmaceutical companies. But, they can't design, conduct, or evaluate the all-important FDA-approved research without the cooperation of experts on human sexuality.

Why Are Sex Researchers Interested in the Pharmaceutical Industry?

As an academic specialty, sexology has long suffered from failure to thrive, and thus it is not difficult to understand why sexologists might be enormously attracted and flattered by the sudden attentions of the pharmaceutical industry. To academic administrators and young graduates planning academic careers, sex research has always seemed too risky or "risqué" to be a legitimate specialty. Furthermore, sex is a perennial battleground in the ultrapolitical culture wars, making sex research funding and academic welcome equally insecure. Consequently, sexology has limped along decade after decade with neither academic credibility nor dependable support.

Chronic Problems with Sex Research Legitimacy and Funding
The former editor of *The Journal of Sex Research* has noted that academia boasts few programs of sexuality studies, few tenured professors doing sex

research, few job advertisements for sexologists, few research grants for sexuality studies, and few governmental agencies interested in sex research (Abramson, 1990). A recent overview of the state of sex research in the United States noted its historic limitations as a legitimate academic subject:

> It is often assumed that it is not professionally legitimate to promote or conduct sexuality research for the sole or primary purpose of contributing to existing knowledge about human sexual behaviors in the social science disciplines. . . . The primary outcome of such controversy [over research on sexuality] has been the inconsistent and modest financial support for this work on the part of both the government and the private sector, as well as a hesitancy to publicly promote research. (DiMauro, 1995, p. 11)

Funding for sex research is subject to unpredictable political attack, as was shown recently when the Secretary of Health and Human Services abruptly blocked two large peer-reviewed and approved NIH sex research grants in response to conservative complaints (Laumann, Michael, & Gagnon, 1994; Udry, 1993). On the clinical front, summaries of sex dysfunction outcome research typically bemoan the lack of funding for randomized psychological treatment trials which would support strong claims about the efficacy of sex therapy (Heiman & Meston, 1997; Schover & Leiblum, 1994). As a result of such attacks and funding drought, sexologists are always on the defensive, worried about proving their claims, attracting talented students, and even about keeping their own jobs.

Shrinking University Budgets

The enormous political and economic changes in academia discussed earlier have further pushed sexologists into the arms of the pharmaceutical industry. The former president of Stanford University recently reviewed the steady decline since the 1970s in federal and philanthropic science funding which occurred alongside the steady rise in the costs of science research (Kennedy, 1997). The loss of federal support has sent ripples throughout academia as universities have sought public and private funding for educational programs, athletics, student loans, salaries, buildings, and so forth. Nonremunerative programs in medical schools, including most sex therapy clinics, have been cut back and even cut out as for the first time faculty in medical schools have had to generate their own operating expenses and salaries (Schover & Leiblum, 1994). Slaughter and Leslie (1997) summarized how "colleges and universities try to compensate for diminished government revenues through liaisons with business and industry, through partnerships focused on innovative product development, and through the marketing of education and business services" (p. 1). This entrepreneurial Weltanschauung permeates current universities and medical schools, affecting sexologists along with everyone else.

Stagnation in Sex Therapy

The final reason some sexologists have been attracted to collaborative work with the pharmaceutical industry may be a certain lack of pride within their own clinical ranks (or is it just a high level of honesty?). In a thorough review of the field, Heiman and Meston (1997) concluded that if you use the most stringent standards, criteria published by a task force of the American Psychological Association, "There are almost no psychological treatments for sexual dysfunctions that conform to all the criteria of 'well-established treatments'" (p. 148). They attribute this result to the absence of treatment manuals (a specific APA requirement for treatment evaluation), the lack of control groups, the early domination of the field by the Masters and Johnson approach which delayed more testable approaches, and our old friend, minuscule funding for evaluation research.

Even so, Heiman and Meston (1997) concluded that effective psychological treatments for primary and secondary anorgasmia, erection failure, vaginismus, and premature ejaculation have been shown by numerous pieces of research. They believe that the psychological treatments for other complaints such as hypoactive sexual desire, sexual aversions, dyspareunia, and retarded ejaculation are less clearly effective, and that better diagnostic differentiation as well as treatment development are needed. However, in a point often overlooked, these authors are equally critical of the narrow research designs and assessment instruments used in the evaluation of medical treatments for sexual dysfunctions.

Schover and Leiblum (1994) took a more pessimistic look at the same situation a few years earlier. Critically assessing study results one dysfunction at a time, these authors suggested that sex therapy's effectiveness had been overstated, in part because biological factors may have been underestimated. Of course, these authors also discussed the impossibility of outcome research in a field without adequate funding. Looking more closely at the data in many of the studies with long-term follow-up, Schover and Leiblum (1994) reported that "the most striking finding was that the reversal of specific sexual dysfunctions was modest, but in each case series, most patients maintained improved overall sexual satisfaction" (p. 19). It may be that the value of sex therapy is obscured by research focusing strictly on symptom reversal and using the narrow language of the *Diagnostic and Statistical Manual of Mental Disorders* of the American Psychiatric Association. Broader, qualitative assessment might be more appropriate in delineating the efficacy of sex therapy.

Similar notes were struck in a 1992 review wherein a British psychiatrist praised early sex therapy research, and suggested that attending to the cognitive aspects of sexuality would improve the quality of sex therapy research at the present (Hawton, 1992). However, he gloomily continued, such research is lacking because funds are "virtually unavailable for research in sex therapy" (Hawton, 1992, p. 49).

For various reasons, therefore, sex therapists have found it difficult to produce the kind of unambiguous statistical results which would stand up in a contest of numbers to a medical audience used to evaluating outcomes by rates and percentages. In a widely publicized 1989 *New England Journal of Medicine* paper, urologists legitimated their rejection of the psychotherapeutic approach to treating men's erectile problems with the dismissive claim that "Only a few long-term follow-up studies of sex therapy have been performed, and they suggest a substantial rate of recurrence of impotence with time after sex therapy" (Krane, Goldstein, & DeTejada, 1989, p. 1654). The citation for this assertion was a summary paper in a urology journal which did not have a single citation to the sex therapy literature. Urologists have made the bold but highly self-serving and questionable claim over and over that their medical treatments are the most effective, and have effectively put sex therapists on the defensive.

Thus, one can see how the recent attentions of the pharmaceutical industry must have come as sunlight in winter to sex researchers. Its attractions included personal relationships with enthusiastic and flattering industry colleagues, a constant stream of paid trips to exotic and luxurious places, generous consultant fees, and business-class airplane tickets, all the standard modes of operation in the world of commercial science. Money for laboratories and research assistants, and released time from academic obligations also became available. Seductions and inducements blur with advantages and attractions, but one can see how they all represented a sea change from the past's straitened and stigmatized atmosphere of academic sex research.

How the Interests of Sexology and the Pharmaceutical Industry Conflict

Despite the mutual attraction between sexology and the pharmaceutical industry, there are several major areas where their interests conflict, perhaps irreconcilably. Some of these are conflicts which exist between the drug industry and all scientific or academic areas, but more importantly, there are numerous conflicts specific to the subject of sexuality.

General Conflicts of Interest: Secrecy and Scientific Integrity

The first conflict is over secrecy of scientific results. Industry interests lie in maximizing profit and companies demand secrecy over information they see as essential to profitability. In recent years, in exchange for corporate funding and access to corporate products (e.g., pre-approved drugs), academic scientists (following the practice of scientists employed within companies) have signed proprietary agreements which give corporations ownership over all research information (Blumenthal, Causino, Campbell, & Louis, 1996; Dickson, 1988; Marsa, 1997). Having signed, scientists cannot publish their studies or discuss their findings at scientific meetings without explicit corporate permission (Sindermann & Sawyer, 1997). This business rule, of course, conflicts with the normative structure of science (some would say the sacred obligation of science) wherein the free exchange of ideas is necessary for the growth of a common fund of knowledge, the critique of existing knowledge, and the dissemination of knowledge (Bradley, 1995; Liebenau, 1987; Schaffner, 1992). It's difficult to measure the impact of secrecy, although one suspects that companies are likely to embargo negative results more often than positive results. One British study using research projects approved by a particular institution's ethics committee reported a lower percentage of the pharmaceutical industry-sponsored research ended up published than the non-sponsored research (Wise & Drury, 1996).

Limitations on scientific communication are especially problematic in medical fields, where withholding or delaying information could cause harm. Failure to publish has already become a problem in sexology, insofar as early studies of the impact of Viagra on women, completed in early 1997, have not yet been published as of the date of this manuscript (personal communication, May, 1999).[2] Only one recent study of Viagra in women has been published, using a very small sample and no placebo group, and failing to demonstrate any therapeutic effect (Kaplan et al., 1999).[3]

Maintaining scientific integrity itself is a problem when scientific information is produced under commercial auspices (Bradley, 1995; Huth, 1992). How much does he who pays the piper call the tune—in other words, how much is the choice of methods and subjects, choice of literature to be cited, data collection and organization, and how results are reported and interpreted influenced by the company paying for the research? A recent newspaper exposé revealed that scientific publications are increasingly ghost-written by drug company medical writers (Eichenwald & Kolata, 1999), a shocking revelation to academics trained in the obligations and implicit promises associated with putting one's name on a publication. Journalists, patients, families of patients, students, researchers, and scholars all rely on published scientific studies to light their way into complex fields. If that domain is subject to commercial bias, scientific integrity is deeply compromised.

Because the public (and the media) must try to evaluate potential improprieties, major medical and scientific journals now require disclosure of all funding sources (and other legal/financial arrangements) as part of manuscript review, and require that such information appear when studies are published. A recent sex research study neglected to mention the pharmaceutical company connections of the authors, an omission quickly pointed out by The New York Times (Grady, 1999; Laumann et al., 1999). Concerns about scientific integrity are increasing, as "the pharmaceutical industry and clinical research are so completely intertwined that it is frequently difficult to find experts who are not in some way tied to the industry" (Valenstein, 1998, p. 199).[4]

How can we assess how sex research is affected by pharmaceutical industry sponsorship? The usual method is to compare results of studies funded versus unfunded by industry, a method which has repeatedly found that company-sponsored studies have more outcomes which favor the drugs (Altman, 1997). To take a recent example, a comparison of the results of 91 behavioral studies with and without tobacco industry support showed that industry-supported papers typically showed that nicotine or smoking improved cognitive performance, while non-industry-supported research studies were more nearly split in their conclusions (Turner & Spillich, 1997). Unfortunately, and ironically, too few studies in sex research journals cite any funding to do this kind of comparison at the present.

It will be important to document how inclusive pharmaceutical industry-sponsored research is in its subjects and methods. The clinical trials prior to Viagra's approval excluded gay men, for example, despite the fact that using nitrates for recreational purposes is common in the gay community, and the combination of Viagra and nitrates can be fatal (Kirby, 1998). Moreover, many individuals who are likely to use Viagra were disqualified from the clinical trials because of pre-existing physical conditions (e.g., poorly controlled diabetes, history of alcohol abuse, stroke or heart attack within past six months) (Goldstein et al., 1998). Pfizer representatives said that men taking heart medications were excluded because "we thought they wouldn't be thinking about sex" and their numerous medications might make it difficult to ascertain the effectiveness of Viagra (Brownlee & Schultz, 1999, p. 63). Were these patients excluded because they would have shown less benefit from the drug? Were gay patients excluded because they would give a "sex drug" the wrong public image?

Recognizing that companies are tempted to "introduce new products without exhaustively investigating their potential risks," the FDA has continuously improved its oversight of study design, but the case of sexuality-enhancing drugs provides unprecedented moral and public image challenges (Merrill, 1997, p. 94). Goldstein et al. (1998) reported that only men in stable heterosexual relationships of at least six months' duration were enrolled in the Viagra trials, yet "only 25 percent of the partners completed the optional questionnaire" (p. 1402). No data from even those partners were included in the final drug trials publication. During an informal conversation two months after Viagra's approval, one of the study's main authors acknowledged that women gave lower estimates of the drug's effect on erection than did men, an effect which has recently been replicated with statistical significance (Cohen, 1998; Salonia et al., 1999). There is no requirement that all

collected data be published, and companies may withhold data which under-
cut their claims.

Illustrative Example

A recent publication reported the effects of oral phentolamine on a small
group of women with complaints about sexual arousal (Rosen, Phillips,
Gendrano, & Ferguson, 1999). Phentolamine is an anti-adrenergic compound extensively tested and used in men with erectile complaints. The
laboratory study on six women evaluated their vaginal pulse amplitude and
self-reported arousal in response to erotic videotapes following medication
or placebo intake. Both physiological and self-report changes following
drug intake occasionally reached statistical significance but were highly
variable, as is often reported in such research. It was hard to know what to
conclude from this study, until one read:

> our results should be viewed with caution until replicated in a well-
> controlled, clinical trial. The purpose of this pilot study was to provide
> "proof of principle" for the concept of vasoactive drug therapy in the treat-
> ment of FSAD (female sexual arousal disorder). (Rosen et al., 1999, p. 143)

Proof of Principle is a term for a step in the FDA's drug approval process, a
curiosity in a scientific publication. In other words, the purpose of the study
was to demonstrate that the compound caused effects, which would then
justify further research. Much drug research is like this, driven by companies
needing to establish a product's viability. The science moves farther and farther away from questions and designs motivated by theories about sexuality.

Specific Conflicts Between the
Pharmaceutical Industry and Sexology

In addition to general concerns about the undermining of scientific integrity as a result of relations with the pharmaceutical industry, there are at
least five specific ways that sexuality research in particular would be diminished and threatened as a result of pharmaceutical industry domination.
These arise in part because the goals of pharmaceutical research are ultimately pragmatic (to produce a saleable product), while those of sexology
are intellectual; but more significantly, they arise because the model of sex-

uality used in sexology is broader, deeper, and more inclusive than the model of sexuality in industry-sponsored research.

Bypasses psychological and relational complexity of sexuality. The pharmaceutical industry approaches sex as a physical function, with adequate function of sex organs the bottom line. In typical fashion, for example, the 1989 paper on impotence defines the condition under study as "the consistent inability to achieve or sustain an erection of sufficient rigidity for sexual intercourse" (Krane et al., 1989, p. 1648). There's little attention to the person or couple attached to the penis, or recognition that relational factors might modify the meaning or importance of penile rigidity or sexual intercourse in a couple's sexual script. It would appear that industry-sponsored research wishes simply to wave away the complexities introduced by the psychosocial context of sexuality. By contrast, relationship theorists would argue that laboratory measurement of sexual organ function or self-report of organ function in the home setting offer a hopelessly incomplete sexual picture, and they would predict that drugs developed in such a bubble will be disappointing (Berscheid, 1999).

All current Viagra research proudly uses an "international" self-report questionnaire, the International Index of Erectile Function (IIEF), with impeccable statistical reliability and construct validity (Rosen et al., 1997). This 15-item instrument contains only one question inquiring about satisfaction with the sexual relationship with the partner, although even those results were omitted from the main Viagra report (Goldstein et al., 1998). Erectile dysfunction, a condition in the man's genitalia, has become the only acknowledged focus of interest, focus of evaluation, and focus of treatment. This represents a substantial narrowing from sex therapy—erasing the partner, erasing subjective meaning, and ironically, perpetuating the obsession with penile hardness which many sex therapists have argued is itself a primary cause of sexual unhappiness.

Wise (1999) recently published two cases in which a couple's marital situation deteriorated following the prescription of Viagra. In neither case was the wife involved in any way in the prescription process. Schmidt (1993) argued that in the current sexuopharmacology research atmosphere,

> No thought is given to the question of what meaning the man's impotence
> may have for his emotional equilibrium or his relationship to his partner. If

something does not function properly, then it has to be repaired, as if it were a bit of machinery. (p. 263)

Masks sociocultural factors. Because sexual function is treated as universal and biological in the pharmaceutical industry model, as witness the "International" IIEF, cultural variation in sexual meaning or script is ignored. All erections are the same. Sexology, by contrast, has a rich literature emphasizing the diversity of sexual experiences, activities, and meanings around the world and throughout history. Sex researchers have examined power dynamics of sexuality, developmental continuities and discontinuities of sexuality, the embeddedness of sexuality within cultural systems of gender meaning, the connection of sexuality to leisure and to shifting notions of sexual orientation and gender identity, and so forth. All these issues are crucial to understanding the somato-psychics of sexual experience, yet all are ignored in the tidal wave of reductionism wherein sex is pelvic vascular function.

In the wake of the product innovations for erectile dysfunction, it is no surprise that new women's pelvic vascular sexual dysfunctions have recently been announced by urologists, foretelling a wave of equal-opportunity pharmaceutical research (Goldstein & Berman, 1998; Park et al., 1997). Female genital dysfunction studies started appearing at conferences in early 1999, and although the data are described as preliminary, careful mention is made even in an abstract of how "this technique may prove useful . . . in determining efficacy of vasoactive drugs in this [female] population" (Werbin et al., 1999, p. 178).[5]

Denies sex is socially constructed. Pharmaceutical industry-sponsored research relies on fixed alternative self-report questionnaires such as the IIEF which approach questions about sexuality as if they were factual and unambiguous. Sexologists, especially as a result of fifteen years of AIDS research, have learned that research questionnaires can themselves contribute to the social construction of sexuality by using language such as "intercourse," "sexual satisfaction," and even "get an erection" or "attempt sexual intercourse" in an unproblematic fashion. For example, when the first question of the IIEF asks "How often were you able to get an erection during sexual activity during the past four weeks?" how does the respondent decide whether a particular moment in a kitchen, bedroom, or movie theater constitutes sexual activity? Is anyone interested in the partner's role in the "getting" of an erection? Is anyone interested in whether the sexual activity during the past four weeks was of mutual interest to the man and the partner? Is anyone looking at how participating in a sex research study affected the sexual activity being counted?

Sexuopharmaceutical research treats people's sexuality the way ankle orthopedists treat dancers—completely ignoring how social and cultural processes shape experience and behavior. Now, no one claims that ankle orthopedists need to know much about social and cultural elements of dance to do useful research and intervention. But ankle experts don't describe their interventions as helping with "dance dysfunctions" or "disorders of dancing." And the doctors' role is further reduced because there are plenty of dance coaches and trainers to consult if one is interested in learning about or how to dance. But sex is a different kettle of fish. There are few resources outside the medical model for people to easily consult. In treating sexual dysfunctions as asocial matters of physiology and bodily function, sexuopharmacological research promotes genital function as the centerpiece of sexuality and ignores everything else, disguising the larger contexts of social power (Gagnon & Parker, 1995).

Ignores connections of sex to politics. Feminists are not alone in connecting the reduction of sexuality to genital function to gender politics (Tiefer, 1995). Schmidt (1993) suggests that

> Gazing at the diligence with which urologists, andrologists, surgeons and physiologists pursue the dream of the 'perfect penis' against the backcloth of the social upheavals and the profound changes in gender relations and sexual conduct of the last 20 years, one could conclude that the struggle is not about restoring one man's potency, but a desperate effort to re-establish western male potency in general. In fact it looks like a magic rite symbolically guaranteeing the phallus's immunity from danger in the face of a (slightly) changing power balance of the sexes. (p. 264)

Gender politics are invisible in sexuopharmaceutical research, but other political issues are equally neglected. Medical-model sex research such as that funded by the pharmaceutical industry mystifies sexuality with the technical (or pseudo-technical) language of "erectile apparatus" and "therapeutic management strategies" (Rivas & Chancellor, 1997,

p. 429). Multisyllabic expertise intimidates and exploits people who lack sex education in a political climate where legislative politics has reduced public sex education to abstinence education.

The current American culture combines limited sex education with constant in-your-face sexual sensationalism, stories of sexual violence and disease, and threats to safe and legal abortion. Thus, it should be no surprise that every study shows widespread public sexual ignorance and uncertainty. People are tongue-tied when it comes to reflecting on their own sexual motives or understanding the multitude of options for sexual decision making. Science and health media advise people with sexual dissatisfactions to consult medical experts, and in this way, the pharmaceutical industry benefits from the current politics of sexual ignorance and medicalization.

Threatens liberatory history of sexology. Finally, sex researchers have often allied themselves with liberatory sexual politics that endorsed sexual diversity and self-determination (e.g., Brecher, 1969). Throughout the twentieth century they have often challenged sexual restrictiveness and puritanical values. Feminism continued this tradition by revealing widespread sexual coercion and consequent sexual inhibition (e.g., Heise, 1995; Segal, 1994). The pharmaceutical industry is interested in increased sexual consumerism, but that is not the same as emancipatory sexual politics. Funded research thus far colludes with repressive traditions by excluding gay or single persons from drug trials and by defining satisfaction as the restoration of a phallocentric script. "Informed consent" in such research is a mockery in the face of participants' lack of comprehensive sexual knowledge. Sexual liberation seems limited to providing genital arousal and orgasm through chemistry. The emotional starvation of such sex research is the measure of the Faustian bargain of the sexologists.

Strategies for Sexology to Resist a Pharmaceutical Takeover

There are many ways sexology can resist the domination of the pharmaceutical industry and preserve its independence in education, research, and the making of public sexuality policy.

Research Drug Consequences

Because pharmaceutical industry-funded research is likely to focus only on the most narrow, pragmatic, and technical effects of the sexuopharmaceuticals, it is incumbent on sexologists to train their lenses on three other types of drug effects; psychosocial impact, unintended consequences, and long-term follow-up.

Industry-funded research is generally short term. Of the four drug studies I cited in this paper, one had no follow-up at all as measurement was taken the same day as the drug (Rosen et al., 1999), one looked at effects for three months (Kaplan et al. 1999), one for four months (Salonia et al., 1999), and one for six months (Goldstein et al., 1998). Much of this follow-up time included continuing drug intake. The brief duration of drug study follow-up has been noted before, in contrast with follow-up studies of psychological interventions lasting up to five years after the intervention has ended (Heiman & Meston, 1997). Longer follow-up, especially when focused more broadly than simply on symptom reversal, can reveal effects (both beneficial and detrimental, both anticipated and unforeseen) on sexuality and relationship factors.

The definition of drug effects to be examined is one of the most important aspects of research design. The widely used International Index of Erectile Function (IIEF), with its fixed response options in response to 15 questions, includes "Q1: How often were you able to get an erection during sexual activity? . . . Q2: When you had erections with sexual stimulation, how often were your erections hard enough for penetration? . . . Q3: When you attempted sexual intercourse, how often were you able to penetrate (enter) your partner? . . . Q4: During sexual intercourse, *how often* were you able to maintain your erection after you had penetrated (entered) your partner?" (Rosen et al., 1997, p. 829). In the report of the Viagra clinical trials, drug efficacy was telescoped to questions three and four only, reinforcing the message that the only issue that matters is organ function (Goldstein et al., 1998). In the 1999 study on Viagra and postmenopausal women, a new nine-item fixed-response questionnaire was adapted from the IIEF (Kaplan et al., 1999). Called the FSFI (Female Sexual Function Index), the questionnaire began with the sentence, "Sexual function includes intercourse, caressing, foreplay, and masturbation" (Kaplan et al, p. 485). However, none of the nine questions used the term *sexual function* again, referring instead to *sexual desire* (never defined), *sex life* (never defined), *sexual relationship* (never defined), *sexual intercourse*, and *sexual stimulation* (both defined). Even had the questions incorporated the broader language, however, the questions still would have neglected emotional experience, sensual pleasure, and personal sexual meanings.

Sexologists must use a broad range of quantitative and qualitative research approaches to measure the impact of sexual drugs on feelings and fantasies as well as functions. What did the users (patients and partners) of the drugs anticipate? How did they feel about the experience of using the drug? Whom did they talk to about the experience? What aspects caused lasting concern? How did the sexuopharmaceuticals affect feelings of gender adequacy, vitality, and desirability? What happened to the magical expectations? What was the impact of worry over side effects?

I was surprised to learn how secretive patients were about their penile prostheses in a follow-up study (one to four years post surgery) conducted some years ago (Tiefer, Pedersen, & Melman, 1988). The majority of interviewees, 52 men and 22 partners, had told almost no one about their prosthesis, despite numerous continuing stresses ranging from somatic obsessions to severe marital conflict. While intercourse was often frequent and patients were proud of their performance, men's sexual experience had become less sensual, and women reported ongoing worries over whether the penis would continue to "work." Both partners covertly checked the penis regularly. Sexual scripts were altered in about one quarter of the sample to eliminate partner oral or manual caressing. Open-ended questions revealed that the rewards of the prosthesis were often more psychological than functional (e.g., "I feel like a man again" said by patients not having sexual intercourse). To avoid promoting a mechanistic model of sexuality, it is incumbent on us to inquire about the broad emotional and interpersonal impact of sexuopharmaceuticals.

Challenge Inflated Epidemiology

It is in the interest of the pharmaceutical industry to publicize and inflate the prevalence of sexual dysfunctions,

> a pattern [which] is emerging as a hallmark of the marketing of new treatments. Medical crusaders draw attention to a disease by broadening its definition to include the most mildly affected patients. That boosts demand for new medicines—even for people who, in an earlier era, wouldn't have been considered sick. Much as Prozac has helped turn even ordinary bouts of the blues into a brain disorder treatable with drugs, the new ED [erectile dysfunc-

tion] drugs promise to medicalize age-related sexual decline, blurring the boundary between disease and discontent. (Stipp & Whitaker, 1998, p. 118)

These authors draw attention to the important role of epidemiological studies and epidemiological rhetoric in the sexuopharmacology story. The definition of sexual dysfunction is elastic, ads inclusion criteria can be broad or restrictive. The only random population study on erectile dysfunction, for example, asked men aged 40 to 70 to characterize themselves as completely, moderately, minimally, or not at all impotent (Feldman, Goldstein, Hatzichristou, Krane, & McKinlay, 1994). The Viagra clinical trials paper cited the results of this study, but conflated all categories, as in "The [sic] disorder is age-associated, with estimated prevalence rates of 39 per cent among men 40 years old, and 67 per cent among those 70 years old" (Goldstein et al., 1998, p. 1397). Thus, the clinical trials report increased the prevalence statistics from what had been 10 million in 1989 (Krane et al., 1989, p. 1648) to 30 million in 1998 (Goldstein et al., 1998, p. 1397). Sexologists must recognize the elasticity of prevalence statistics and expose exponential growth numbers as part of industrial public relations.

Recently, the answers to one yes/no survey question in a large, representative, population-based study of sexual practices (Laumann, Gagnon, Michael, & Michaels, 1994) were reanalyzed in a drug industry-supported study to emphasize the prevalence of sexual dysfunction, which was characterized as an "important health problem" in "urgent need for population-based data concerning [its] prevalence, determinants, and consequences" (Laumann et al., 1999, p. 537). The complex statistical manipulations require sophisticated examination, which is probably why the extensive media coverage usually went no farther than quoting the first sentence of the abstract's results, "Sexual dysfunction is more prevalent for women (43%) than men (31%)" (Laumann et al., 1999, p. 537). "Sexual dysfunction," as a single category, is probably as meaningless to a sexologist as "illness" might be to a physician or "ignorance" to an educator, but it is far from meaningless to marketers.

Thus far, sexologists have not challenged the escalating statistics. Perhaps this results from our long-held belief that sexual problems (including but far from limited to sexual dysfunctions) are common, but hidden, and that it would be a better world if people were more able to acknowledge and seek help for their sexual dissatisfactions. Benevolent intentions, however, can be co-opted by industry-related interests to increase market demand, and sexologists must monitor how their data, methods, and interpretations are used.

Resist Oversimplification of Sexuality

Pharmaceutical industry-sponsored sex research treats sex as a far simpler aspect of life than does sexology, a trend in evidence since urologists began to dominate erectile dysfunction discourse at the beginning of the 1990s. In response to the National Institute of Health's 1992 Consensus Development Conference Report on Impotence, sexologist-psychiatrist Bancroft commented, with admirable British understatement, that the report's discussion of psychology was "breathtakingly inadequate" (Bancroft, 1993, p. 205). Similarly, a Dutch psychologist-sexologist pointed out that "In the section on diagnostic procedures 14 lines are devoted to sexual history, and 77 lines to an evaluation of the anatomical and physiological substrate of sexual function," adding, "this is clearly out of balance" (Everaerd, 1993, p. 220).

The trend towards oversimplifying sexuality by ignoring or minimizing the psychosocial aspects is abetted by a dearth of sophisticated sexological research methods, a legacy of the shortage of funding and academic legitimacy discussed earlier. Survey methods are perhaps most advanced, driven by policy interests in sexually transmitted diseases and adolescent pregnancy (Bancroft, 1999). But even highly quantitative methods can explore sexuality as a part of social life, as shown in the important Chicago study (Laumann, Gagnon, et al., 1994). Also, numerous qualitative methods are emerging that will allow better research on relational factors in sexuality. For example, Clement (1999) recently described efforts to analyze and code narratives of sexual interactions as a new way to study sexual scripts, and Gavey and McPhillips (1999) used discourse analysis to examine women's contradictory feelings about condoms. Feminist research, with its emphasis on methods that allow individuals to use their own language and frameworks, will offer insights into sexuality in real life. Phenomenological and narrative research on sex therapy, for example, would make more visible the complexities of sexual relationships and allow sexologists to defend the complexity and range of sexual experience, as well as the central importance of meaning to the experience of sexuality.

We must recognize that part of the public appeal of the urologist-pharmaceutical industry model of sexuality is that bypassing sexual psychology holds out the hope of simple solutions and uses medical model language to relieve people of responsibility for their problems (Tiefer, 1986a). But, people often suspect that this simplification is a trick, and I have found that presenting the complexity of sexuality in humanistic language resonates with people's wishes and romantic experiences, and engages their affect and imagination in ways that can overcome the appeal of reductionism.

Professional Education and Regulation

We have entered a new era of research ethics (Schaffner, 1992). Integrity guidelines have been established in many areas of funded research that can help researchers and funders alike (Bradley, 1995). These will continue to evolve as new questions are raised about conflicts of interest, academic publishing pressures, academic entrepreneurship, needs for disclosure, and so forth (Hersen & Miller, 1992). Sex researchers, newcomers in the world of commercial funding opportunities, need ethical and historical education about academic and scientific standards. Industry support of conferences and educational materials must be limited, as it seems that despite the language of "unrestricted educational grants," pharmaceutical representatives now attend sexuality conferences they sponsor and can intrude on participants' collegial experiences.[6]

Sexologists can play an important role in educating physicians about a role for the new sexuopharmaceuticals in the context of a more complex understanding of sexuality, although pharmaceutical industry sponsorship of such educational presentations would be problematic. Psychobiosocial sexuality research can be published in primary care journals along with lists of resource materials for physicians. Sexologists can develop consultation services to primary care physicians and committees to review sexuopharmaceutical advertisements. Professional sexuality research organizations can join the legion of scientific research organizations in developing, disseminating, and enforcing standards of responsible research conduct (Frankel, 1993).

Conclusion

With the advent of sexuopharmaceutical drugs and their tremendous public and commercial interest, sexology has entered a new era. I started by saying that this paper was an essay on family values, insofar as I see the professional and academic family of sexology threatened by commercial co-optation. Of course this isn't the first time, nor will it be the last, that a family's values are threatened by the temptations of money. Either sexologists respond to the new ethical and methodological challenges by defending and promoting their own professional expertise, theoretical insights, and independent goals, or they will be co-opted by the powerful engine of commercialization. Collaborative research is possible, but only with equal attention to values based in the sexological paradigm. If sexology loses its independent status, the public will have even fewer places to turn for sexual enlightenment free from commercial or political bias.

Notes

1. The first international conference of the International Association for the Study of Sexuality, Culture, and Society was held in Amsterdam in 1998; the journal *Sexualities: Studies in Culture and Society* began publishing in 1998.

2. These data were finally presented in public for the first time in June, 2000. The senior author said that the company, which owned the data, had sent her preliminary information one week before the conference presentation, but that she still did not have access to all the raw data (Laan, et al., 2000).

3. Several other small studies have since been published, again with negative results.

4. An important editorial in *The New England Journal of Medicine* must be read by all interested in these academic-industry conflicts of interest (Angell, 2000).

5. One year later, July, 2000, we are seeing such studies filling sessions at the annual American Urological Association conference, and the beginnings of a new urology subspecialty in female sexual dysfunction.

6. Cf. my unpublished policy statement, "No free lunch: Recommendations for the Society for the Scientific Study of Sex regarding pharmaceutical company sponsorship, April 22, 2000."

part five

THE CREATION OF FSD

Female sexual dysfunction (FSD) is the newest chip off the sex and medicalization block. It's an amazing amalgam of everything I have been thinking about for my whole career—medicalization, sexuality theory and practice, feminism, social construction, gender politics, women's sexual problems and treatments, professionalization—and to be truthful, for the past five years I have been giddy with pleasure at watching a story unfold that I understand and in which I have a role to play. Here's the short version of what's happening (a much longer version is in Tiefer, 2001).

Following the 1998 FDA (Food and Drug Administration) approval of Viagra, the drug for men's erectile dysfunction (ED), journalists began asking "Where is the Pink Viagra? Where is the sex drug for women?" Having written about the medicalization of men's sexual problems for over ten years, I heard bells ring. I knew that either a new women's disease would have to be "discovered" to take advantage of the great marketing opportunity provided by the success of Viagra or existing women's sexual problems would have to be repackaged and medicalized.

Sure enough, the next year a Boston urologist who had been active on the ED front organized a large conference on women's sexual problems and tried to start a new medical organization. He had the support of the drug industry, and he succeeded the next year. Enthusiastically backed by drug industry money, innumerable professional and scientific conferences have now been held on "FSD," and we are well on our way to having a new medicalized perspective on women's sexuality.

In response to these developments, I convened a group of feminist social scientists and psychotherapists in 2000 to challenge all this medicalization, and the articles in this section were written as I pursued the
campaign we designed. Although I had thought of myself as an activist before, it was only within academia, not in the public sphere. Now, however,
I sought out opportunities to speak to journalists and get my message out to
the public. I have participated in vicious debates as well as thoughtful discussions, and the new era of medicalization for women's sexuality is really
just beginning. We called our campaign "A New View for Women's Sexual
Problems" and you can follow its progress on http://www.fsd-alert.org. I
hope these articles encourage you to challenge some of what's coming
down the pike that alleges to benefit women. Things are more complicated
than they look, and it is a genuine watershed moment in the social construction of sex.

chapter 1

"FEMALE SEXUAL DYSFUNCTION" ALERT: A NEW DISORDER INVENTED FOR WOMEN

Dear readers of *Sojourner*, the Boston women's newspaper:

We've all heard that sexuality is socially constructed, but it's rare to actually witness the process in action. Well, such a moment is coming to Boston, Massachusetts, in late October 1999, in the form of a scientific conference sponsored by Boston University's School of Medicine through its departments of Continuing Education and Urology. The conference, from October 22 to 24, is entitled "New Perspectives in the Management of Female Sexual Dysfunction." It will be held at the Swissôtel and registration costs $495 for physicians and $395 for others (gasp). A business meeting will be held to discuss and vote on creating a new organization to address this supposed dysfunction, and the whole ball of wax has been underwritten by "unrestricted educational grants" from several pharmaceutical companies (bingo!).

I am a feminist and psychologist who has specialized in sexuality for the past 30 years. (I got my Ph.D. at UC/Berkeley in 1969.) As a researcher and therapist working in two New York City medical school departments of urology during the 1980s and 1990s, I witnessed first-hand a phase in the social construction of sexuality that in 1986 I called "In Pursuit of the Perfect Penis: The Medicalization of Men's Sexuality." The climax of this phase, long in preparation, burst upon the public in March 1998, when Pfizer pharmaceutical company's erection-enhancing drug, Viagra, was approved by the FDA.

Now we are witnessing the next phase of this process, as pharmaceutical companies gear up for research on women. But what vision of women's sexuality will be promoted by such work? Which women will be involved? What are appropriate norms for women's sexual function, for subjective experience, for satisfaction? Can there even be norms when the broad diversity of women's sexual interests has been documented by decades of feminist writing and research? Indeed, my belief is that this new "female sexual dysfunction" (just a new term for "frigidity"?) is being invented at this very moment and that it represents a serious challenge for feminists.

Let's just briefly turn to the key clues indicating that we are watching the calculated invention of a new disorder that serves many financial and professional constituencies—but not necessarily the interests of women. Urology (clue one) is a subdivision of surgery focusing on diseases of the bladder, kidneys, and genital structures. Urologists' interest in sexual problems (principally erection problems) over the past two decades comes at a time of changing demographics, changing medical economics, and changing sexual norms. To briefly summarize these changes, the population has been aging, physicians and others squeezed by managed care have been searching for more profitable opportunities, and the notion that everyone is entitled to and expecting good sex till the day they die is increasingly popular.

Research on men's sexuality was at first subject to the same poor funding and professional skepticism as other sex research. However, urologists were used to working in conjunction with industries (surgical equipment and drug manufacturers, for example), and the pharmaceutical industry itself (ever since the Reagan years) had been in a phase of deregulation and active growth.

Thus, the 1980s saw many medical conferences on research on erections, always held in exotic locations and luxurious hotels (clue two) with high registration fees (clue three), along with organizations supporting that research (e.g., Society for the Study of Impotence) (clue four) and journals devoted to their publication (e.g., *International Journal for Impotence Research*). The government put the imprimatur on this research when, in 1992, the National Institutes of Health (NIH) held a consensus development conference on erection problems that was organized by urologists. Designating "erectile dysfunction" a serious public health concern, the government gave notice that erection problems would be taken seriously and implied that big profits could be made from aggressive investment. Fast forward and Viagra becomes one of the biggest news stories of 1998.

And, a small voice asks, where were women in this story of triumph and advancement? What did these two decades of effort on the industrial, medical, urological, scientific, and federal front do for women? I'd like to know the answer myself, because I certainly haven't been able to find it in the scientific literature, or while attending conferences, or even in working in urology departments themselves. Women are largely disinvited from the consulting rooms where erections are treated, and their opinions and concerns about men's erections have almost never been studied. Although satisfying women sexually is the alleged purpose of all the erectile research and repair (in fact, gay men were excluded from the Viagra drug trials), none of the research ever inquired what women wanted or needed sexually. Having an erection so men can feel equal to other men seems more what's really going on. I'll never forget the patient who told me that he wanted treatment for his erection problems so that he could go into a bar and feel as good as the other guys. The impact of all these long-lasting hard erections on women's anatomy, women's preferences, and women's well-being is unknown.

A new day dawns, however, this month in Boston, as the same team that brought you Viagra and the many Viagra-wannabees now turns its searchlight on women. Already there have been years of unpublished work on Viagra with women using brief questionnaires to measure outcome (as in sexual performance by men), and years of work with female animals examining their clitoral and vaginal arteries for signs of the same sort of blockages urologists liked to claim caused erection problems for men. The direction these researchers are now heading seems pretty predictable. The invitation for the upcoming meeting was sent to "health care disciplines": "basic science, diabetology, endocrinology, engineering (sic), family practice, primary care medicine, gerontology, gynecology, nursing, pharmacology, psychology, psychiatry, rehabilitation medicine, urology, and vascular surgery." Absent were women's medicine, gay and lesbian medicine, adolescent medicine, women's studies, lesbian studies, bisexual and transgender studies, social science, sociology, medical sociology, anthropology, medical anthropology, history, history of medicine, cultural studies, film studies, ethnic studies, and so on. Whose interests will be served by this Boston meeting and any new organization that emerges from it? What points of view will be presented and what points of view ignored? Which women will be discussed in this meeting and organization, and what will be known about their lives and their sexualities?

It seems clear that the purpose of this conference on "New Perspectives in the Management of Female Sexual Dysfunction" is to promote the medicalization of women's sexuality—a process of establishing universal norms, and then declaring all variations disordered and in need of treatment. We can expect then the usual medical sequelae: expensive meetings, books and journals underwritten by drug companies, new disorders discovered to be treated by expensive drugs, health and medical journalists alerting the public to new disorders and their quick-fix cures, drug company-sponsored epidemiological studies creating and identifying new markets, urgent government and commercially funded consensus conferences. Meanwhile, the factors which account for the lion's share of women's sexual problems (economic, social, political) will be ignored, denied, avoided, and generally said to be "not about sexuality." In other words, medicalization is fundamentally about normal vs. abnormal function, and fundamentally about defining that in terms of physical performance. As best I can tell, that is what this conference will celebrate, and promote.

As I said, it's a privilege to get to see social construction in action. And it'll be fun to see what difference a feminist welcoming committee will make. A dozen or so feminists have reserved modestly priced rooms at a nearby hotel. We intend to challenge the pharmaceutical fashioning of female bodies in a number of creative ways. If you would like to be a member of the welcoming committee, or make a donation, please contact me by e-mail at ltiefer@mindspring.com.

A NEW VIEW OF WOMEN'S SEXUAL PROBLEMS BY THE WORKING GROUP ON A NEW VIEW OF WOMEN'S SEXUAL PROBLEMS[1]

In recent years, publicity about new treatments for men's erection problems has focused attention on women's sexuality and provoked a competitive commercial hunt for "the female Viagra." But women's sexual problems differ from men's in basic ways which are not being examined or addressed.

We believe that a fundamental barrier to understanding women's sexuality is the medical classification scheme in current use, developed by the American Psychiatric Association (APA) for its *Diagnostic and Statistical Manual of Disorders (DSM)* in 1980, and revised in 1987 and 1994. It divides (both men's and) women's sexual problems into four categories of sexual "dysfunction": sexual desire disorders, sexual arousal disorders, orgasmic disorders, and sexual pain disorders. These "dysfunctions" are disturbances in an assumed universal physiological sexual response pattern ("normal function") originally described by Masters and Johnson in the 1960s. This universal pattern begins, in theory, with sexual drive, and proceeds sequentially through the stages of desire, arousal, and orgasm.

In recent decades, the shortcomings of the framework, as it applies to women, have been amply documented. The three most serious distortions produced by a framework that reduces sexual problems to disorders of physiological function, comparable to breathing or digestive disorders, are:

1. A false notion of sexual equivalency between men and women. Because the early researchers emphasized similarities in men's and women's physiological responses during sexual activities, they concluded that sexual disorders must also be similar. Few investigators asked women to describe their experiences from their own points of view. When such studies were done, it became apparent that women and men differ in many crucial ways. Women's accounts do not fit neatly into the Masters and Johnson model; for example, women generally do not separate "desire" from "arousal," women care less about physical than subjective arousal, and women's sexual complaints frequently focus on "difficulties" that are absent from the DSM. (See Tiefer, 1991c, Basson, 2000, Frank, Anderson, and Rubinstein, 1978, Hite, 1976, Ellison, 2000, etc.)

   Furthermore, an emphasis on genital and physiological similarities between men and women ignores the implications of inequalities related to gender, social class, ethnicity, sexual orientation, etc. Social, political, and economic conditions, including widespread sexual violence, limit women's access to sexual health, pleasure, and satisfaction in many parts of the world. Women's social environments thus can prevent the expression of biological capacities, a reality entirely ignored by the strictly physiological framing of sexual dysfunctions.

2. The erasure of the relational context of sexuality. The American Psychiatric Association's DSM approach bypasses relational aspects of women's sexuality, which often lie at the root of sexual satisfactions and problems—e.g., desires for intimacy, wishes to please a partner, or, in some cases, wishes to avoid offending, losing, or angering a partner. The DSM takes an exclusively individual approach to sex, and assumes that if the sexual parts work, there is no problem; and if the parts don't work, there is a problem. But many women do not define their sexual difficulties this way. The DSM's reduction of "normal sexual function" to physiology implies, incorrectly, that one can measure and treat genital and physical difficulties without regard to the relationship in which sex occurs.

3. The leveling of differences among women. All women are not the same, and their sexual needs, satisfactions, and problems do not fit neatly into categories of desire, arousal, orgasm, or pain. Women differ in their values, approaches to sexuality, social and cultural backgrounds, and current

situations, and these differences cannot be smoothed over into an identical notion of "dysfunction"—or an identical, one-size-fits-all treatment.

Because there are no magic bullets for the socio-cultural, political, psychological, social, or relational bases of women's sexual problems, pharmaceutical companies are supporting research and public relations programs focused on fixing the body, especially the genitals. The infusion of industry funding into sex research and the incessant media publicity about "breakthrough" treatments have put physical problems in the spotlight and isolated them from broader contexts. Factors that are far more often sources of women's sexual complaints—relational and cultural conflicts, for example, or sexual ignorance or fear—are downplayed and dismissed. Lumped into the catchall category of "psychogenic causes," such factors go unstudied and unaddressed. Women with these problems are being excluded from clinical trials on new drugs, and yet, if current marketing patterns with men are indicative, such drugs will be aggressively advertised for all women's sexual dissatisfactions.

A corrective approach is desperately needed. We propose a new and more useful classification of women's sexual problems, one that gives appropriate priority to individual distress and inhibition arising within a broader framework of cultural and relational factors. We challenge the cultural assumptions embedded in the DSM and the reductionist research and marketing program of the pharmaceutical industry. We call for research and services driven not by commercial interests, but by women's own needs and sexual realities.

Sexual Health and
Sexual Rights: International Views

To move away from the DSM's genital and mechanical blueprint of women's sexual problems, we turned for guidance to international documents. In 1974, the World Health Organization held a unique conference on the training needs for sexual health workers. The report noted: "A growing body of knowledge indicates that problems in human sexuality are more pervasive and more important to the well-being and health of individuals in many cultures than has previously been recognized." The report emphasized the importance of taking a positive approach to human sexuality and the enhancement of relationships. It offered a broad definition of "sexual health" as "the integration of the somatic, emotional, intellectual, and social aspects of sexual being."[2]

In 1999, the World Association of Sexology, meeting in Hong Kong, adopted a Declaration of Sexual Rights.[3] "In order to assure that human beings and societies develop healthy sexuality," the Declaration stated, "the following sexual rights must be recognized, promoted, respected, and defended":

- The right to sexual freedom, excluding all forms of sexual coercion, exploitation and abuse;
- The right to sexual autonomy and safety of the sexual body;
- The right to sexual pleasure, which is a source of physical, psychological, intellectual and spiritual well-being;
- The right to sexual information . . . generated through unencumbered yet scientifically ethical inquiry;
- The right to comprehensive sexuality education;
- The right to sexual health care, which should be available for prevention and treatment of all sexual concerns, problems, and disorders.

Women's Sexual Problems: A New Classification

Sexual problems, which The Working Group on A New View of Women's Sexual Problems defines as discontent or dissatisfaction with any emotional, physical, or relational aspect of sexual experience, may arise in one or more of the following interrelated aspects of women's sexual lives.

I. Sexual Problems Due to Socio-Cultural, Political, or Economic Factors

    A. Ignorance and anxiety due to inadequate sex education, lack of access to health services, or other social constraints:

        1. Lack of vocabulary to describe subjective or physical experience.

        2. Lack of information about human sexual biology and life-stage changes.

        3. Lack of information about how gender roles influence men's and women's sexual expectations, beliefs, and behaviors.

4. Inadequate access to information and services for contraception and abortion, STD prevention and treatment, sexual trauma, and domestic violence.

B. Sexual avoidance or distress due to perceived inability to meet cultural norms regarding correct or ideal sexuality including:

1. Anxiety or shame about one's body, sexual attractiveness, or sexual responses.

2. Confusion or shame about one's sexual orientation or identity, or about sexual fantasies and desires.

C. Inhibitions due to conflict between the sexual norms of one's subculture or culture of origin and those of the dominant culture.

D. Lack of interest, fatigue, or lack of time due to family and work obligations.

II. Sexual Problems Relating to Partner and Relationship

A. Inhibition, avoidance, or distress arising from betrayal, dislike, or fear of partner, partner's abuse or couple's unequal power, or arising from partner's negative patterns of communication.

B. Discrepancies in desire for sexual activity or in preferences for various sexual activities.

C. Ignorance or inhibition about communicating preferences or initiating, pacing, or shaping sexual activities.

D. Loss of sexual interest and reciprocity as a result of conflicts over commonplace issues such as money, schedules, or relatives, or resulting from traumatic experiences, e.g., infertility or the death of a child.

E. Inhibitions in arousal or spontaneity due to partner's health status or sexual problems.

III. Sexual Problems Due to Psychological Factors

A. Sexual aversion, mistrust, or inhibition of sexual pleasure due to:

1. Past experiences of physical, sexual, or emotional abuse.

2. General personality problems with attachment, rejection, cooperation, or entitlement.

3. Depression or anxiety.

B. Sexual inhibition due to fear of sexual acts or of their possible consequences, e.g., pain during intercourse, pregnancy, sexually transmitted disease, loss of partner, loss of reputation.

IV. Sexual Problems Due to Medical Factors

Pain or lack of physical response during sexual activity despite a supportive and safe interpersonal situation, adequate sexual knowledge, and positive sexual attitudes. Such problems can arise from:

A. Numerous local or systemic medical conditions affecting neurological, neurovascular, circulatory, endocrine or other systems of the body;
B. Pregnancy, sexually transmitted diseases, or other sex-related conditions.
C. Side effects of many drugs, medications, or medical treatments.
D. Iatrogenic conditions.

Conclusion

This document is designed for researchers desiring to investigate women's sexual problems, for educators teaching about women and sexuality, for medical and nonmedical clinicians planning to help women with their sexual lives, and for a public that needs a framework for understanding a rapidly changing and centrally important area of life.

Notes

For further information about the Campaign for A New View of Women's Sexual Problems, to obtain additional copies of this document, or to make a tax-deductible financial contribution, please contact: Campaign for a New View, 163 Third Ave., PMB #183, New York, NY 10003, USA, or Ltiefer@Mindspring.com

1. Linda Alperstein, Carol Ellison, Jennifer R. Fishman, Marny Hall, Lisa Handwerker, Heather Hartley, Ellyn Kaschak, Peggy Kleinplatz, Meika Loe, Laura Mamo, Carol Tavris, Leonore Tiefer.

2. WHO Technical Report, series Nr. 572, 1975. Full text available http://www2.hu-berlin.de/sexology.

3. Full text available on the website listed in footnote 3 and also on http://www.tc.umn.edu/~colem001/was/wdeclara. It is published in E. M. L. Ng, J. J. Borras-Valls, M. Perez-Conchillo, and E.Coleman (eds.) (2000) *Sexuality in the New Millennium*. Bologna, Italy: Editrice Compositori.

chapter 3

THE SELLING OF
"FEMALE SEXUAL DYSFUNCTION"

This first conference on female sexual dysfunction (FSD) [held in Boston, 1999] offers researchers and clinicians an important opportunity to add to the already sizable literature on contemporary women's sexual problems. However, this opportunity is threatened by commercial domination and an excessively narrow biomedical focus which neglects the research and theory growing out of 30 years of feminist scholarship. More than lip service needs to be paid to the importance of interdisciplinary understanding. The commercial cart cannot be permitted to pull the empirical and theoretical horses, as happened in the impotence/erectile dysfunction field. FSD is at a crossroads, and the women's movement is watching.

I come to this meeting as a sex researcher, clinical psychologist, and as a member of what the Director of the National Institute of Health (NIH) Office of Research on Women's Health, Dr. Vivian Pinn, characterizes as "the women's advocacy community" (i.e., a feminist). I wanted to bring that special insider/outsider perspective and message because we are at an important point in the history of sex and the history of women.

Those gathered here have an opportunity to make substantial contributions to the ongoing story of women's sexuality. But, as a sexologist and a feminist, I am concerned that this new group and area of specialization may not succeed in avoiding the temptations of simplistic models and simplistic solutions for women's very complex sexual dilemmas.

I am especially concerned because of the experience of the impotence/erectile dysfunction field. I do not want to happen to the women's sexuality field what happened at the 1992 NIH consensus development conference on impotence. I don't want to wake up a couple of years from now and find a sexuality report about women that is as limited and biased as the one produced about men (NIH, 1993). Topics other than the strictly biomedical were given very short shrift, and there was no opportunity for insight from most areas within sexology. I participated in that conference, and I don't want that disappointing chapter repeated with women.

We must acknowledge that the difficulty of designing meaningful sex research is partly due to the poor preparation available to current clinical sex researchers. In addition, many clinical sex researchers are uncomfortable with real-life sexuality. They avoid looking too closely at the psychology of sexuality. They protect themselves with standardized questionnaires translated into many languages and by sticking strictly to a vocabulary of acts. Perhaps researchers are embarrassed to ask about what people feel and want sexually, about what sexuality means in people's lives and relationships. Researchers avoid inquiring too closely about how eroticism is connected to deeply personal longings for affirmation, to the avoidance of inner doubt, to the need for power, and to a secure sense of identity. Researchers talk instead about sexual desire, arousal, and activity as if these were natural and universal, spontaneous and standardizable, comparable in people and rats.

Sexual psychology is not the only area that researchers resist looking at too closely. They also view sexual culture, especially the workings of gender as a major element in sexual culture, as a threatening topic. Gender is complicated; it's not just a label that refers to how people with different genitals are socialized. Gender is fundamentally about how power works in society, and here I can only refer interested sex researchers to the ever-growing literature on gender and sexuality for further elaboration (Lancaster & di Leonardo, 1997).

As a feminist scholar, I am shocked when I hear the repeated claim by researchers in this new field of female sexual dysfunction (FSD) that there's been no research on women's sexuality. There are truckloads and warehouses full of research on women's sexuality detailing how gender and sexuality intertwine to make the history of women's sexual experience the story of diverse forms of suppression and resistance. For 25 years the women's health movement and the feminist therapy movement have perfected treatments for women's sexual complaints, focusing on psychoeducation, assertiveness training, corrective physiology education, body image reclamation, masturbation education, and work on shame and other forms of inhibition (Daniluk, 1998; McCormick, 1994; Tiefer, 1996b). Given the disregard of this literature by the "new" researchers, do you wonder why feminists like Judy Norsigian of the Boston Women's Health Collective have been so ready to express their concerns about this conference in the *Boston Globe* (Kong, 1999)?

Sexual benefits are ubiquitously promised to women by many sectors of society, especially those that stand to make a profit. "Wear these clothes . . . use this face cream . . . swallow a few of these pills." Fortunately, women started not only the women's liberation movement, but the consumer movement. The new FSD initiative will have to prove its good intentions are more than just a rhetorical front.

Perhaps this helps explain to you why I and some other feminists took the extraordinary and audacious step of using the press to put some pressure on this meeting (Tiefer, 1999b). We want it to live up to its potential of offering a new initiative for research, not just multidisciplinary window-dressing for either commercial interests whose only goal is profit or careerism uninformed by a larger vision of women's social predicaments.

As both a feminist and sister researcher, then, let me call on you to include these five issues in your research:

1. Study all the consequences, both the benefits and the harms, of your interventions. The erectile dysfunction movement was poor at this.
2. Abjure a vision of women's sexuality that standardizes sexuality and neglects how social class, sexual orientation, religion, race, and nationality don't just affect, but literally coconstruct, the meaning of genital acts and the experience of sexual subjectivity. There's a large body of literature on the social construction of sexuality and I have prepared a bibliography for those interested.
3. Be alert to the insidious dangers of commercialization of your research. Sex sells. If you didn't know it before Viagra, you know it now. But, we are not in the retail business. Try to keep the new FSD society out of the pockets of the pharmaceutical industry. Remember what your mother taught you—there's no free lunch.
4. Be alert to how the pressures of industry affect the design and conduct of sexuopharmacological research, influencing categories in epidemiological

research so as to expand the potential market for drug products, drawing inclusion criteria so as to eliminate participants unlikely to show positive results, and designing outcome measures so as to maximize positive results (Tiefer, 2000). These factors can have misleading and damaging impact on people who use the drug products after the trials are over.

5. Open your meetings for true interdisciplinary collaboration. Make sure you have a sliding fee scale, liberal scholarship opportunities, affordable housing, and student work exchange.

6. Finally, 25 years of feminist research has taught us a great deal about the complex methods, concepts, and politics involved in research on gender, which can immeasurably enrich research on women's sexual problems and complaints. There is no need to reinvent the wheel, and political pressure will no longer permit bypassing it.

chapter 4

BOOK REVIEW:
A NEW SEXUAL WORLD—NOT!

Review of *For Women Only: A Revolutionary Guide to Over-coming Sexual Dysfunction and Reclaiming Your Sexual Life* by Laura and Jennifer Berman with Elisabeth Bumiller (New York, Henry Holt & Co., 2001).

Meet the Berman sisters, Laura and Jennifer. One a Ph.D. in sex education, one an M.D. in urology. Both thirty-something moms. You've seen them on *Oprah* and in *Vogue*—white, blond, thin, perfect teeth, perfect pearls, always smiling. The Bermans, promoted by public relations money from the pharmaceutical industry, are having their 15 minutes of fame as the poster-women of the new pharmacological management of women's sexuality, and now you can read their book (written with, probably by, journalist Elisabeth Bumiller), *For Women Only: A Revolutionary Guide to Overcoming Sexual Dysfunction and Reclaiming Your Sexual Life*.

The Bermans' popularity is largely a public relations phenomenon, but their book is worth reviewing to show how their neo-medical point of view signifies another turn in the ever-changing reframing of women's sexuality. It's a perpetual revolution, ladies, and we must know which way the wind blows lest we get blown down, over, or worst of all, back. We're dealing here with the old one-two punch—the politics of patriarchy and the politics of profit. Cultural analysts have identified expert-author advice books such as this one as primary influences on the regulation of sexual norms over the last century. The heavily biomedical twist to *For Women Only* adds a new, conservative chapter to this genre, and looks to me like an attempt simultaneously to affirm and undermine feminist claims to women's self-determination.

Five minutes in the U.S.A. reveals that consumer culture is conflicted about sex. On the one hand, commercial media promote an anarchic cafeteria of sexual styles and satisfactions, while on the other hand, deviation from norms of sexual attractiveness, sexual partnering and correct orgasmic performance continues to be stigmatized. The American public, lacking the kind of Scandinavian or Dutch comprehensive sex education that permits ease with the subject of sex, remains confused and insecure. Who really knows about sex? Where should one turn for advice? There are zillions of new web sites, magazine articles, and products that all ratchet up the hype: sex is great, orgasm is mind-blowing, use it or lose it, know yourself, don't be a freak. But the cacophony just adds to people's anxiety. The confusion is especially intense for LGBT folk, who have double the challenge to read between lines, deconstruct, and find personal relevance in hyped prime-time sex that uses their sexuality only to accessorize the straight message. Little attention is paid to diversity or subjectivity in either the straight or bent world, and everyone suffers.

The message of the Bermans' book is that satisfactory sex is largely a matter of correct physical function (arousal and orgasm), and that there's more to know about (and worry about) in your genital neuroanatomy and blood flow than you've ever dreamt of. The reader learns this as the Bermans describe the experience of women going through the routine two-day workup at their new UCLA Women's Sexual Health Clinic. They indicate that women of all sexual orientations are welcome, and I think it is important to understand how, in the Bermans' medical world, all vulvas are the same, and all women attached to them deserve the same medical approach. This, of course, is both deeply respectful and ignorant.

We begin on page one with "Nicole," a 40-year-old Kentuckian, who read about the Bermans in a magazine article and came for a consultation because she had "no interest in sex." I'm going to describe Nicole's workup (the routine, two-appointment Berman workup) in detail, and then analyze it, because the workup shows how the medical model represented by the Bermans "manages" sex, whether gay or straight.

Nicole began her workup on the first day by completing several short questionnaires asking her to rate her sexual desire, ability to become aroused, level of lubrication, genital sensations, ability to reach orgasm, pain during intercourse, satisfaction with sex partner's sexual stimulation techniques, and feelings of emotional intimacy during sex. (Probably a lesbian patient would receive the same forms and "simply" be instructed to omit the intercourse questions.) Then Nicole was interviewed for 45 minutes by Laura Berman, the sex educator and therapist. Nicole said she thought her sex problems followed laser surgery for vulvar skin cancer three years previously. She disclosed her current use of Paxil for depression, her conservative sexual upbringing, her lifelong difficulty with sex unless she drank alcohol, her non-masturbation history, her fear of vibrators and her male partner's recent intermittent impotence. Many interesting elements here, but medical model workups, like thousand-mile auto checkups, require that the candidate move swiftly along from test to test, so that the mechanic/healer can get the "whole picture."

Without missing a beat, Nicole is next shuttled off to Jennifer, the urologist, for a "full gynecological and urological exam" including medical history (we learn of a long history of bladder infections), extensive blood work (several hormone measures), genital anatomy exam, vaginal pH test, clitoral and labial sensation test using a small vibrator device called a biothesiometer (Jennifer tells Nicole her labial sensation is low), vaginal muscle test done by slowly inflating a balloon device in the vagina, ultrasound to visualize clitoral and labial bloodflow, and internal vaginal and uterine bloodflow test with a vaginal "tampon" device. All these measures were in the normal range, Jennifer says. Lesbian patients might find the attention to vaginal normalcy less than maximally relevant, but my guess is that Jennifer Berman, like most M.D.s, would feel that a complete assessment of all functional parts is necessary. The focus is on function, not pleasure, after all, and the medical model requires all parts to function before a patient can pass the exam.

Next Nicole gets a vibrator and a pair of 3-D surround sound video glasses and watches an erotic video while genitally stimulating herself in private for 15 minutes. Jennifer tells her "that the goal is to become maximally aroused so we can get the best measurements." Afterward, Nicole "shyly" reports that she liked the vibrator, but there's no time to get into that. Back to Jennifer's consulting room to get on the table and repeat all the clitoral, labial, and vaginal measures now that Nicole's self-stimulation has produced some genital blood flow. Quite a first day in L.A.

Back in Laura Berman's office, Nicole asked what the authors say is the "single most common question in our practice: 'Do you think it's in my head?'" They give what is probably their most common answer, "Absolutely not," soothing Nicole by saying that there was no doubt the genital surgery had "affected the sensory nerves to her labia and minor branches of the clitoris, making it difficult for her to become maximally aroused and have an orgasm." They add that there are obvious relationship issues and traumatic emotional consequences of her cancer diagnosis and genital surgery.

The next day Nicole returns and gets some (amount undisclosed) Viagra one hour before repeating all the tests and measures. She has an orgasm while using the vibrator while watching the erotic movie. Way to go, Nicole! "She left our clinic with a prescription for Viagra, which she now takes on a regular basis, and was referred to a trained sex therapist in her hometown." Read the lines, and read between the lines, and you will understand what is going on in the contemporary management of women's sexual dissatisfactions.

Let's analyze some of the elements of Nicole's workup sequence to see what I mean by reading between the lines.

1. Nicole reads about the Bermans in a magazine (she reads magazines and believes in them, magazines select and recommend medico-expert sexual authority). Nicole was able to afford a trip to L.A. and a 2-day consultation. Good insurance or a hefty bank account, assertive, able to travel, can leave her job, her family didn't prevent her. This is not true for all the women who'll read this book or watch the Bermans on *Oprah*, that's for sure.

2. Nicole is welcomed as a patient, alone, at the L.A. clinic. Sex is constructed as an individual matter in the medical world view, but it may be completely the wrong model for some people or couples or life stages. The idea that sexuality is something co-constructed, like friendship, rather than something "inside" each individual, is alien to the medical model.

3. The Bermans' narrative tells us that Nicole is 40, a bank loan officer and from Kentucky, but we learn nothing about her marital status (almost all patients in the book are heterosexual and partnered, but in the postfeminist age, actual marital status is unimportant), nationality, ethnicity, social class, level of education, religion, etc. These factors are unimportant in the universal-body medicalized mentality, and the fact that they are not mentioned causes the reader of this book not to think about them, either.

4. The workup begins with short questionnaires that presume shared meanings of words like desire, arousal and satisfaction. In fact, we don't all agree what such words mean, but medical questionnaires teach women to think of their sexual lives in medical language, leaving out issues of love, spirituality, or multiple motives. The sex to be discussed is a mechanically complex, but conceptually uncomplicated, process. Filling out these questionnaires prepares women to accept doctors' sexuo-mechanical world view, which wouldn't bother me so much if we also had culturally validated humanistic sex experts to consult.

5. In Nicole's 45-minute interview with Laura Berman, Nicole discusses her sex history within the professional's framework. Having myself conducted thousands of these brief, clinic interviews in more than a decade's hospital employment, I learned a lot about people in them, but the constraints of time eventually led me to be less and less interested in the nuances, since I wouldn't have time to follow up in any meaningful way. I began simply looking for red flags. Since this is Nicole's only opportunity (maybe in her whole life) for an extensive sex discussion with a person comfortable talking about sex, the brevity is a tragic tease.

6. The medical tests conducted by Jennifer Berman are a fascinating combination of science and mumbo-jumbo. Most of the tests have no valid norms at the present time, so there is no way to know what the measurements mean. Again, as in her interview with Laura Berman, Nicole exposes her sexuality to an expert and asks for guidance about norms, but gets back bland medical reassurance unsupported by sexual science. The impact on the reader of all this scientificism is likely to be especially disturbing, creating insecurity about the health of her own vaginal pH, vaginal muscles, clitoral blood flow, etc. This is another tragic tease.

7. The directed masturbation is probably worth the price of Nicole's air travel, though I doubt it's what her insurance company thinks it is paying for. Nothing like a little implosion now and again to introduce women to sexual possibilities they never learned about at home. Of course, learning about vibrators and self-stimulation may be less novel to lesbian patients. Nicole's masturbation is better with Viagra on the second day? Maybe. I wonder if just doing it twice was the crucial matter. After all, Nicole had never laid hands on one of these devices before. This is another tragic moment, when Nicole is led to believe that Viagra has helped her, so now she takes it on "a regular basis." Nicole, are you listening? Throw those pills away! The FDA has not approved Viagra for use by women, and there is no evidence from your workup that you actually need it.

8. Most cases presented in the book are unresolved, as is Nicole's. There is practically no long-term follow up anywhere. Most women leave with prescriptions for testosterone or DHEA (a type of male hormone) or Viagra, some leave with some psychological insights and recommendations for further therapy, but the Bermans offer no information on how the sex lives of most of the women and couples work out.

The Bermans want their book to be reassuring and encouraging to women, and I think most readers will learn something. There's lots of interesting information about sexual development, communication between partners, and sexual psychology. There's lots of interesting information about sexual biology, too, although it's mixed in with untested nouveau ideas about soy, testosterone, and the all-important genital blood flow. It would be hard for most readers to separate out the valid from the speculative. The book has lots of interesting genital diagrams, though you can find them in plenty of feminist books. Jennifer Berman talks about how pelvic surgery is often done without regard to the sexual consequences for women and how she is determined to do some relevant research on this. That's good. I hope she writes about this after she has some data.

There are lengthy descriptions of all the new (as-yet untested and unapproved) pills, cream, potions, and patches, but you can find these in a minute on the Internet. Though the Bermans frequently pay lip service to the value of psychological treatments in helping women with sexual dissatisfaction, they recommend that almost everyone should take supplementary androgen of one sort or another. The one lesbian case they discuss (1 page out of 246) gets a little communication skill training and a little testosterone supplement. We are told the couple's sexual relationship improved "tremendously." In their resource pages, only one lesbian resource is listed (GLOBAL—Gay and Lesbian Organizations Bridging across the Lands).

I suppose this book will come and go while *Our Bodies, Ourselves* and its various teammates (e.g., *Ourselves Growing Older*) continue to sell, be taught, get translated, and evolve. I sincerely hope so. But I am greatly concerned by the huge amount of marketing that's going on around the new pharmaco-medicalization approach to women's sexual lives. Pfizer and the other mega-companies are enormously involved in the sexuality education of medical students and in postgraduate continuing medical education. Doctors are learning to ask a few simple questions and prescribe drugs. I think this is crazy, but maybe it's just me. New drugs are sexy, and new sex drugs are really sexy, and it's hard to fight the trend.

Extensive knowledge about sexual experience, especially from the subjective and interpersonal dimensions, is simply not being developed. Health and science journalists are ill-trained to challenge the new drug claims, and just saying no gets boring. The average citizen has no idea of the immense profitability of blockbuster drugs and what companies will do to have them succeed. The discourse of sexual rights as the route to sexual emancipation and pleasure is growing in other parts of the world (Latin America, Africa, Asia, and Eastern Europe, in particular), and I predict that this direction will offer more emancipating opportunities than the medicalized discourse so prominent in the United States. I hope the Bermans' book will be read and deconstructed widely by people interested in the social construction of sexuality. As a text, it's fascinating. As an advice book, it worries me greatly.

THE PINK VIAGRA STORY: WE HAVE THE
DRUG, BUT WHAT'S THE DISEASE?

Ever since Viagra put a spring in the step of millions of
impotent men after coming onto the market in March
[1998], attention has been focused on the more mysterious
key to sexual gratification among women. (Campbell, 1998)

Another way to put this would be, "Ever since Viagra proved to the
pharmaceutical industry that contemporary sexual confusions and dissatisfactions could be medicalized and marketed (to the sweet cash register ring of
billions of dollars and Euros), companies have been searching for some way
to make women into sex problem consumer-patients." News media around
the world have tirelessly chronicled the "hunt for the female Viagra,"[1] which,
as of the date of this writing (June, 2003), still lacks a definitive quarry.

The problem has been that before pink Viagras or other such products
could be tested, approved, and sold to the public, there had to be clarity on
exactly what disease or disorder the drug would be treating. And despite
huge industry expense and the involvement of multitudes of doctors, marketers, and health journalists, there has been no consensus on a targetable
women's sexual disorder that could work for the industry as men's erectile
dysfunction had.

Clarifying women's sexual function and dysfunction has become not
only complicated, but contentious, and therein lies an interesting story
about sexuality, medicalization, globalization, and feminism.

Sexuality in
Contemporary Life and Culture

Sexual options become more interesting every day. Now we have reality shows on television that not only showcase sexual attractiveness, but feature real (maybe) longing, lust, pursuit, rejection, and jealousy along with the endless expanses of flesh. For seemingly insatiable audiences of men and women, gay and straight, old and young, mass media offer a continuous Roman orgy.

Background social shifts such as increased longevity, a new freedom of choice about relationships, and new goals for recreation and physical well-being set the stage for changes in sexual life. Publicity about HIV-AIDS and campaigns against international sexual trafficking make the public aware of how diverse and driven sexual life can be. And then there are the ever present stories about celebrities' sexual lives which have filled the press since the time of penny papers. Results of social science surveys, perhaps stimulated by publicity about new drugs and the apparent primacy of sexual life for the ubiquitous celebrities, show that ordinary people expect more in the way of perfect performance from their sexual lives than they used to.

Ironically, all this sexuality promotion coexists with only the most rudimentary sexuality education in most regions save Scandinavia and Northern Europe. The idea of comprehensive sexuality education that would include an understanding of identities, bodies, and relationships, introduce cross-cultural variation, and dispassionately describe value systems is certainly lacking in the U.S. and U.K. People are somehow supposed to be able to figure out the vicissitudes of sexual life from their own experience, the teachings of family and other authorities, and the hyped and confusing messages from the media. Good luck.

Midwifing "Female Sexual Dysfunction"

The dilemmas and anxieties of contemporary sexual life create a variety of markets, not least of which is a medical market for obtaining sexual information and managing sexual uncertainty and dissatisfaction. As women's sexual entitlement (at least in industrialized nations) grew through the 1970s and 1980s, women were freer to pursue sex—but what sex would they pursue? What forms would satisfaction take?

Orgasm widely became the presumed measure of women's satisfaction in both feminist writing and sex research by the middle 1970s. Revoking Freud's dismissal of clitoral pleasure was a major feminist triumph and segued into the assumption that orgasm should be as important and valued for women as it is for men. Some feminists argued that orgasm could become a new tyranny and source of pressure, but sexual self-determination without goalposts was too anarchic to become popular.

By the late 1990s, physicians gathered at meetings sponsored by the pharmaceutical industry to discuss the complaints they were hearing from women about low sexual interest and difficulty with arousal and orgasm. In some cases, these seemed to be women with a history of disease or medical treatment (surgery, chemotherapy) who felt newly emboldened to raise sexual complaints and newly hopeful about medical remedies. In most cases, however, these were women whose complaints lacked identifiable medical causes, whose expectations had been raised by the media, who had partners who expected more from them, and who turned for advice and relief to physicians as a result of "disease awareness campaigns" that suggested doctors had much to offer in the way of sexual health.

Instead of taking the new public interest in women's sexual life as an opportunity for collaborative research with feminist scholars, social scientists, and relationship experts, however, leading physicians and sexologists allowed themselves to be drawn into a narrowly focused industry-dominated perspective whose sole purpose was developing a medical sexual rhetoric suited for new diagnoses and new drugs. By 1998, experts in secret industry-sponsored meetings were refining a list of sexual disorders for women—too little desire, problems with arousal and orgasm, pain—basically the same list as for men—that made sex into a medical function like digestion, and opened the gates to over-the-counter and prescription-only products. The list of disorders became a new problem, "female sexual dysfunction," and journalists began to follow the story of the search for its treatments with articles like "Rx for Sex," "The Science of 'O'," "Designing Women," and "The Search for the Lady Viagra."[2]

The Medical
Steamroller Meets a Bump in the Road

Unexpectedly, however, there were problems in the drug development process, and after five years of intense effort, surprised physicians and researchers are now saying that women's sexual function and satisfaction is mysterious, complicated, and certainly different from men's (Duenwald, 2003). The favorite slide at sexology conferences around the world these days shows two metal boxes, one with a single up and down switch, and the other with many knobs and buttons of different shapes and sizes. The first box is labeled "men's sexuality" and the second, "women's sexuality." Does this sound familiar—"What DO women want?"

The stumbling block turned out to involve both diagnosis and new drug evaluation. The drug evaluation problem was what outcome measure to use in clinical trials for women. For erectile problems in men, drug companies basically just asked "Is it harder?" and "Does it last longer?" The answers were quantifiable and statistics could be used to show whether drugs "worked" or not. But, lacking a penis or other visible sign of sexual functioning, women's sexual satisfactions turned out to be more difficult to measure. Should success of a drug for women be gauged by more orgasms? More sexual encounters? Higher self-reported arousal or pleasure?

The U.S. Food and Drug Administration says it will reject purely physical measures like genital temperature and bloodflow in assessing drug trial results. But it also will reject purely subjective measures like "enjoys sex more." The smart money is on statistically validated questionnaires that combine event-counting and subjective assessment. The first drug to consistently and reliably reduce "sexual distress" in women with defined complaints of sexual arousal or desire will probably be approved to treat "female sexual dysfunction."

But the bigger problem has turned out to be channeling women's sexual complaints into specific diagnoses—hence the many knobs and buttons. It turns out that the list of sexual disorders for women developed in the industry-sponsored meetings—too little desire, problems with arousal and orgasm, pain—don't work too well. There are no unambiguous biological measures to slot women into one category or another, and women's own descriptions of arousal and desire often overlap. Many women report several complaints. Moreover, although drugs tested so far frequently affect genital measures of blood flow, they don't improve sexual distress and satisfaction ratings. This has led to scientists' epiphany that women's sexual lives are contextualized, that is, that sexual experience depends as much or more on social context (relationship, cultural background, past sexual experiences) as on genital functioning. This is news?

Towards a Progressive Perspective of Sexual Problems

The explanation that "women are different" has both advantages and disadvantages for progressive sexual medicine. Looking at social context could bring awareness and attention to issues of sexual abuse and assault, insecure body image, anxiety and depression, lack of sexual knowledge and access to reproductive health care, and the many ways in which male supremacy still thrives in sexual life. Improving these "contextual" matters will unquestionably improve women's sexual opportunities for pleasure and satisfaction. I suspect clinical trials repeatedly report equivalent responses to placebos and to active drugs because of the sex education and encouragement that are part of the trial.[3] I would think a doctor with a clipboard cooing, "Gee, that's great, let's see how you do next week," could go a long way in correcting a disadvantageous context—at least temporarily.

Eventually, researchers might recognize that sexual life is contextualized for both men and women, and that men are not simply sexual robots. Men's social privilege allows their context to be invisible, like being a fish in water or a rich shopper in Saks Fifth Avenue. Cultural entitlements for men to be sexual and scripts that call for men to initiate sexual encounters favor men's arousal. Similarly, the "coital imperative" and the active role men take in sex make it likely that men will regularly experience pleasure and orgasm in their encounters. Men aren't lucky in their biology; they have the context going for them.

The disadvantage of the new "women are different" rhetoric, of course, is that it naturalizes the categories of "men" and "women," produces endless ghastly sociobiologizing, and may never lead physicians and researchers to the awareness that sexual life is contextualized for everyone. Women's sexuality can be ghettoized by any theory, and I can imagine a generation of experts in new women's sexual health centers teaching the "men are from Mars, women are from Venus" philosophy that women's sexuality is relational and contextual and touchy-feely. That would be terrible.

Backlash Against Big Pharma

The global pharmaceutical industry is extremely large, wealthy, and powerful. A temporary delay in developing the perfect outcome measure for drug trials or in creating workable diagnostic categories for recruiting patients for those trials may be no more than just a temporary delay. It may be—it probably will be—that in a year or two, female arousal and desire drugs will be as widely available and as widely praised as Viagra and the Viagra wannabees now emerging from Lilly and Bayer.

But, the search for the Pink Viagra is occurring just as a new backlash against the global pharmaceutical industry is picking up steam. Editorials in medical journals (e.g., "Is academic medicine for sale," in the 2000 *New England Journal of Medicine*) and entire issues of the *British Medical Journal* (e.g., April 13, 2002 on "Too Much Medicine" and May 31, 2003 on "No Free Lunch") indicate that aspects of the medical community are opposed to excessive pharmaceutical industry involvement in advertisement, medical research, training, organizations, publications, and continuing education.[4]

This backlash dovetails with the analysis and critique of "medicalization" over the past several decades within sociology, the women's health movement, the "anti-psychiatry" movement, and newly, from cultural historians examining the social construction of illness and disease. All these scholars argue that the medical model, with its hallmark elements of mind-body dualism, universalism, individualism, and biological reduction, is not well suited to many of the challenges of contemporary life and suffering.

Yet, at the same time, patient advocacy groups are clamoring for medical legitimacy, increased funding and research, and, above all, new drug treatments. And the drug industry continues to expand.

Allying with the backlash, I convened a "Campaign for a new view of women's sexual problems" in 2000 to provide a feminist anti-medicalization perspective in the debate about "female sexual dysfunction."[5] Salvation is in the struggle, they say, but I still think I'll live to see that pink pill.

Notes

1. Many "Pink Viagra" stories, especially ones including critique, are listed on and linked to http://www.fsd-alert.org/press.html.

2. See footnote 1.

3. A recent American Urological Association conference abstract (May, 2003) reported that a cream for FSD improved things 50–60% depending on dose, but the placebo improved things 54%. A high placebo rate is true in the erectile dysfunction literature, also.

4. Many links to medical literature publications on the backlash against the pharmaceutical industry can be found in section IV on http://www.fsd-alert.org/links.html.

5. http://www.fsd-alert.org.

CONCLUSION: WE NEED
THEORY, WE NEED POLITICS

I got into sexology accidentally, and it has taken me many years to get the big picture of the sexuality knowledge-making players and their interests, roles of mass media, what's true and what's tradition, and the way social construction works. The story of sex, as with any social construction, is constantly evolving, and that makes understanding it difficult.

As sexual excitement, desire, and activities come to be more highly valued in society, our understanding needs to incorporate the effects of more hyperbolic media expert messages, more advertised products to promote sexual excitement, changes in role model behavior, etc. That's how social construction works. Just because you understand that something isn't "natural" or part of some evolutionary drive doesn't mean you actually get how it *does* work. To understand sexual excitement, for example, you need to understand how psychology, biology and society interact and change. Expectations play such a large role that it helps to grasp the sociology of consumption, the backdrop recent history of patents and governmental deregulation, and how people from different backgrounds read and internalize cultural messages about identity and social worth. Students often ask me where to go to train to become a sexologist. There is no easy answer because sexuality is a multidisciplinary construction. Start someplace, I say, get good at it, and keep moving.

Accepting the premise that sexuality is socially constructed is just the beginning. I could tell you so many clinical stories that would show how the myth of naturalism kept people ignorant of the very factors that would make their sexual lives happier. Yet, these same people cling to the myth of naturalism defensively, i.e., so as to avoid having to admit their true fears, hopes, insecurities, or examine where they come from and how they can change.

Well, a couple of clinical anecdotes will have to suffice (details disguised, as is usual in these matters). Consider John, a young man who has satisfactory erections when he masturbates, but mostly non-erections when he is with his girlfriend, Mary, due to his anxieties about failure, commitment, and loss of control (though he is unaware of all of this at the beginning). Mary has never confronted such a problem, and her personality and values make her react very tensely. She was raised in a strict religious home and is both embarrassed to discuss sex with John and ambivalent about "too much time" spent in sexual acts other than no-hands intercourse. Also, she is somewhat of a perfectionist who takes everything as criticism. Thus, despite all evidence to the contrary, she feels John's problem must be her fault ("is he really attracted to me?") and she is defensive and resentful about cooperating in sex therapy treatment. John doesn't "believe" in psychology, and anxiously forgets many of the ideas about relaxation, communication, and sensuality that he reads in the self-help books the therapist assigns. Viagra "works" for him physically, but Mary "knows" when he takes it because his face gets flushed, and she gets angry because she feels pressured to have sex on his schedule. Almost a year of weekly sessions devoted to unpacking each of these elements is required as their love life gradually becomes fun and intimate rather than a source of despair and irritation.

Or, consider Michael (or Eric or Carl or Ellen or Jennifer -ñ I have seen many cases just like this), a person who is very interested in sex when a relationship is new, but who loses interest after about a year and actually develops an aversion to making love with the otherwise dear partner. In the past the person regarded the loss of sexual interest as a signal to move on, but now s/he is beginning to think maybe there's more to it. Often, both partners are in their 30s and wanting to be in a committed relationship. The loss of sexual interest is a mystery. Resolving the problem takes excavating individual and couple meanings of pleasure, safety, commitment, habits, expectations, discomforts, etc. Some couples end up together (and much closer) and others learn that their partner choices came from weakness and fear.

Well, this isn't a textbook on sex therapy. It's a book that attempts to complicate the popular sexual picture and offer some new directions. There's so much work that needs to be done. Bring on those little sex bookmobiles I mentioned in the introduction. Elect those pro-sex-research politicians. Roll back the cozy corporate-academic relationships. Get rid of those lying ads for magic pills, patches, and potions. Figure out how those gender theories actually apply to your sexual desires. Well, it's what I would recommend, at least. If you have a better idea, let me know.

REFERENCES

Abramson, P. R. (1990). Sexual science: Emerging discipline or oxymoron? *Journal of Sex Research* 27, 147–165.

Altman, L. K. (April 29, 1997). Experts see bias in drug data. *New York Times*, pp. C1, C8.

American Psychiatric Association (APA) (1952). *Diagnostic and Statistical Manual of Mental Disorders*. Washington, D.C.: APA.

_____. (1968). *Diagnostic and Statistical Manual of Mental Disorders*, 2nd ed. Washington, D.C.: APA.

_____. (1980). *Diagnostic and Statistical Manual of Mental Disorders*, 3rd ed. Washington, D.C.: APA.

_____. (1987). *Diagnostic and Statistical Manual of Mental Disorders*, 3rd rev. ed. Washington, D.C.: APA.

_____. (1994). *Diagnostic and Statistical Manual of Mental Disorders*, 4th ed. Washington, D.C.: APA.

Angell, M. (2000). Is academic medicine for sale? *New England Journal of Medicine* 342, 1516–1518.

Ansell, J. S. (1987). Trends in urological manpower in the United States in 1986. *Journal of Urology* 138, 473–476.

Arno, P. S. and Feiden, K. L. (1992) *Against the Odds: The story of AIDS drug development, politics and profits*. New York: HarperCollins, Inc.

Aron, C. S. (1999). *Working at Play: A history of vacations in the United States*. New York: Oxford University Press.

Aronowitz, R. A. (1998). *Making Sense of Illness: Science, society and disease*. New York: Cambridge University Press.

Ballance, R. H. (1996). Market and industrial structure. In P. Davis, ed., *Contested Ground: Public purpose and private interest in the regulation of prescription drugs*. New York: Oxford University Press, pp. 95–108.

Bancroft, J. (1989). *Human Sexuality and Its Problems*, 2nd ed. Edinburgh: Churchill-Livingstone. (1st ed. published in 1983.)

_____. (1993). But what is psychogenic erectile dysfunction? *International Journal of Impotence Research* 5, 205–206.

_____. ed. (1999). *Researching Sexual Behavior*. Bloomington: Indiana University Press.

Barbach, L. G. (1975). *For Yourself: The fulfillment of female sexuality*. New York: Signet.

Barnes, B., Bloor, D., and Henry, J. (1996). *Scientific Knowledge: A sociological analysis*. Chicago: University of Chicago Press.

Barreca, R. (ed.) (1996). *The Penguin Book of Women's Humor*. New York: Penguin Books.

Barsky, A. J. (1988). *Worried Sick: Our troubled quest for wellness*. Boston: Little, Brown.

Basson, R. (2000). The Female Sexual Response revisited. *Journal of the Society of Obstetrics and Gynecology of Canada* 22, 383–387.

Basson, R., Berman, J., Burnett, A., Derogatis, L., Ferguson, D., Fourcroy, J., Goldstein, I., Grazziottin, A., Heiman, J., Laan, E., Leiblum, S., Padma-Nathan, H., Rosen, R., Segraves, K., Segraves, R. T., Shabsigh, R., Sipski, M., Wagner, M., and Whipple, B. (2000). Report on the International Consensus Development Conference on Female Sexual Dysfunction: Definitions and classifications. *Journal of Urology* 163, 888–893.

Baxendale, Hadley V. (1974). *Are Children Neglecting Their Mothers?* Garden City, N.Y.: Doubleday & Co., Inc.

Bayer, R. (1981). *Homosexuality and American Psychiatry.* New York: Basic Books.

Beach, F. A. (1956). Characteristics of masculine "sex drive." In M. R. Jones, ed., *Nebraska Symposium on Motivation.* Lincoln: University of Nebraska Press.

Bem, S. L. (1981). Gender schema theory: A cognitive account of sex typing. *Psychological Review* 88, 354–364.

_____. (1993). *The Lenses of Gender: Transforming the debate on sexual inequality.* New Haven: Yale University Press.

Bennett, P. and Rosario, V. A., eds. (1995). *Solitary Pleasures: The historical, literary, and artistic discourses of eroticism.* New York: Routledge.

Berscheid, E. (1999). The greening of relationship science. *American Psychologist* 54, 260–266.

Birke, L. (1986). *Women, Feminism and Biology: The feminist challenge.* New York: Methuen.

Blakeslee, S. (1993). New therapies are helping men to overcome impotence. *New York Times,* June 2, section C, p. 12.

Blaun, R. (1987). Dealing with impotence. *New York,* March 30, pp. 50–58.

Bleier, R. (1986). Sex differences research: Science or belief? In R. Bleier, ed., *Feminist Approaches to Science.* New York: Pergamon.

Bloch, M., and Bloch, J. H. (1980). Women and the dialectics of nature in 18th century French thought. In C. P. MacCormack and M. Strathern, eds., *Nature, Culture and Gender.* Cambridge: Cambridge University Press.

Blumenthal, D., Causino, N., Campbell, E. and Louis, K. S. (1996). Relationships between academic institutions and industry in the life sciences—An industry survey. *The New England Journal of Medicine* 334, 368–373.

Boswell, J. (1990). Concepts, experience and sexuality. *differences* 2, 67–87.

Boyle, M. (1993). Sexual dysfunction or heterosexual dysfunction? *Feminism and Psychology* 3, 73–88.

Bradbury, P. (1985). Desire and pregnancy. In A. Metcalf and M. Humphries, eds., *The Sexuality of Men.* London: Pluto Press.

Bradley, S. G. (1995). Conflict of interest. In F. L. Macrina, ed., *Scientific Integrity: An introductory text with cases.* Washington, D.C.: American Society for Microbiology Press, pp. 161–181.

Brecher, E. M. (1969). *The Sex Researchers.* Boston: Little, Brown & Co.

Brecher, R., and Brecher, E., eds. (1966). *An Analysis of Human Sexual Response.* New York: Signet.

Brody, J. (1988). Personal health. *New York Times,* August 12, section B, p. 4.

Brown, L. S. (1994). *Subversive Dialogues: Theory in feminist therapy.* New York: Basic Books.

Brownlee, S. and Schultz, S. (1999). Dying for sex: The FDA approved Viagra quickly— perhaps too quickly. *U.S. News & World Report,* January 11, p. 62–66.

Bülbül (1973). *I'm Not for Women's Lib . . . but.* Stanford, Cal.: New Seed Press.

Burck, C. & Daniel, G. (1990) Feminism and Strategic Therapy: Contradiction or complementarity. In R. J. Perelberg & A. C. Miller, eds., *Gender and Power in Families.* New York: Routledge.

Burnham, J. C. (1987). *How Superstition Won and Science Lost: Popularizing science and health in the United States.* New Brunswick: Rutgers University Press.

Burris, A. S., Banks, S. M., and Sherins, R. J. (1989). Quantitative assessment of nocturnal penile tumescence and rigidity in normal men using a home monitor. *Journal of Andrology* 10, 492–497.

Buss, D. M. (1994). *The Evolution of Desire: Strategies of human mating.* New York: Basic Books.

Butler, J. (1990). *Gender Trouble: Feminism and the subversion of identity*. New York: Routledge.

Campbell, M. (July 19, 1998). Women's love drug better than Viagra. *Sunday Times of London*, p. 21.

Caplan, P. (1995). *They Say You're Crazy*. Reading, MA: Addison-Wesley.

Caporael, L. R., and Brewer, M. B. (1991). The quest for human nature: Social and scientific issues in evolutionary psychology. *Journal of Social Issues* 47, 1–9.

Carlson, N. R. & Johnson, D. A. (1975) Sexuality Assertiveness Training: A workshop for women. *Counseling Psychologist* 5, 53–59.

Carlson, R. (1971). Where is the person in personality research? *Psychological Bulletin* 75, 203–219.

Chapkis, W. (1986). *Beauty Secrets: Women and the politics of appearance*. Boston: South End Press.

Christensen, C. (1995) Prescribed Masturbation in Sex Therapy: A critique. *Journal of Sex and Marital Therapy* 21, 87–99.

Churcher, S. (1980). The anguish of the transsexuals. *New York*, June 16, pp. 40–49.

Cline, S. (1993). *Women, Passion and Celibacy*. New York: Carol Southern Books.

Clement, U. (1990). Surveys of heterosexual behavior. *Annual Review of Sex Research* 1, 45–74.

_____ (1999). Coding interactional sexual scripts. In J. Bancroft, ed., *Researching Sexual Behavior*. Bloomington: Indiana University Press, pp. 341–345.

Cohen, J. (July 6, 1998). Anticlimax department: At the urologists' convention, Viagra's unsung expert witnesses. *The New Yorker*, p. 26.

Conrad, P., and Kern, R., eds. (1981). *The Sociology of Health and Illness: Critical perspectives*. New York: St. Martin's Press.

Conrad, P., and Schneider, J. W. (1980). *Deviance and Medicalization: From badness to sickness*. St. Louis: C. V. Mosby.

Corner, G. W. (1961). Foreword. In W. C. Young, ed., *Sex and Internal Secretions*, vol. 1, 3rd ed. Baltimore: Williams and Wilkins.

Crawford, R. (1977). You are dangerous to your health: The ideology and politics of victim blaming. *International Journal of Health Services* 7, 663–680.

Daniluk, J. C. (1998). *Women's Sexuality Across the Life Span*. New York: Guilford Press.

Davidson, J. K. & Darling, C. A. (1993). Masturbatory guilt and sexual responsiveness among post-college-age women: Sexual satisfaction revisited. *Journal of Sex and Marital Therapy* 19, 289–300.

Davis, M. S. (1993). *What's So Funny? The comic conception of culture and society*. Chicago: University of Chicago Press.

DeLamater, J. (1981). The social control of sexuality. *Annual Review of Sociology* 7, 263–290.

Diamond, J. M. (1997). *Why Is Sex Fun? The evolution of human sexuality*. New York: HarperCollins.

Dickson, D. (1988). *The New Politics of Science*. Chicago: The University of Chicago Press.

DiMauro, D. (1995). *Sexuality Research in the United States: An assessment of the social and behavioral sciences*. New York: The Social Science Research Council.

Dodson, B. (1974) *Liberating Masturbation*. Union, N.J.: Survey Research Corporation.

_____ (1987). *Sex for One: The Joy of Selfloving*. New York: Crown.

_____ (1991). *Selfloving: A video portrait of a women's sexuality seminar*. Available from www.bettydodson.com.

Duenwald, M. (2003). Effort to make sex drug for women challenges experts. *New York Times*, March 25, p. F5.

Duggan, L. (1990). Review essay: From instincts to politics: Writing the history of sexuality in the US. *Journal of Sex Research* 27, 95–109.

Ehrenreich, B., and English, D. (1978). *For Her Own Good: 150 years of the experts' advice to women*. Garden City, N.Y.: Anchor Press/Doubleday.

Ehrenreich, B., Hess, E., and Jacobs, G. (1986). *Re-making Love: The feminization of sex*. Garden City, N.Y.: Anchor Press, Doubleday.

Eichenwald, K. and Kolata, G. (May 16, 1999). Drug trials hide conflicts for doctors. *New York Times*, pp. 1, 35–36.

Elliott, M. (1985). The use of "impotence" and "frigidity": Why has "impotence" survived? *Journal of Sex and Marital Therapy* 11, 51–56.

Ellison, C. (2000). *Women's Sexualities: Generations of women share intimate secrets of sexual self-acceptance.* Oakland, Cal.: New Harbinger.

Everaerd, W. (1993). Erectile knowledge: Fact and fiction. *International Journal of Impotence Research* 5, 219–220.

Featherstone, M., Hepworth, M., and Turner, B. S., eds. (1991). *The Body: Social process and cultural theory.* Newbury Park, Cal.: Sage Publications.

Federation of Feminist Women's Health Centers (1981). *A New View of a Woman's Body.* New York: Simon & Schuster.

Feldman, H. A., Goldstein, I., Hatzichristou, D. G., Krane, R. J., and McKinlay, J. B. (1994). Impotence and its medical and psychosocial correlates: Results of the Massachusetts male aging study. *Journal of Urology* 151, 54–61.

Ferenz, L. (1997). Ethical considerations of federal guidelines and models of moral responsibility governing neuropharmacologic research. In M. Hertzman and D. E. Feltner, eds., *The Handbook of Psychopharmacology Trials: An overview of scientific, political, and ethical concerns.* New York: New York University Press, pp. 23–45.

Festinger, L. (1954). A theory of social comparison processes. *Human Relations* 7, 117–140.

Fine, M., and Gordon, S. M. (1989). Feminist transformations of/despite psychology. In M. Crawford and M. Gentry, eds., *Gender and Thought: Psychological perspectives.* New York: Springer-Verlag.

Flax, J. (1987). Postmodernism and gender relations in feminist theory. *Signs* 12, 621–644.

Ford, C. S., and Beach, F. A. (1951). *Patterns of Sexual Behavior.* New York: Harper and Row.

Foucault, M. (1978). *The History of Sexuality, Vol. 1, An introduction.* New York: Pantheon. (Originally published in 1976.)

Foucault, M., and Sennett, R. (1982). Sexuality and solitude. *Humanities in Review* 1, 3–21.

Frank, E., Anderson, C., and Rubinstein, D. (1978). Frequency of sexual dysfunction in "normal" couples. *New England Journal of Medicine* 299, 111–115.

Frankel, M. S. (1993). Professional societies and responsible research conduct. In National Academy of Sciences, ed., *Responsible Science: Ensuring the integrity of the research process, vol. II.* Washington, D.C.: National Academy Press.

Freedman, E. B., and D'Emilio, J. (1988). *Intimate Matters: A history of sex in America.* New York: Harper and Row.

Friedan, B. (1976). *It Changed My Life: Writings on the women's movement.* New York: Random House.

Gagnon, J. H. (1973). Scripts and the coordination of sexual conduct. *Nebraska Symposium on Motivation* 21, 27–60.

_____. (1977). *Human Sexualities.* Glenview, Ill.: Scott, Foresman.

_____. (1979). The interaction of gender roles and sexual conduct. In H. A. Katchadourian, ed., *Human Sexuality: A developmental perspective.* Berkeley: University of California Press.

_____. (1985). Attitudes and responses of parents to pre-adolescent masturbation. *Archives of Sexual Behavior* 14, 451–466.

Gagnon, J. H. and Parker, R. G. (1995). Conceiving sexuality. In R. G. Parker and J. H. Gagnon, eds., *Conceiving Sexuality: Approaches to sex research in a postmodern world.* New York: Routledge, pp. 3–16.

Gagnon, J. H., and Simon, W. (1969). Sex education and human development. In P. J. Fink and V. O. Hammet, eds., *Sexual Function and Dysfunction.* Philadelphia: F. A. Davis.

_____. (1973). *Sexual Conduct: The social sources of human sexuality.* Chicago: Aldine.

Gartrell, N. & Mosbacher, D. (1984). Sex differences in the naming of children's genitals. *Sex Roles* 10, 867–876.

Geertz, C. (1980). Sociosexology. *New York Review of Books*, January 24, pp. 3–4.

Gergen, K. J. (1985). The social constructionist movement in modern psychology. *American Psychologist* 40, 266–275.

Gilligan, C. (1982). *In a Different Voice*. Cambridge, Mass.: Harvard University Press.

Goldstein, I. and Berman, J. R. (1998). Vasculogenic female sexual dysfunction: Vaginal engorgement and clitoral erectile insufficiency syndromes. *International Journal of Impotence Research*, 10 suppl. 2, S84–90.

Goldstein, I., Lue, T. F., Padma-Nathan, H., Rosen, R. C., Steers, W. D., and Wicker, P. A., for the Sildenafil study group. (1998). Oral sildenafil in the treatment of erectile dysfunction. *New England Journal of Medicine* 338, 1397–1404.

Grady, D. (1999). Sure, we've got a pill for that. *New York Times*, February 14, sect. 4, P. 1, 5.

Green, R., and Wiener, J. (1980). *Methodology in Sex Research*. Report No. 80–1502. Washington, D.C.: Department of Health and Human Services.

Greer, G. (1971). *The Female Eunuch*. New York: McGraw-Hill.

Guba, E. G. (1990). *The Paradigm Dialog*. Newbury Park, Cal.: Sage Publications.

Hall, D. L. (1974). Biology, sex hormones and sexism in the 1920s. *Philosophical Forum* 5, 81–96.

Hall, L. A. (1991). *Hidden Anxieties: Male sexuality, 1900–1950*. Cambridge, Eng.: Polity Press.

Hall, M. (1993) Why limit me to ecstasy: Toward a positive model of genital incidentalism among friends and other lovers. In E. D. Rothblum & K. A. Brehony, eds., *Boston Marriages: Romantic but asexual relationships among contemporary lesbians*. Amherst: University of Massachusetts Press.

Hall, S. S. (1998). Our memories, our selves. *New York Times Magazine*, February 15, pp. 26–33, 49, 56.

Hamilton, C. (2000). *Our Syndromes, Ourselves*. Kansas City: Andrews McMeel Publishing.

Haraway, D. (1986). Primatology is politics by other means. In R. Bleier, ed., *Feminist Approaches to Science*. New York: Pergamon.

_____ (1991). *Simians, Cyborgs and Women: The reinvention of nature*. New York: Routledge.

Hawton, K. E. (1985). *Sex Therapy*. Oxford: Oxford University Press.

_____ (1992). Sex therapy research: Has it withered on the vine? *Annual Review of Sex Research* 3, 49–72.

Healy, D. (1998). *The Anti-Depressant Era*. Cambridge, Mass.: Harvard University Press.

Heiman, J. R. and Meston, C. M. (1997). Empirically validated treatment for sexual dysfunction. *Annual Review of Sex Research* 8, 148–194.

Heimel, C. (1991). *If You Can't Live With Me, Why Aren't You Dead Yet?* New York: HarperCollins.

Heise, L. (1995). Violence, sexuality and women's lives. In R. G. Parker and J. H. Gagnon, eds. *Conceiving Sexuality: Approaches to sex research in a postmodern world*. New York: Routledge, pp. 109–134.

Hersen, M. and Miller, D. J. (1992). Future directions: A modest proposal. In D. J. Miller and M. Herson, eds., *Research Fraud in the Behavioral and Biomedical Sciences*. New York: John Wiley & Sons. pp. 225–263.

Hightower, J. (1975). *Eat Your Heart Out: Food profiteering in America*. New York: Crown Publishers, Inc.

Hite, S. (1976). *The Hite Report*. New York: Macmillan.

_____. (1987). *Women and Love: A cultural revolution in progress*. New York: A. Knopf.

Hoch, Z., Safir, M., Peres, Y., and Shepher, J. (1981). An evaluation of sexual performance: Comparison between sexually dysfunctional and functional couples. *Journal of Sex and Marital Therapy* 7, 195–206.

Hollender, M. H. & Mercer, A. J. (1976). Wish to be held and wish to hold in men and women. *Archives of General Psychiatry*, 33, 49–51.

hooks, b. (1984). *Feminist Theory, from Margin to Center*. Boston: South End Press.

_____. (1989). *Talking Back: Thinking feminist, thinking black*. Boston: South End Press.

Hornstein, G. (1989). Quantifying psychological phenomena: Debates, dilemmas and implications. In J. G. Morawski, ed., *The Rise of Experimentation in American Psychology*. New Haven: Yale University Press.

Hubbard, R. (1990). *The Politics of Women's Biology*. New Brunswick: Rutgers University Press.

Hurlburt, D. F. (1991). The role of assertiveness in female sexuality: A comparative study between sexually assertive and nonassertive women. *Journal of Sex and Marital Therapy* 17, 183–190.

Huth, E. J. (1992). Conflicts of interest in industry-funded clinical research. In R. G. Spece, D. S. Shimm, and A. E. Buchanan, eds., *Conflicts of Interest in Clinical Practice and Research*. New York: Oxford University Press, pp. 389-406.

Irvine, J. M. (1990). *Disorders of Desire: Sex and gender in modern American sexology*. Philadelphia: Temple University Press.

_____. (2002). *Talk about Sex: The Battles over Sex Education in the United States*. Berkeley: University of California Press.

Jackson, M. (1984). Sexology and the universalization of male sexuality (from Ellis to Kinsey and Masters and Johnson). In L. Coveney, M. Jackson, S. Jeffreys, L. Kaye, and P. Mahoney, eds., *The Sexuality Papers*. London: Hutchinson.

Jeffords, S. (1989). *The Remasculinization of America: Gender and the Vietnam War*. Bloomington: Indiana University Press.

Jordanova, L. (1989). *Sexual Visions: Images of gender in science and medicine between the 18th and 20th centuries*. Madison: University of Wisconsin Press.

Kabalin, J. N., and Kessler, R. (1989). Penile prosthesis surgery: Review of ten year experience and examination of reoperations. *Urology* 33, 17–19.

Kaplan, H. S. (1979). *Disorders of Sexual Desire*. New York: Brunner/Mazel.

Kaplan, S. A., Reis, R. B., Kohn, I. J., Ikeguchi, E. F., Laor, E., Te, A. E. and Martins, A. C. P. (1999). Safety and efficacy of sildenafil in postmenopausal women with sexual dysfunction. *Urology* 53, 481–486.

Kaschak, E. and Tiefer, L., eds. (2001). *A New View of Women's Sexual Problems*. Binghamton, N.Y.: Haworth Press.

Kaslow, F. W., ed. (1996). *Handbook of Relational Diagnosis and Dysfunctional Family Patterns*. New York: John Wiley & Sons.

Katchadourian, H. A. (1979). The terminology of sex and gender. In H. A. Katchadourian, ed., *Human Sexuality: A comparative and developmental perspective*. Berkeley: University of California Press.

Kaufman, G. and Blakely, M. K., eds. (1980). *Pulling Our Own Strings: Feminist humor and satire*. Bloomington: Indiana University Press.

Kennedy, D. (1997). *Academic Duty*. Cambridge, Mass.: Harvard University Press.

Kessler, S. J., and McKenna, W. (1985). *Gender: An ethnomethodological approach*. Chicago: University of Chicago Press. (Originally published in 1978.)

Kilmann, P. R., Boland, J. P., Norton, S. P., Davidson, E., and Caid, C. (1986). Perspectives of sex therapy outcome: A survey of AASECT providers. *Journal of Sex and Marital Therapy* 12, 116–138.

Kinsey, A. C., Pomeroy, W. B., and Martin, C. E. (1948). *Sexual Behavior in the Human Male*. Philadelphia: W. B. Saunders Co.

Kinsey, A. C., Pomeroy, W. B., Martin, C. E., and Gebhard, P. H. (1953). *Sexual Behavior in the Human Female*. Philadelphia: W. B. Saunders Co.

Kirby, D. (May 3, 1998). Viagra wants to be (taken) alone. *New York Times*, sect. 14, p. 6.

Kirkeby, H. J., Andersen, A. J., and Poulsen, E. U. (1989). Nocturnal penile tumescence and rigidity: Translation of data obtained from normal males. *International Journal of Impotence Research* 1, 115–125.

Kitzinger, C. (1987). *The Social Construction of Lesbianism*. Newbury Park, Cal.: Sage Publications.

Klass, A. (1975). *There's Gold in Them Thar Pills: An inquiry into the medical-industrial complex*. Harmondsworth, Eng.: Penguin.

Kong, D. (1999). Doubts heard over sexual dysfunction gathering. *Boston Globe*, October 22, pp. B1, B6.

Kramon, G. (1989). Psychiatric care: Orphan of insurance coverage. *New York Times*, November 7, section B, p. 16.

Krane, R. J., Goldstein, I., and DeTejada, I. S. (1989). Impotence. *New England Journal of Medicine* 321, 1648–1659.

Laan, E., van Lunsen, R. H. W., Everaerd, W., Heiman, J. R., and Hackbert, L. (June, 2000). The effect of sildenafil on women's genital and subjective sexual response. Paper presented at the International Academy of Sex Research, Paris, France.

Laan, E. and Everaerd, W. (1995). Determinants of female sexual arousal: Psychophysiological theory and data. *Annual Review of Sex Research* 6, 32–76.

Ladas, A. K., Whipple, B., and Perry, J. D. (1982). *The G Spot and Other Recent Discoveries About Human Sexuality*. New York: Holt, Rinehart and Winston.

Lancaster, R. N. and diLeonardo, M., eds. (1997). *The Gender/Sexuality Reader*. New York: Routledge.

Langreth, R. (1998). Prescriptions and hot products aid drug firms. *Wall Street Journal*, January 28.

Larson, M. S. (1977). *The Rise of Professionalism: A sociological analysis*. Berkeley: University of California Press.

Laumann, E. O., Gagnon, J. H., Michael, R. T., and Michaels, S. (1994). *The Social Organization of Sexuality: Sexual practices in the United States*. Chicago: University of Chicago Press.

Laumann, E. O., Michael, R. T., and Gagnon, J. H. (1994). A political history of the national sex survey of adults. *Family Planning Perspectives* 26, 34–38.

Laumann, E. O., Paik, A. & Rosen, R. C. (1999). Sexual dysfunction in the United States. *Journal of the American Medical Association* 281, 537–544.

Laws, S. (1990). *Issues of Blood: The politics of menstruation*. New York: Columbia University Press.

Lehrman, N. (1970). *Masters and Johnson Explained*. Chicago: Playboy Press.

Leiblum, S. R. & Rosen, R. C. (eds.) (1989). *Principles and Practice of Sex Therapy: Update for the 1990s*. New York: Guilford Press.

Lerner, H. G. (1976). Parental mislabeling of female genitals as a determinant of penis envy and learning inhibitions in women. *Journal of the American Psychoanalytical Association* 24, 269–283.

LeVay, S. & Valente, S. M. (2002). *Human Sexuality*. Sunderland, Mass.: Sinauer Associates.

Levine, J. (1992). *My Enemy, My Love: Man-hating and ambivalence in women's lives*. New York: Doubleday.

_____ (2002). *Harmful to Minors: The perils of protecting children from sex*. Minneapolis: University of Minnesota Press.

Lewinsohn, R. (1958). *A History of Sexual Customs*. New York: Harper and Row.

Liebenau, J. (1987). *Medical Science and Medical Industry: The formation of the American pharmaceutical industry*. Baltimore: Johns Hopkins University Press.

Lipman, S. (1991). *Laughter in Hell: The use of humor during the holocaust*. Northvale, N.J.: Jason Aronson, Inc.

Lloyd, G. (1984). *The Man of Reason: "Male" and "female" in Western philosophy*. Minneapolis: University of Minnesota Press.

LoPiccolo, J. (1977). The professionalization of sex therapy: Issues and problems. *Society* 14, 60–68.

_____. (1978). Direct treatment of sexual dysfunction. In J. LoPiccolo and L. LoPiccolo, eds., *Handbook of Sex Therapy*. New York: Plenum Press.

_____ (1992) Postmodern sex therapy for erectile failure. In R. C. Rosen & S. R. Leiblium, eds., *Erectile Disorders: Assessment and Treatment*. New York: Guilford Press.

Lowe, M., and Hubbard, R., eds. (1983). *Woman's Nature: Rationalizations of inequality*. New York: Pergamon Press.

MacKenzie, B., and MacKenzie, E. (1988). *It's Not All in Your Head*. New York: E. P. Dutton.

MacKinnon, C. A, (1987). A feminist/political approach. In J. H. Geer and W. T. O'Donohue, eds., *Theories of Human Sexuality*. New York: Plenum Press.

McCormick, N. B. (1994). *Sexual Salvation: Affirming women's sexual rights and pleasures.*
Westport, Conn.: Praeger.

McLaren, A. (1999). *Twentieth-Century sexuality: A history.* Oxford: Blackwell Publishers.

Marsa, L. (1997). *Prescription for Profits: How the pharmaceutical industry bankrolled the unholy
marriage between science and business.* New York: Scribner's.

Martin, B. (1993). The critique of science becomes academic. *Sciences, Technology and Human Values* 18, 247–259.

Maslow, A. H. (1966). *The Psychology of Science.* New York: Harper and Row.

Masters, W. H., and Johnson, V. E. (1966). *Human Sexual Response.* Boston: Little, Brown.

_____. (1970). *Human Sexual Inadequacy.* Boston: Little, Brown.

_____. (1976). *The Pleasure Bond.* New York: Bantam Books.

_____. (1979). *Homosexuality in Perspective.* Boston: Little, Brown.

Mead, M. (1955). *Male and Female: A study of the sexes in a changing world.* New York: Mentor.

Melman, A., Tiefer, L., and Pedersen, R. (1988). Evaluation of first 406 patients in urology
department based center for male sexual dysfunction. *Urology* 32, 6–10.

Mentor Corporation. (n.d.). *A Guide for Setting Up Educational Seminars.* Goleta, Cal.:
Mentor Corporation.

Merrill, R. A. (1997). FDA regulation of clinical drug trials. In M. Herzman and D. E. Feltner, eds., *The Handbook of Psychopharmacology Trials: An overview of scientific, political,
and ethical concerns.* New York: New York University Press, pp. 61–99.

Metcalf, A., and Humphries, M., eds. (1985). *The Sexuality of Men.* London: Pluto Press.

Miller, P. Y., and Fowlkes, M. R. (1980). Social and behavioral construction of female sexuality. *Signs* 5, 783–800.

Millman, M., and Kanter, R. M., eds. (1975). *Another Voice: Feminist perspectives on social
life and social science.* Garden City, N.Y.: Doubleday.

Mindess, H. (1971). *Laughter and liberation.* Los Angeles: Nash.

Mishler, E. G. (1981). Viewpoint: Critical perspectives on the biomedical model. In E. G.
Mishler, L. R. AmaraSingham, S. T. Hauser, R. Liem, S. D. Osherson, and N. E. Waxler,
Social Contexts of Health, Illness and Patient Care. Cambridge: Cambridge University Press.

Modleski, T. (1984). *Loving with a Vengeance: Mass-produced fantasies for women.* New York:
Methuen.

Morrow, D. J. (1998). From lab to patient, by way of your den. *New York Times*, June 7, section 3, pp. 1, 10–11.

Mosher, D. (1991). Macho men, machismo and sexuality. *Annual Review of Sex Research* 2,
199–243.

Moynihan, R. (2003). The making of a disease: Female sexual dysfunction. *British Medical
Journal* 326, 45–47.

Myers, J. E. (1999). *A Treasury of Victorious Women's Humor.* Springfield, Ill.: Lincoln-
Herndon Press, Inc.

National Institutes of Health (NIH) (1992). Consensus Development Conference Statement on Impotence. Office of Medical Applications of Research. Bethesda, Md.: NIH.

National Institutes of Health (NIH) (1993). Consensus Development Conference Statement on Impotence. *International Journal of Impotence Research* 5, 181–199.

Naunton, E. (1989). Answers to impotence: Support groups IA and I-Anon offer hope to
the millions. *Sunday New York Daily News*, April 9.

Nelkin, D. (1987). *Selling Science: How the press covers science and psychology.* New York: W.
H. Freeman.

Nelkin, D., and Tancredi, L. (1989). *Dangerous Diagnostics: The social power of biological information.* New York: Basic Books.

New psychiatric syndromes spur protest. (1985). *New York Times*, November 19, section C,
p. 16.

Nestle, M. (2002). *Food Politics: How the food industry influences nutrition and health*. Berkeley: University of California Press.

Ng, E. M. L., Borras-Valls, J. J., Perez-Conchillo, M., and Coleman, E. (eds.). (2000). *Sexuality in the New Millennium*. Bologna, Italy: Editrice Compositori.

O'Donohue, W. & Geer, J. H. (eds.) (1993). *Handbook of Sexual Dysfunctions: Assessment and treatment*. Boston: Allyn and Bacon.

Organization helps couples with impotence as problem. (1984). *New York Times*, June 24, section 1, pt. 2, p. 42.

Ortner, S. B., and Whitehead, H., eds. (1981). *Sexual Meanings: The cultural construction of gender and sexuality*. Cambridge: Cambridge University Press.

Osherson, S. D., and AmaraSingham, L. (1981). The machine metaphor in medicine. In E. G. Mishler, L. AmaraSingham, S. T. Hauser, R. Liem, S. D. Osherson, and N. E. Waxler, eds., *Social Contexts of Health, Illness and Patient Care*. Cambridge: Cambridge University Press.

Padgug, R. A. (1979). On conceptualizing sexuality in history. *Radical History Review*, no. 20, 3–23.

Park, K., Goldstein, I., Andry, C., Siroky, M. B., Krane, R. J., and Azadzoi, K. M. (1997). Vasculogenic female sexual dysfunction: The hemodynamic basis for vaginal engorgement insufficiency and clitoral erectile insufficiency. *International Journal of Impotence Research* 9, 27–37.

Parlee, M. B. (1987). Media treatment of premenstrual syndrome. In B. E. Ginsburg and B. F. Carter, eds., *Premenstrual Syndrome: Ethical and legal implications in a biomedical perspective*. New York: Plenum.

Payer, L. (1992). *Disease-Mongers: How doctors, drug companies, and insurers are making you feel sick*. New York: Wiley & Sons.

Peplau, L. A., and Gordon, S. L. (1985). Women and men in love: Gender differences in close heterosexual relationships. In V. E. O'Leary, R. K. Unger, and B. S. Wallston, eds., *Women, Gender and Social Psychology*. Hillsdale, N.J.: Lawrence Erlbaum Associates.

Person, E. S. (1980). Sexuality as the mainstay of identity: Psychoanalytic perspectives. *Signs* 5, 605–630.

Petras, J. W. (1973). *Sexuality in Society*. Boston: Allyn and Bacon.

Petrou, S. P., and Barrett, D. M. (1991). Current penile prostheses available for the treatment of erectile dysfunction. *Problems in Urology* 5, 594–607.

Pleck, J. H., Sonenstein, F. L., and Ku, L. C. (1993). Masculine ideology and its correlates. In S. Oskamp and M. Costanzo, eds., *Gender Issues in Contemporary Society*. Newbury Park, Cal.: Sage Publications.

Plummer, K., ed. (1981). *The Making of the Modern Homosexual*. London: Hutchinson.

_____. (1982). Symbolic interactionism and sexual conduct: An emergent perspective. In M. Brake, ed., *Human Sexual Relations: Towards a redefinition of sexual politics*. New York: Pantheon.

Poll shows widespread use of three major impotence treatments. (1993). *AUA Today*, May, p. 6.

Potter, J., and Wetherell, M. (1987). *Discourse and Social Psychology: Beyond attitudes and behavior*. London: Sage.

Pryor, D. (1997). The pharmaceutical companies. In M. Hertzman and D. E. Feltner, eds., *The Handbook of Psychopharmacology Trials: An overview of scientific, political, and ethical concerns*. New York: New York University Press, p. 46- 60.

Rado, S. (1949). An adaptational view of sexual behavior. In P. Hoch and J. Zubin, eds., *Psychosexual Development in Health and Disease*. New York: Grune and Stratton.

Rhode, D. L., ed. (1990). *Theoretical Perspectives on Sexual Difference*. New Haven: Yale University Press.

Riessman, C. K. (1983). Women and medicalization: A new perspective. *Social Policy* 14, 3–18.

Ritzer, G. (1996). *McDonaldization of Society*, rev. ed. Thousand Oaks, Cal.: Pine Forge Press.

Rivas, D. A. and Chancellor, M. B. (1997). Management of erectile dysfunction. In M. L. Sipski and C. J. Alexander, *Sexual Function in People with Disability and Chronic Illness: A health professional's guide*. Gaithersburg, Md.: Aspen Publishers, Inc., pp. 429–464.

Robbins, T. (1999). *From Girls to Grrlz: A history of comics from teens to zines*. San Francisco: Chronicle Books.

Robinson, P. (1976). *The Modernization of Sex*. New York: Harper and Row.

Rosen, R. C., and Leiblum, S. R. (1992a). Erectile disorders: An overview of historical trends and clinical perspectives. In R. C. Rosen and S. R. Leiblum, eds., *Erectile Disorders: Assessment and treatment*. New York: Guilford.

––––––, eds. (1992b). *Erectile Disorders: Assessment and treatment*. New York: Guilford.

––––––, eds. (1995). *Case Studies in Sex Therapy*. New York: Guilford Press.

Rosen, R. C., Phillips, N. A., Gendrano, N. C., and Ferguson, D. M. (1999). Oral phentolamine and female sexual arousal disorder: A pilot study. *Journal of Sex and Marital Therapy* 25, 137–144.

Rosen, R. C., Riley, A., Wagner, G., Osterloh, I. H., Kirkpatrick, J., and Mishra, A. (1997). The international index of erectile function (IIEF): A multidimensional scale for assessment of erectile dysfunction. *Urology* 49, 822–830.

Rosenthal, E. (1989). Innovations intensify glut of surgeons. *New York Times*, February 9, section C, p. 1.

Rosenthal, R. (1966). *Experimenter Effects in Behavioral Research*. New York: Appleton-Century-Crofts, 1966.

Rosenthal, R., and Rosnow, R. L. (1969). The volunteer subject. In R. Rosenthal and R. L. Rosnow, eds., *Artifact in Behavioral Research*. New York: Academic Press.

Rothblum, E. D. and Brehony, K. A. (eds.) (1993). *Boston Marriages: Romantic but asexual relationships among contemporary lesbians*. Amherst: University of Massachusetts Press.

Rowe, K. (1995). *The Unruly Woman: Gender and the genres of laughter*. Austin: University of Texas Press.

Rubin, G. (1984). Thinking sex: Notes for a radical theory of the politics of sexuality. In C. S. Vance, ed., *Pleasure and Danger: Exploring female sexuality*. Boston: Routledge and Kegan Paul.

Sahli, N. (1984). *Women and Sexuality in America: A bibliography*. Boston: G. K. Hall and Co.

Salonia, A., Montorsi, F., Maga, T., Bua, L., Guazzoni, G., Barbieri, L. Graziottin, A., and Rigatti, P. (1999). Patient-partner satisfaction of sildenafil treatment in evidence-based organic erectile dysfunction. *Journal of Urology* 161S, 213.

Sarnoff, S. & Sarnoff, I. (1979). *Sexual Excitement, Sexual Peace*. New York: M. Evans and Co.

Sarrel, L., and Sarrel, P. (1983). How to have great new sex with your same old spouse. *Redbook*, March, pp. 75–77, 172.

Sayers, J. (1982). *Biological politics: Feminist and anti-feminist perspectives*. London: Tavistock publications.

Schaffner, K. F. (1992). Ethics and the nature of empirical science. In D. J. Miller and M. Herson, eds., *Research Fraud in the Behavioral and Biomedical Sciences*. New York: John Wiley & Sons. pp. 17–33.

Schiavi, R. C. (1988). Nocturnal penile tumescence in the evaluation of erectile disorders: A critical review. *Journal of Sex and Marital Therapy* 14, 83–97.

Schiavi, R. C., Schreiner-Engel, P., Madeli, J., Schanzer, H., and Cohen, E. (1990). Healthy aging and male sexual function. *American Journal of Psychiatry* 147, 766–771.

Schiebinger, L. (1986). Skeletons in the closet: The first illustrations of the female skeleton in 18th century anatomy. *Representations* 14, 42–82.

Schlosser, E. (2002). *Fast Food Nation: The dark side of the all-American meal*. New York: HarperCollins Perennial.

Schmidt, G. S. (1983a). Foreword. In J. Bancroft, *Human Sexuality and Its Problems*. Edinburgh: Churchill-Livingstone.

––––––. (1993). A backlash disguised as progress. *International Journal of Impotence Research* 5, 263–264.

Schnarch, D. (1991). *Constructing the Sexual Crucible*. New York: Norton.

Schneider, B. E., and Gould, M. (1987). Female sexuality: Looking back into the future. In B. B. Hess and M. M. Ferree, eds., *Analyzing Gender: A handbook of social science research*. Newbury Park, Cal.: Sage Publications.

Schover, L. R. and Leiblum, S. R. (1994). Commentary: The stagnation of sex therapy. *Journal of Psychology & Human Sexuality* 6, 5–30.

Schur, E. M. (1984). *Labeling Women Deviant: Gender, stigma, and social control*. New York: Random House.

Scott, S., and Morgan, D., eds. (1993). *Body Matters: Essays on the sociology of the body*. London: Falmer Press.

Sedgwick, E. K. (1995) Jane Austen and the masturbating girl. In P. Bennett & V. A. Rosario, eds., *Solitary Pleasures: The historical, literary, and artistic discourses of eroticism*. New York: Routledge.

Segal, L. (1983). Sensual uncertainty, or why the clitoris is not enough. In S. Cartledge and J. Ryan, eds., *Sex and Love: New thoughts on old contradictions*. London: The Women's Press.

_____ (1994). *Straight Sex: The politics of pleasure*. London: Virago Press.

Segraves, R. T. (1998). Editorial: Pharmacological era in the treatment of sexual disorders. *Journal of Sex & Marital Therapy* 24, 67–68.

Seidler, V., ed. (1992). *Men, Sex and Relationships: Writings from Achilles Heel*. New York: Routledge.

Shapiro, J. (1980). The battle of the sexes. *Science* 207, 1193–1194.

Sharlip, I. (1989). Editorial. *International Journal of Impotence Research* 1, 67–69.

Shepard, A. (1994). *Cartooning for suffrage*. Albuquerque: University of New Mexico Press.

Sherif, C. (1979). Bias in psychology. In J. A. Sherman and E. T. Beck, eds., *The Prism of Sex: Essays in the sociology of knowledge*. Madison: University of Wisconsin Press.

Simon, W. (1973). The social, the erotic, and the sensual: The complexities of sexual scripts. *Nebraska Symposium on Motivation* 21, 61–82.

_____. (1989). Commentary on the status of sex research: The postmodernization of sex. *Journal of Psychology and Human Sexuality* 2, 9–37.

Simon, W., and Gagnon, J. H. (1986). Sexual scripts: Permanence and change. *Archives of Sexual Behavior* 15, 97–120.

Sims, M. (1982). *On the Necessity of Bestializing the Human Female*. Boston: South End Press.

Sindermann, C. J. and Sawyer, T. K. (1997). *The Scientist as Consultant*. New York: Plenum Trade.

Slaughter, S. (1993). Beyond basic science: Research university presidents' narratives of science policy. *Science, Technology, and Human Values* 18, 278–302.

Slaughter, S. and Leslie, L. L. (1997). *Academic Capitalism: Politics, policies, and the entrepreneurial university*. Baltimore: Johns Hopkins University Press.

Snitow, A., Stansell, C., and Thompson, S. (1983). *Powers of Desire: The politics of sexuality*. New York: Monthly Review Press.

Soble, A. (1987). Philosophy, medicine and healthy sexuality. In E. E. Shelp, ed., *Sexuality and Medicine, vol. 1, Conceptual roots*. Dordrecht, Holland: D. Reidel Publishing Co.

Spark, R. F., White, R. A., and Connolly, P. B. (1980). Impotence is not always psychogenic: Newer insights into hypothalamic-pituitary-gonadal dysfunction. *Journal of the American Medical Association* 243, 750–755.

Spitzer, R. L., Williams, J. B. W., and Skodol, A. E. (1980). DSM-III: The major achievements and an overview. *American Journal of Psychiatry* 137, 151–164.

Stein, H. F. (1987). Polarities in the identity of family medicine: A psychocultural analysis. In W. J. Doherty, C. E. Christianson, and M. B. Sussman, eds., *Family Medicine: The maturing of a discipline*. New York: The Haworth Press.

Steinem, G. (1980). If men could menstruate: A political fantasy. In G. Kaufman & M. K. Blakely, eds., *Pulling Our Own Strings: Feminist humor and satire*. Bloomington: Indiana University Press, pp. 25–26.

Stipp, D. (1987). Research on impotence upsets idea that it is usually psychological. *Wall Street Journal*, April 14, pp. 1, 25.

Stipp, D. and Whitaker, R. (1998). The selling of impotence. *Fortune*, March 16, pp. 115–124.

Stock, W. (1984). Sex roles and sexual dysfunction. In C. S. Widom, ed., *Sex Roles and Psychopathology*. New York: Plenum Press.

Sulloway, F. J. (1979). *Freud: Biologist of the mind*. New York: Basic Books.

Symons, D. (1979). *The Evolution of Human Sexuality*. New York: Oxford University Press.

Tavris, C. (1992). *The Mismeasure of Woman*. New York: Simon & Schuster.

_____. (2001). *Psychobabble and Biobunk: Using psychology to think critically about issues in the news*. 2nd edition. Upper Saddle River, N.J.: Prentice-Hall.

Tavris, C., and Sadd, S. (1977). *The Redbook Report on Female Sexuality*. New York: Delacorte Press.

Teitelman, R. (1994). *Profits of Science: The American marriage of business and technology*. New York: Basic Books.

Tepper, M. S. (1999). Attitudes, beliefs, and cognitive processes that may impede or facilitate sexual pleasure in people with spinal cord injury. University of Pennsylvania dissertation for the Ph.D. in Education.

Tiefer, L. (1978). The context and consequences of contemporary sex research: A feminist perspective. In W. McGill, D. Dewsbury, and B. Sachs, eds., *Sex and Behavior: Status and prospectus*. New York: Plenum Press.

_____. (1986a). In pursuit of the perfect penis: The medicalization of male sexuality. *American Behavioral Scientist* 29, 579–599. (Reprinted in the first edition of *Sex Is Not a Natural Act*.)

_____. (1986b). "Am I Normal?": The question of sex. In C. Tavris, ed., *Everywoman's Emotional Well-Being*. Garden City, N.Y.: Doubleday. (Reprinted in this volume.)

_____. (1987). Social constructionism and the study of human sexuality. In P. Shaver and C. Hendrick, eds., *Sex and Gender*. Newbury Park, Calif.: Sage Publications. (Reprinted in this volume.)

_____. (1988a). A feminist critique of the sexual dysfunction nomenclature. *Women and Therapy* 7, 5–21.

_____. (1988b). A feminist perspective on sexology and sexuality. In M. M. Gergen, ed., *Feminist Thought and the Structure of Knowledge*. New York: New York University Press.

_____. (1990a). Gender and meaning in the DSM-III and DSM-III-R sexual dysfunctions. Paper delivered at American Psychological Association, Boston, August. (Reprinted in this volume.)

_____. (1990b). Sexual biology and the symbolism of the natural. Paper presented at the International Academy of Sex Research, Sigtuna, Sweden, and subsequently published (in German translation) in *Zeitschrift für Sexualforschung* 4 (1991), 97–108. (Reprinted in this volume.)

_____. (1991a). Commentary on the status of sex research: Feminism, sexuality and sexology. *Journal of Psychology and Human Sexuality* 4, 5–42.

_____. (1991b). New perspectives in sexology: From rigor (mortis) to richness. Plenary address given to the Society for the Scientific Study of Sex, New York, 1990, and subsequently published in *Journal of Sex Research* 28 (1991), 593–602. (Reprinted in the first edition of *Sex Is Not a Natural Act*.)

_____. (1991c). Historical, scientific, clinical and feminist criticisms of "the human sexual response cycle" model. *Annual Review of Sex Research* 2, 1–23. (Reprinted in this volume.)

_____. (1992a). Nomenclature and partner issues. Paper presented at National Institutes of Health Consensus Development Conference on Impotence, Bethesda.

_____. (1992b). Critique of the DSM-IIIR nosology of sexual dysfunctions. *Psychiatric Medicine* 10, 227–245.

_____. (1992c). Feminism and sex research: Ten years' reminiscences and appraisal. In J. C. Chrisler and D. Howard, eds., *New Directions in Feminist Psychology*. New York: Springer Publishing Co.

———. (1995). *Sex Is Not a Natural Act, and Other Essays.* Boulder: Westview Press. (First edition of this book.)

———. (1996a). The Medicalization of Sexuality: Conceptual, normative, and professional issues. *Annual Review of Sex Research* 7, 252–282.

———. (1996b). Towards a Feminist Sex Therapy. *Women and Therapy* 19, 63–64. (Reprinted in this volume.)

———. (1997). Sexual biology and the symbolism of the natural. In M. M. Gergen and S. N. Davis, eds., *Toward a New Psychology of Gender: A reader.* New York: Routledge, pp. 363–374.

———. (1999a). Challenging Sexual Naturalism, the Shibboleth of Sex research and Popular Sexology. In D. Bernstein, ed., *Gender and Motivation* (vol. 45 of *Current Theory and Research in Motivation*). Lincoln: University of Nebraska Press, pp. 143–172.

———. (1999b). "Female Sexual Dysfunction" Alert: A New disorder invented for women. *Sojourner: The Women's Forum,* October, p. 11. (Reprinted in this volume.)

———. (2000). Sexology and the Pharmaceutical Industry: The threat of cooptation. *Journal of Sex Research* 37, 273–283. (Reprinted in this volume.)

———. (2001). Arriving at a "new view" of women's sexual problems: Background, theory, and activism. In Kaschak, L. and Tiefer, L., eds., *A New View of Women's Sexual Problems.* Binghamton, N.Y.: Haworth. Pp. 63–98.

Tiefer, L., and Melman, A. (1983). Interview of wives: A necessary adjunct in the evaluation of impotence. *Sexuality and Disability* 6, 167–175.

Tiefer, L., Moss, S., and Melman, A. (1991). Follow-up of patients and partners experiencing penile prosthesis malfunction and corrective surgery. *Journal of Sex and Marital Therapy* 17, 113–128.

Tiefer, L., Pedersen, B., and Melman, A. (1988). Psychosocial follow-up of penile prosthesis implant patients and partners. *Journal of Sex and Marital Therapy* 14, 184–201.

Toufexis, A. (1988). It's not "all in your head." *Time,* December 5, p. 94.

Trilling, L. (1950). The Kinsey Report. In L. Trilling, ed., *The Liberal Imagination: Essays on literature and society.* Garden City, N.Y.: Doubleday Anchor.

Turner, C. & Spillich, G. J. (1997). Research into smoking or nicotine and human cognitive performance: Does the source of funding make a difference? *Addiction* 92, 1423–1426.

Udry, J. R. (1993). The politics of sex research. *Journal of Sex Research* 30, 103–110.

Unger, R. K. (1983). Through the looking-glass: No wonderland yet! (The reciprocal relationship between methodology and models of reality). *Psychology of Women Quarterly* 8, 9–32.

Valenstein, E. S. (1998). *Blaming the Brain.* New York: The Free Press.

Valverde, M. (1987). *Sex, Power, and Pleasure.* Philadelphia: New Society Publishers.

Vance, C. S. (ed.) (1984). *Pleasure and Danger: Exploring female sexuality.* Boston: Routledge and Kegan Paul.

Verhulst, J., and Heiman, J. R. (1988). A systems perspective on sexual desire. In S. R. Leiblum and R. C. Rosen, eds., *Sexual Desire Disorders.* New York: Guilford Press.

Vicunus, M. (1982). Sexuality and power: A review of current work in the history of sexuality. *Feminist Studies* 8, 133–156.

Wagner, G., and Kaplan, H. S. (1992). *The New Injection Treatment for Impotence.* New York: Brunner Mazel.

Walby, S. (1993). 'Backlash' in historical context. In M. Kennedy, C. Lubelska, & V. Walsh, eds., *Making Connections: Women's studies, women's movements, women's lives.* London: Taylor & Francis, pp. 79–89.

Weber, J. and Barret, A. (1998). The new era of lifestyle drugs. *Business Week,* May 11, Cover, 92–98.

Weeks, J. (1981). *Sex, Politics, and Society: The regulation of sexuality since 1800.* London: Longman.

———. (1982). The development of sexual theory and sexual politics. In M. Brake, ed., *Human Sexual Relations: Towards a redefinition of sexual politics.* New York: Pantheon.

_____. (1985). *Sexuality and Its Discontents: Meanings, myth, and modern sexualities.* London: Routledge and Kegan Paul.

Weisstein, N. (1973). Introduction. In E. Levine, *"All She Needs . . . ".* New York: Quadrangle/The New York Times Book Co.

Werbin, T., Salimpour, P., Berman, L., Krane, R. J., Goldstein, I., and Berman, J. (1999). Effect of sexual stimulation and age on genital blood flow in women with sexual arousal disorder. *Journal of Urology* 161S., 178.

Whatley, M. H. and Henken, E. R. (2001). *Did You Hear About the Girl Who? Contemporary legends, folklore and human sexuality.* New York: New York University Press.

Williams, R. (1976). *Keywords: A vocabulary of culture and society.* New York: Oxford University Press. (Rev. ed. published in 1983.)

Willis, E. (1988). Feminism, moralism, and pornography. In K. Ellis, B. Jaker, N. D. Hunter, B. O'Dair, and A. Tallmer, eds., *Caught Looking: Feminism, pornography, and censorship.* Seattle: The Real Comet Press.

Wise, P. and Drury, M. (1996). Pharmaceutical trials in general practice: The first 100 protocols. An audit by the clinical research ethics committee of the Royal College of General Practitioners. *BMJ* 313, 1245–1248.

Wise, T. N. (1999). Psychosocial side effects of sildenafil therapy for erectile dysfunction. *Journal of Sex and Marital Therapy* 25, 145–150.

Wolf, N. (1991). *The Beauty Myth.* New York: William Morrow.

Zilbergeld, B. (1999). *The New Male Sexuality,* revised. New York: Bantam Books.

_____. (1992). The man behind the broken penis: Social and psychological determinants of erectile failure. In R. C. Rosen and S. R. Leiblum, eds., *Erectile Disorders: Assessment and treatment.* New York: Guilford.

INDEX